THE HOLLYWOOD REPORTER
STAR PROFILES

THE *Hollywood* REPORTER

★STAR★
★PROFILES★

GENERAL EDITOR
★MARC WANAMAKER★

Octopus Books

This book was devised and produced
by Multimedia Publications (UK) Ltd

Editor: Richard Rosenfeld
Text Editor: Maggie Daykin
Production: Arnon Orbach
Design: Graham Mitchener
Picture Research: Dave Kent,
Sheila Corr

Contributors:
Lindsey Boyd
Minty Clinch
W. Stephen Gilbert
Marianne Gray
Curtis Hutchinson
Mark Lewis
Jane Root

First published 1984 by
Octopus Books Limited
59 Grosvenor Street
London W1

ISBN 0 7064 2253 8

Typeset by Rowland Phototypesetting
(London) Limited
Colour origination by The Clifton
Studio Limited, London
Printed in Spain by Mateu Cromo
Artes Graficas, Madrid

Contents

Introduction 6

Woody Allen 8
Julie Andrews 10
Fred Astaire 12
Lauren Bacall 14
Brigitte Bardot 16
John Barrymore 18
Warren Beatty 20
Ingrid Bergman 22
Humphrey Bogart 24
Clara Bow 26
Marlon Brando 28
James Cagney 30
Charlie Chaplin 32
Maurice Chevalier 34
Sean Connery 36
Gary Cooper 38
Joan Crawford 40
Bing Crosby 42
Bette Davis 44
Doris Day 46
James Dean 48
Robert de Niro 50
Marlene Dietrich 52
Faye Dunaway 54
Clint Eastwood 56
W. C. Fields 58
Errol Flynn 60
Henry Fonda 62
Jane Fonda 64
Clark Gable 66
Greta Garbo 68
Judy Garland 70
Lillian Gish 72
Betty Grable 74
Cary Grant 76
Gene Hackman 78
Jean Harlow 80
Rita Hayworth 82
Audrey Hepburn 84
Katharine Hepburn 86
Charlton Heston 88
Dustin Hoffman 90
Bob Hope 92
Boris Karloff 94
Buster Keaton 96
Gene Kelly 98

Grace Kelly 100
Alan Ladd 102
Hedy Lamarr 104
Burt Lancaster 106
Charles Laughton 108
Vivien Leigh 110
Jack Lemmon 112
Carole Lombard 114
Sophia Loren 116
Lee Marvin 118
Groucho Marx 120
James Mason 122
Steve McQueen 124
Robert Mitchum 126
Marilyn Monroe 128
Paul Newman 130
Jack Nicholson 132
David Niven 134
Laurence Olivier 136
Al Pacino 138
Gregory Peck 140
Mary Pickford 142
Anthony Quinn 144
Robert Redford 146
Burt Reynolds 148
Edward G. Robinson 150
Ginger Rogers 152
Mickey Rooney 154
George C. Scott 156
Peter Sellers 158
Sissy Spacek 160
Sylvester Stallone 162
Barbara Stanwyck 164
James Stewart 166
Meryl Streep 168
Barbra Streisand 170
Gloria Swanson 172
Elizabeth Taylor 174
Spencer Tracy 176
John Travolta 178
Lana Turner 180
Rudolph Valentino 182
John Wayne 184
Orson Welles 186
Mae West 188

Index 190

Introduction

In 1913, Cecil B. De Mille took the westbound train to the end of the line, and found himself in Hollywood. It was not, at first sight, a cataclysmic discovery, merely a ranch that had grown into a small pastoral town in the Southern Californian desert. Where there was irrigation, there were groves of oranges and avocados. Where there wasn't, there was sand. Hardly the place you would expect to become the headquarters of the world's greatest dream factory. Yet, in seven short years, the major studios had established themselves in the wilderness and the production schedules ran to 800 films a year.

Imported stars

The stars were their raw material, and they were imported from around the globe. There were the Englishmen, Charlie Chaplin, Charles Laughton, Boris Karloff and Cary Grant; the Europeans, Edward G. Robinson, Hedy Lamarr, Greta Garbo and Marlene Dietrich; the native born New Yorkers, James Cagney and Humphrey Bogart. Katharine Hepburn and Bette Davis steamed in from privileged New England, Buster Keaton, Gene Kelly, Jean Harlow and Fred Astaire from the wastes of middle America, Clara Bow and John Barrymore from Brooklyn.

They had nothing in common except luck, the magic ingredient that raised them above the masses and made them rich beyond the dreams of avarice. Some were beautiful, some handsome, some educated, some intelligent, some indeed were talented, but even the combination of all these qualities was no guarantee of success in a town motivated by sex, money and the illusion of glamour. A shopgirl, like Texas-born Lucille Fay Le Sueur, could re-christen herself Joan Crawford and ride high for five decades by changing her image to suit the times, but a classical actor like Laurence Olivier was apt to find himself back in London before you could say "cut".

In those early days before the Second World War, when silent pictures were giving way to talkies, being a star was a hazardous affair. On the surface it looked fine. Each actor vied with his peers to build a bigger and better mansion overlooking the gold paved streets of Hollywood from the more salubrious environs of Bel Air and Beverly Hills. Within those well guarded walls, there were marble halls and swimming pools, baseball parks and riding stables. Yachts and limousines and servants were theirs to command.

The problem was that the stars were locked into their gilded cages, and the only way out was down. The villain of the piece was the studio, rapacious, monopolistic and dictatorial. Olivier put his finger on an essential truth when he described acting as a "masochistic form of exhibitionism, not quite the occupation of an adult". Hollywood agreed with him and treated its stars like the children it trained them to be.

Having taken the elementary precaution of tying any promising newcomer into a seven year exclusive contract, it proceeded to rip them off systematically. Cagney, a Warner Brothers' trouper, had their number, for what it was worth. "Making pictures was a fatiguing business," he has explained, "and I was kept plenty busy, and I mean literally to all hours. Frequently we'd work to three or four in the morning. I'd look over and there'd be the director, sitting with his head thrown back. He was tired ; we were all tired. This was the kind of pressure the studio put on us because they wanted to get the thing done as cheaply as possible. At times we started at nine in the morning and worked straight through to the next morning. We were completing in 17 days, 19 days, 21 days. Hell, we could have phoned them in."

Fast moving hoofer

Many of the stars would have found it less gruelling if they'd had any say in how the films should be cast or made or even how their own parts should be interpreted, but independent thought was strictly forbidden. A 1930s Cagney film had Jimmy as a fast talking gangster, or occasionally as a fast moving hoofer, and it grossed at least a million dollars from its minimal investment. The other stars worked to a similar bottom line. Their studios got rich and so did they, but they didn't have to be happy. And, for the most part, they weren't.

In this fickle world, where everyone was only as good as their last picture, the most popular safety valves were drink and marriage. Alcohol might ruin a profile and with it a career, as John Barrymore and Errol Flynn discovered, but it deadened the dull routine of intensive work interspersed with long periods of leisure. Marriage was the accepted antidote to loneliness and aging, but only rare was it of the "till death us do part" variety. More often it was a liaison of convenience, subject to intolerable temptation every time a new leading lady or leading man came on the scene.

The pattern was very predictable. Two young hopefuls with stars in their eyes would meet and fall in love. One would make it, the other wouldn't, and the one that did would begin to think it was possible to do better. A few weddings later and it would become clear the wrong decision had been made, but by that time the habit of playing the mating game was too deeply ingrained. Five visits to the altar were not uncommon with aging actors taking glamorous brides along with their toupees, while actresses clung to the remnants of youth with the assistance of face lifts and young studs.

Since World War II, the studio system has broken down, aided and abetted by determined performers such as Burt Lancaster and Kirk Douglas who set up their own production companies in the 1950s and made their pictures stick. Today's actors don't like to be called stars, despite their licence to pick and choose their parts. Once they're established, they can write their own scripts, direct their own films and paddle their own canoes, provided they can show a profit. Robert Redford, Paul Newman, Clint Eastwood, Jane Fonda and Sylvester Stallone are the new leaders of the pack. They don't

stand before a camera for less than a million dollars, unless it be in the cause of Art, and then only if the product pleases. They know that power is money, and they have plenty of both.

Off screen, alcohol has rather gone out of fashion, caught in the pincer movement between drugs and the fanatical Fonda-esque pursuit of the body beautiful, but marriage is still in there fighting for its rights. And still losing, especially in the Southern Californian divorce courts which makes costly claims on one in three liaisons. In this, at least Hollywood and its stars still lead the world.

Woody Allen

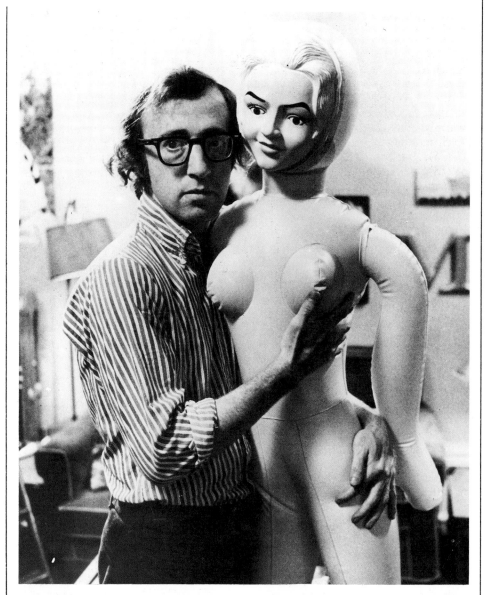

America's best loved neurotic, Allen Stewart Konigsberg, describes himself as being incapable of enjoying anything. He elaborates: he hates the countryside, alcohol, marriage, meeting people, vacations and everything to do with films except writing the scripts. But the image doesn't quite fit.

Once a month, for the past 10 years, he has played the clarinet in a small jazz bar in Manhattan, unpaid Listening to, and performing, the music of Gershwin and Fats Waller seem to be the two great loves of his life. And the background music for his films reflects this interest.

Stand-up comedian

Woody Allen, as we all know him, first saw the light of day in the rough end of Brooklyn on December 1, 1935. As a child he hated school, the only satisfaction it gave him was in being allowed to develop an early talent for writing funny stories and jokes, which he sold—quite profitably—to New York newspapers.

After graduation, Allen worked as a full-time writer for Sid Caesar and other leading stars of American TV comedy until he could summon up enough courage to tell his own jokes, as a stand-up comedian in New York's *Bitter End* and *Blue Angel* night clubs.

Failed marriages

He married young. He was just 19, and his bride—Harlene Rosen—16. The marriage lasted five, squabble-filled years, Allen later dismissing it with a typically sardonic remark: "We pondered whether to take a vacation or get a divorce. We decided that a trip to Bermuda would be over in two weeks, but a divorce is something you always have."

His second marriage, to Louise Lasser, his co-star in *Bananas* (1971), lasted only two years. Although he now looks back on both marriages as failures, Allen remains on friendly terms with both ex-wives.

What's New Pussycat (1965), introduced him to the film world. He

A twentieth-century sex comedy from the man who made neurosis his own: **Bananas** *(1971), with Woody Allen and friend (top right); in drag (right).*

8

was invited to write the script as well as being offered a part in it, but subsequently disowned the film. An appearance in the Bond spoof *Casino Royale* (1967), is another experience that he now seems keen to forget.

His real break came with his script for *Take the Money and Run* (1969), in which he took the lead role. Also, as he says, "Some very brave people let me direct it." This paved the way for Allen to make those bitingly satirical, yet warmly human films with which he is so closely associated: *Love and Death* (1975); *Annie Hall* (1977); *Interiors* (1978); *Manhattan* (1979); *A Midsummer Night's Sex Comedy* (1982) and, his masterpiece, *Zelig* (1983). His performance as Leonard Zelig, the mysterious Jew from New York, was described as that of "a genius and an enthusiast" and the film "brilliantly marshaled and directed".

Private life

Allen shields his private life from publicity extremely well, but it is, of course, well known that Diane Keaton was his constant companion for a number of years, and, like the lovers they played in *Annie Hall*, they were unable to resolve their differences. Eventually, they went their separate ways, though he has never lost his tender feeling for her, nor she for him. Now, the usually zany and flippant comedian says of her: "She increased my affection, feelings and understanding for women and made me see how appealing the female sex is. Through her I got my insight into them."

Certainly, the female characters in his films became notably more three-dimensional. Allen denies that *Annie Hall* is autobiographical but,

when drawn, admits that most of his films are based on real-life experiences.

After his close relationship with Keaton, he was understandably reluctant to embark on another. As he describes that period, he "dated around, living with girls from two days to two weeks" and "having sex only with people I liked a lot". Certainly he liked Mia Farrow a lot—enough to buy her a delightful weekend house

Below: *Discussing the shape of things to come with Diane Keaton in* **Interiors** *(1978), his first serious drama.*
Bottom: *Sounding off as edgy New York writer Isaac Davis in* **Manhattan** *(1979).*

on Long Island and a $35 000 sable coat. Allen is not exactly known for his philanthropy, so such lavish gifts signaled that marriage was in the air. Indeed it was set for November, 1982, but Allen called it off at the eleventh hour when the story was leaked to the press.

The enigma

Allen remains very much an enigmatic and elusive figure, to the extent of refusing to collect the awards the film industry has bestowed on him, including two Oscars for *Annie Hall*—one for his directing, the other for his first-class screenplay.

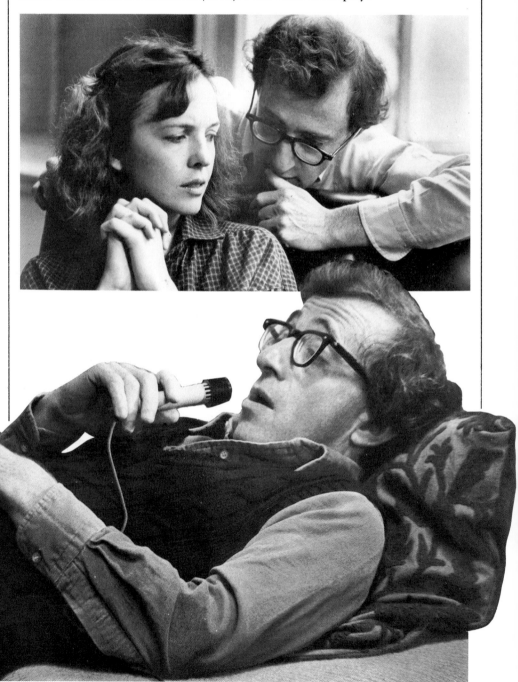

Julie Andrews

To the millions of moviegoers who saw *The Sound of Music* and *Mary Poppins* (both released in 1965), Julie Andrews will always remain a well-scrubbed, rather asexual girl-next-door.

Julie sees herself differently, and has almost made a career out of trying to erase this image and replace it with something a little raunchier. But way back in *Torn Curtain* (1966), even the skills of Alfred Hitchcock—a master at revealing the fire beneath the ice-cool image of a succession of "refined" beauties—could not get the "Joan Collins" out of her. Andrews was wooden and ill at ease throughout.

Goody two shoes

More recently she has become bolder, baring her breasts in *S.O.B.* (1981) and playing a transvestite nightclub singer in the very well received *Victor/Victoria* (1982). Even these later films have failed to break the mold however. Like it or not, she is still the fans favorite Goody Two Shoes. And it seems that the reason this wholesome image has stuck like glue is that the real Julie Andrews *is* charming, funny and a little prim, just like the roles that launched her career.

In an industry where sexual scandal, adultery and divorce are now all too common, she writes children's books, looks after her family—which includes two adopted Vietnamese orphans—and lives a life of something approaching domestic bliss. She has been married to the same man, film director Blake Edwards, for over 15 years, which is something approaching a miracle in Hollywood.

Childhood debut

But Julie's life has not been without the occasional wrinkles. Born in Surrey, England in 1935, she was only four when her parents decided to divorce.

From then on she spent most of her time on the move, traveling with her mother and stepfather's vaudeville act round end-of-the-pier shows. She was just 13 when she made her own stage debut. In the same year she met the 13-year-old Tony Walton, later to make his mark as a stage designer, and destined to become her first husband.

Her career blossomed and she was a

The well-scrubbed, wholesome image of Hollywood's favorite girl next door (left) took quite a battering. First came the cleavage in **Darling Lili** (1970), directed by Blake Edwards (below), before being replaced in 1982 by the stunning leggy transvestite club singer (above) in **Victor/Victoria**.

smash success as Eliza in both the Broadway and London stage productions of *My Fair Lady*. It seemed inevitable that she would be asked to star in the film version, but the plum part went to Audrey Hepburn. Andrews, now married to Walton, was pointedly absent from the glittering first night but, true to form, she was angry when Audrey did not receive an Oscar nomination. "It wasn't Audrey who passed me over when they were casting," she said and then went on to collect the best actress award herself, for *Mary Poppins*.

Fame and marriage

The Sound Of Music and international acclaim followed, Andrews moved to Hollywood, while Walton stayed with his work in New York. Walton stayed where his work was—in New York. For a time they wrote constantly, as well as sending each other longer letters recorded on tape. But the separation began to take its toll on their marriage. Walton insisted that she shouldn't mope at home and Andrews began to be seen at parties, squired by a number of eligible Hollywood bachelors, including rising young director Blake Edwards.

Mental cruelty

In 1967 Andrews filed for divorce on the ground of mental cruelty. Until this day, however, she has always refused to discuss exactly what this entailed. "It was a personal disaster," she says. "Day after day I would go off to my room and cry for hours. It was such a shock that I needed a psychiatrist to help calm me."

Things started to go badly in other ways too: her next film *Star!* (1968) was an expensive flop. Rumors of temperament on the set began to circulate and the press blamed her for the break-up of the Blake Edwards' marriage. Julie describes the period as "a long tunnel", from which she only emerged with the help of her analyst and Blake, whom she married in 1969.

It has been an exceptionally happy marriage, however. "Why do I love Blackie?" she asks herself, using her pet-name for her husband. "I like what he is. He is very good for me, he is straight and pulls me up when I go straying into something that is wrong for me. Life is tremendous fun with him. And, I find him very attractive." All in all, just what Mary Poppins would have ordered.

Fred Astaire

Late last century, Frederic Austerlitz —a young subaltern in the Austro-Hungarian army—was jailed for grinning at his brother, who also happened to be his senior officer. He should have saluted, not grinned at him! When Frederic was released he resigned his commission and emigrated to the States, where he met and married schoolteacher Ann Geilus. Thus their son, the greatest popular dancer the world has known, was born an American; otherwise the history of the Hollywood musical might have been very different.

Unbelievably, young Fred's first 32 years were overshadowed by his elder sister, Adele. It was her precocious dancing talent that persuaded their proud parents to put Adele and Fred on the stage, with the new surname of Astaire, taken from their grandmother's family.

Pitched into vaudeville, their experience and polish were unrivaled by the time they reached their twenties. They were leading Broadway stars throughout the 1920s and many of their successes were the musicals that Fred would later film.

Friend of Royalty

When they visited England, they were taken up by the fashionable set—Fred became a close friend of his near-contemporary the Prince of Wales, later Edward VIII. But on stage, Adele was always the senior partner until, following *The Band Wagon* in 1931, she retired to marry into the English aristocracy.

Gay Divorcee was Astaire's first and last Broadway show without his sister. Then he, too, married—a divorcee, and heiress to a rumored $20 million—and moved to Hollywood.

Fred's racket

An earlier screen test had elicited the famous verdict: "Can't act. Slightly bald. Can dance a little." Fred himself commented, "I was a weird-looking character but you didn't have to be a handsome dog. That's not my racket."

Fred's racket was dancing, and this time he was luckier. After a brief appearance in a Joan Crawford vehicle, he was cast as second lead in the RKO picture *Flying Down to Rio* (1933), opposite a youngster he had worked with in New York, Ginger Rogers. Their dance duet, introduced by Ginger saying, "We'll show 'em a thing or three," stole the picture. As RKO wired Astaire, "It was a colossal success stop offering seven year contract stop." With his legs now insured for $300 000 the cycle of 10 Fred and Ginger movies had begun.

A high flying 1930s hoofer in uniform (left); *and going through his paces in* **The Gay Divorcee** (1934), *with Ginger Rogers* (below).

It was a chemistry that worked. As Katharine Hepburn put it, "He gave her class and she gave him sex." But sex is usually more popular than class. Temporarily assigned another partner, Astaire experienced the first flop in his career, and RKO quickly remixed the proven formula.

Relentless perfectionist

Though their screen personalities meshed so well, the pair were forever denying press stories that they were either in love or at each other's throats; the actual relationship seems to have been cool. Ginger was a competent hoofer—"a Charleston dancer" in Fred's slightly ungallant phrase—but she had ambitions, not only as a dancer but also as an actress. She doubtlessly felt held back as Fred's partner. He was a relentless perfectionist and worrier —"Moaning Minnie" Adele always called him. Genuinely shy and self-effacing, he never quite believed in himself as a movie star.

As if to demonstrate that their partnership was strictly business, Ginger still refers to him as "Mr Astaire", and was conspicuously absent from the 1981 ceremony at which the American Film Institute honoured him with its Life Achievement Award, an all-star occasion.

With the partnership finally ended, Astaire's career drifted in the 1940s. He moved from studio to studio, from screen partner to screen partner, toying with the idea of retirement.

Indian summer

But at MGM a new enthusiasm for and expertise in musicals was developing under a brilliant producer called Arthur Freed. When his leading dance star Gene Kelly broke an ankle

Above: *Activity is the key to longevity as Astaire proves at home in 1978, a year before his eightieth birthday.*

preparing *Easter Parade* (1948), Freed coaxed Astaire from his racehorses to take over.

The flame rekindled, Astaire enjoyed an Indian summer, playing lover-as-father-figure to young ballerinas like Cyd Charisse in *The Band Wagon* (1953) and Leslie Caron in *Daddy Long Legs* (1955), charming *ingénues* like Audrey Hepburn in one of his finest films, *Funny Face* (1957), and Vera-Ellen in *The Belle of New York* (1952). On television he found perhaps

his most dynamic partner of all, Barrie Chase.

Suddenly widowed in 1954, Fred lived with his mother until her death at 97. His career continued with occasional acting roles and he danced one more time as Kelly's co-narrator on *That's Entertainment II* (1976). Though he was appalled to see himself, no-one else could fault him, at 77 still fleet of foot, deft and elegant.

After squiring a succession of young women, including Frank Sinatra's younger daughter, Fred entered his eighties married to a 35-year-old jockey. The couple live privately in Beverly Hills.

Lauren Bacall

Lauren Bacall was just 19 when she made her Hollywood debut in *To Have and Have Not* (1944), but it was to be the biggest success of her career. In a publicity campaign carefully orchestrated by Warner Brothers and director Howard Hawks—and inspired by her sultry on-screen persona—she became known as "The Look". She later revealed that "The Look" originated because she was so nervous during filming that she had to keep her head down to prevent it from trembling. However, that pose—chin lowered, eyes raised seductively—became her trademark.

Born in 1924 in New York City, and christened Betty Perske, she attended the American Academy of Dramatic Arts, making her Broadway debut in 1942. In March 1943 she appeared on the cover of the magazine *Harper's Bazaar* and was noticed by Howard Hawks' wife, who showed the picture to her husband. He summoned Bacall to Hollywood, and within a month she had started work on *To Have and Have Not*, opposite Humphrey Bogart.

One-track mind

The chemistry between Bogart and Bacall was dynamic. They fell in love on screen and off, and on the film's release in 1944 it was evident to all that the many sexual innuendoes in their scenes together reflected their real feelings. Bacall had always had a one-track mind when it came to what she called her "crushes", but she had not previously had an affair. Taking on the worldly Bogart at first caused her anguish because he could not make a clean break from third wife Mayo Methot, whose extreme jealousy was inflamed by a drink problem.

Though the two lovers tried to keep their liaison a secret, it attracted attention almost from the start and so displeased Hawks that he tried to pair off Bacall with Clark Gable instead! But Bogart obtained his divorce and "Slim" and "Steve" (they adopted in real life the names they had used in the film that brought them together) were married in May 1945, when she was 20 and he 45.

As a couple their publicity value was immense, but the critics never liked Bacall as much again and she fast gained a reputation as a rebel, being

Above: *The sultry teenage beauty that captured Humphrey Bogart's heart.*

suspended a dozen times by Warner Brothers for refusing parts. However, she did get to play opposite Bogart in three more films, most notably in *The Big Sleep* (1946). Their marriage, too, thrived. A son, Stephen, and a daughter, Leslie, were born.

When the House Un-American Activities Committee investigations into Hollywood began in 1947, she and Bogart were among a group of celebrities that flew to Washington to make a formal protest. This was the start of her involvement in politics as an active Democrat.

Throughout the early 1950s she had several flirtations with other men, though none serious enough to threaten her marriage. Democratic

presidential candidate Adlai Stevenson was the focus of her energies for a time and she worked for his (unsuccessful) campaign, causing Bogart a little jealousy. Composer Leonard Bernstein was another brief infatuation.

Turbulent affair

Bacall's happy marriage ended tragically, however, when she was only 32. Bogart was operated on for cancer in March 1956, without success, and she nursed him devotedly until he died nearly a year later.

The shock of his death has reverberated throughout her life, but at the time she needed an object for her affections and within a few months was involved in a turbulent relationship with Frank Sinatra. This time friends were doubtful of a happy outcome and they were right—Sinatra's

volatile nature could not cope with her increasing dependence. He did ask her to marry him, but blamed her when news of their engagement was leaked to the press. He called it off and ignored her whenever they met for the next six years—behaviour which she has never forgiven.

Working back in the New York theater, she met and fell in love with Jason Robards, in whom many saw a close resemblance to Bogart. Robards was unpredictable and a heavy drinker, but she was determined not to let these problems jeopardize their life together. Robards' second wife filed suit for adultery, citing Bacall. When the

Left: *A little larger than life to publicize* **To Have and Have Not** *(1944).*
Below: *Playing happy families, with Bogart and son Stephen in 1949.*
Bottom: *A brief lull in her turbulent friendship with Frank Sinatra, in 1957.*

couple married in Mexico in July 1961, Bacall was four months pregnant; their son Sam was born in December. But from the start things did not run smoothly and they separated long before their divorce in 1969.

Recognition—and a snub

Bacall always wanted to be acknowledged in her own right and not just as Bogart's widow. Her part in the Broadway musical *Applause* which won her a Tony award in 1970 was therefore one of her most satisfying professional achievements. She became involved with her much younger co-star Len Cariou, but he left the show after a year.

Plans to marry tough-guy Harry Guardino were called off in 1983 and, in the same year, there was a post-script to her old affair with Sinatra—at a showbiz party "old blue eyes" reportedly snubbed her one more time.

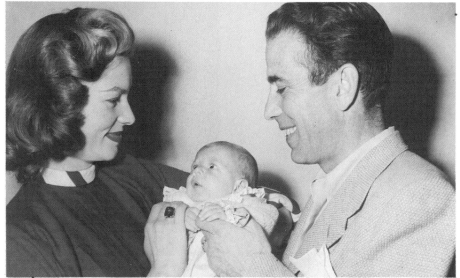

Brigitte Bardot

For two successive generations, the provocative, pouting sex-kitten has been the personification of female sexuality on and off screen—enticing bait for the succession of men in her private and cinematic life.

Bardot's personal life has always aroused more interest than her films. Wherever she goes, the press follows, eager for a new story about her often turbulent sex-life: three marriages, divorces, suicide attempts and stormy love-affairs. Even at 50, Bardot still makes the headlines.

Ugly duckling

Her story is that of Cinderella in reverse: the rich girl who went to the ball, only to find emptiness and disillusion. Born on September 28, 1934, the daughter of a wealthy industrialist, Bardot went to a private school where she showed a certain flair for dancing. She describes herself then as "ugly with thin hair. I wore spectacles and a brace on my teeth."

At 15 she appeared on the cover of *Elle*, France's leading fashion magazine, and Roger Vadim—her future husband and mentor—was transfixed by her sultry image. Despite opposition from her parents, he married her three years later, but not before Bardot had made her first suicide bid while he was away filming in the South of France.

She became an international star in *And God Created Woman* (1956), but the subsequent limelight proved such a strain on her already fragile marriage that the couple divorced in 1957.

Love lesson

Bardot consoled herself in a romantic interlude with actor Jean-Louis Trintignant, but when he received his call-up papers, she publicly announced that she would not spend the next 18 months as a grass-widow. Trintignant walked out of her life.

Nonplussed, Bardot threw herself into her work as never before, but the bedroom scene in *La Femme et le Pantin* (1958) just wouldn't go right. After two hours of fruitless romping, Julien Duvivier, the director, told the

Right: A characteristic pose from the privileged sex kitten who took the world by storm in the early 1950s.

scantily dressed starlet how to make love to her Spanish co-star Antonio Vilar. "Let me make love my own way," she snapped. "*I* know how to make love."

There followed a romance with Sacha Distel, then marriage to her handsome co-star in *Babette Goes to War* (1959), Jacques Charrier.

By 1960 Bardot knew she would never become a *great* actress and told reporters, "This Brigitte Bardot I have created is a monster. She is not me." Then, during the making of one of her best films, *La Vérité* (1960) Bardot fell in love again, with co-star Sami Frey. But on her twenty-sixth birthday she swallowed some sleeping-pills and slashed her wrists. She was rushed to hospital just in time. The following year, her marriage to Charrier ended.

Then, during the 1963 Cannes Film Festival, Brigitte met a handsome Brazilian car dealer, Bob Zaguri, who whisked her off to Rio. Again, it was fated not to last. In 1966, Bardot was in a St Tropez restaurant with Zaguri when in walked Vadim with one of Europe's most eligible bachelors, the wealthy German industrialist Günther Sachs, who soon won Bardot's heart. They were married in Las Vegas but, despite her efforts to lead a life more suited to her new title of Countess, a deepening rift between them became apparent during the filming of *Shalako* (1968). Bardot remarked, "Günther is dry, artificial, always obsessed with

Above: *Bardot, aged 30, displays her charms in a* **Ravishing Idiot** *(1964).* Below: *The bashful bride-to-be, before she married Jacques Charrier in 1959.*

Above: *An impassioned plea on behalf of animals from their new champion.*

making an impression." The couple were divorced in 1969.

Patrique Gilles, a 23-year-old student, provided a welcome distraction for Bardot. He appeared in her next film, *Les Femmes* (1969), in the role he was all too soon to play in real life, Bardot's discarded lover.

Naked uproar
In 1973, Vadim cast her in his film *Don Juan*, and she made headlines again. Her naked love scene with Jane Birkin caused an uproar. But at 38, Bardot could still display a 35-23-35 figure, the same measurements as in 1952, the year of her first film.

By 1974, the seemingly ageless Bardot had formed yet another romantic attachment, this time with the Czechoslovakian sculptor Miroslav Brozek, "Now I'd just adore to be his wife. I am available. If he needs me, I'm there." They split up after a happy relationship of almost five years, which left her quite philosophical: "With my experience, I say you can never count on a man. I give myself completely in love and when I discover I get nothing in return, nothing is the same."

On the night of her forty-ninth birthday party she once again attempted suicide, was discovered by her gardener and rushed to the Oasis Clinic, St Tropez.

Now recovered, what has Bardot in store for us? Another film? Possibly. Another conquest? Of that there can be no doubt.

John Barrymore

Few stars have fallen so completely, and from such a great height, as John Barrymore. In 1925 he was at his peak: a triumphant Hamlet on the London stage and, at 43, about to become a romantic screen swashbuckler to rival Fairbanks. Ten years later he was in the grip of alcoholism, his memory deserting him and the celebrated matinee-idol-looks which had earned him the nickname of the "Great Profile", grown puffy and blurred almost beyond recognition.

Alcohol and illness

Displaying an early sense of timing, Barrymore came into the world on St Valentine's Day 1882. He was born into a theatrical family—both his parents were actors—and after dabbling in journalism, followed his brother Lionel and sister Ethel on to the boards in 1903. The same year his father suffered a complete mental collapse and two years later died in New York's Bellevue Hospital. In the 1930s, when alcoholism and failing memory began to torment him, Barrymore was haunted by his father's illness.

Barrymore's stage breakthrough came in 1909, in a light comedy, *The Fortune Hunter*. Already, he was drinking heavily and, according to his biographer Gene Fowler, succeeded in "smelling more of alcohol than fame" until Galsworthy's *Justice* established him as a dramatic actor. By then he had also made his screen debut in *An American Citizen* (1913), the first of a series of athletic comedy-thrillers.

A bravura performance in *Dr Jekyll and Mr Hyde* (1920), in which Barrymore achieved a remarkable on-screen transformation without the aid of make-up, gained him world acclaim.

Stormy marriages

The year 1920 also saw his marriage to the poetess Michael Strange, a remarkable character with "the face of a Romney portrait and the spirit of a US Marine". It was but the second of four stormy marriages. Many years later Barrymore recalled, "I never

Top Right: The profile that launched the screen lover of a generation.
Right: At home with Dolores Costello, one of four wives, and their daughter.

married any of my wives—they married me."

In 1924 he arrived in Hollywood to play the title role in Warners' *Beau Brummel*. This led to an affair with his co-star, the ravishing 17-year-old Mary Astor and a contract with Warner Brothers at the immense fee of $76 250 a picture.

Next came *The Sea Beast* (1926), an adaptation of *Moby Dick*. Vying with the great white whale for Barrymore's attention was his beautiful co-star Dolores Costello. Barrymore became infatuated with her and a year later, filming *When A Man Loves* (1927), deliberately threw away scene after scene in order to build up her performance. She went to the altar with him in 1928, but life with the star proved something of a trial. In the early 1930s, when he was desperately trying to control his alcoholism, he was reduced to drinking perfume from Costello's dressing table.

Hard drinking

In 1927, Barrymore moved to United Artists at a fee of $150 000 a film, but as fast as the money came in he spent it. His rambling estate, "Bella Vista", consisted of no less than 16 separate buildings containing 45 rooms. A dozen servants tended the two swimming pools, trout pond, bowling green, skeet-shooting range and aviary, whose exotic inhabitants included Barrymore's pet vulture Maloney.

Hard-drinking guests—of whom there was no shortage—could drown their sorrows in a replica English pub or a genuine frontier saloon shipped all

Below: *Almost the end for the ruined alcoholic as he "spanks" wife Elaine in* **My Dear Children** *(1940).*

the way from Alaska.

Thanks largely to his mellifluous voice and his perfect profile, Barrymore stayed at the top for another five years. In 1932, five films netted him $375 000, and in MGM's *Grand Hotel*, opposite Greta Garbo, he gave one of his finest performances. But drink was taking its toll. He had developed a paunch, and a dewlap under his chin; his glazed eyes were sinking into nests of wrinkles and his voice became increasingly slurred.

Off the set, however, he still played the Great Lover. In her first film, *A Bill of Divorcement* (1932), Katharine Hepburn was cast as his daughter. After the first day's shooting, Barrymore invited her to his dressing room where he received her, naked except for his socks. As she shrank back, he exclaimed, "My dear, any young girl would be thrilled to make love to the great John Barrymore." "Not me," cried Hepburn.

Fading idol

In *Dinner at Eight* (1933), he came close to playing himself, a fading matinee idol. In the same year, drink finally exacted a terrible price. During the shooting of a scene for *Counselor-at-Law* (1933) his memory deserted him; after 56 takes he still could not get it right. Next day he played it perfectly, but the writing was on the wall. There was a final brilliant performance, with Carole Lombard, in *Twentieth Century* (1934) and then decline.

By the end of the decade he was relegated to supporting roles and leads in B movies, relying heavily on huge prompt cards. Occasionally he rallied. In *Midnight* (1939) he gave a charming performance, although co-star Mary Astor later recalled that throughout the shooting he had little or no idea of what the film was about.

During the last three years of his life he kept going by parodying his own image. With fourth wife, Elaine Barrie, he toured in a grisly play *My Dear Children* and audiences flocked to see the former great star fluff his lines and fall over the furniture. In *The Great Profile* (1940), he was a broken-down old ham actor and on Rudy Vallee's radio show played stooge to guests such as Groucho Marx. One night Mary Astor spotted him alone in a corridor of the radio studio, sagging against a wall like someone "who just couldn't walk another step". He died, poverty stricken, in 1942.

Warren Beatty

As the Bachelor King of Hollywood, Warrèn Beatty gained the reputation of being a modern Don Juan. Some of the world's most beautiful women—Joan Collins, Natalie Wood, Leslie Caron, Julie Christie, Jane Seymour, Kate Jackson and Diane Keaton—fell for his smooth brand of irresistible masculine charm.

Recluse
Since turning 40, however, Beatty has become something of a recluse, though still concerned to preserve on celluloid his boyish good looks. For the film *Heaven Can Wait* (1978) he is reported to have insisted on countless retakes and soft-focus close ups. Away from film-making, he now spends a lot of time alone, surrounded by his books. He seems finally to have outgrown the heady days of parties at

Above: *The face that launched celebrated love affairs*.

Playboy boss Hugh Hefner's luxury mansion, surrounded by a bevy of attentive and adoring beauties.

Born in March 1937, Beatty is the younger brother of actress Shirley MacLaine. Their mother worked as a drama coach and, while he was still at school, Warren appeared in some of the amateur stage productions she directed.

However this childhood training did not lead him straight into the theater. He worked in the construction business for a time before taking drama lessons and breaking into television. The doors to the big time opened with his starring role in Broadway's *A Loss of Roses*.

He moved to Hollywood in 1960, making his big-screen debut in

Splendour in the Grass (1961). With his unique charisma and youthful looks reminiscent of James Dean, he soon won the attention of his leading lady, Natalie Wood, who left her husband, Robert Wagner, to live with Beatty. But the time was not right for him to settle down to a serious commitment. Soon he was involved with the beautiful French actress Leslie Caron, and this led to a divorce case in which he was named co-respondent.

Playboy parody
International fame followed in the wake of his portrayal of gangster Clyde Barrow in the runaway success *Bonnie and Clyde* (1967). It was largely thanks to Beatty that the film was made. He had been approached by the scriptwriters and, fired with enthusiasm, produced the film as well

as taking on the very demanding role of Barrow.

One of Beatty's most popular and successful screen roles poked fun at his Hollywood playboy image. This was his Beverly Hills hairdresser-cum-superstud in *Shampoo* (1975), in which he bedded Goldie Hawn, Lee Grant, Carrie Fisher and Julie Christie all in a single day . . . the film was made shortly after the break-up of his off-screen relationship with Christie.

In 1975, the Hollywood grapevine buzzed with the news that Beatty had at last been hooked and intended to marry singer Michelle Phillips. Beatty, who had spent the previous few years living in hotels, had bought her a magnificent house in a secluded area of Beverly Hills. He did not move in however, and the affair came to an end three years later.

Breaking new ground

His most publicized affair was with Oscar-winning actress Diane Keaton. The couple were constantly photographed together and rumours of an impending marriage became stronger when it was announced they would star in *Reds* (1981). The film broke new ground in Hollywood popular entertainment for its historical accuracy in tracing the career of John Reed, a founder of the American Communist party.

Many welcomed *Reds* as the final proof that McCarthyism in Hollywood was dead: for the first time, a Hollywood film portrayed communists as people like any other. Reed was shown to be a well-meaning American, opposed to the exploitation of the working class of America – and not a dangerous and ruthless agent with

Above Left: *A moment of intimacy with Faye Dunaway for the virile anti-hero of* **Bonnie and Clyde** *(1967), the film that put Beatty's name in lights and triggered his career as a producer.* Above: *With Diane Keaton, Beatty's co-star in* **Reds** *(1981), a film he co-scripted, produced, directed.*

Moscow's interests at heart.

Beatty's commitment to the project was total—not only did he play Reed, he also produced, directed and co-scripted the film.

Reds was summed up as "not only putting a new perspective on history as seen through the eyes of Hollywood, but doing it in a new way, thus pushing back the boundaries of American commercial cinema". No mean achievement—or accolade—for a former playboy.

Ingrid Bergman

When producer Hal B. Wallis bought the play *Everybody Goes to Rick's* he intended it for Ronald Reagan and Ann Sheridan. Then he realized that it would be a much better vehicle for Humphrey Bogart. A Bogart-Sheridan teaming would be old hat. But Ingrid Bergman, Hollywood's favorite new romantic actress, who was under contract to David O. Selznick, was available.

Bergman found Selznick vague about the Warner project. "I don't quite know what the story is," he told her, "but I'm glad you're going to be beautifully dressed and you'll have a beautiful entrance." When filming began, she was none the wiser. The script arrived a day at a time and nobody knew how the picture would end. In such hit or miss fashion does Hollywood sometimes make a masterpiece, for the film was *Casablanca* (1943) and it put Bergman and Bogart among the immortals.

This success led to Bergman being given the role she most wanted—Maria in *For Whom the Bell Tolls* (1943). It was this role, in a movie that now seems dated and ponderous, for which she received an Oscar nomination rather than for her luminous presence in *Casablanca*. But both parts called on her to suffer doomed love, and this particular theme, in all its variations— forbidden love, impossible love, exploited love—rapidly became Bergman's speciality.

Destined for Hollywood

She was born August 29 1915 in Stockholm and, before her teens had lost her German mother, her father and, subsequently, the aunt who had brought her up. A lonely, withdrawn child, she fell in love with the theater and, at 17, became a student at the Royal Dramatic Theater School in Stockholm. Within two years, she had broken into films, making 11 in 6 years. The sixth, *Intermezzo* (1936), brought her international recognition. One famous showbusiness newspaper reported: "Ingrid Bergman's star is destined for Hollywood."

Selznick brought her to Hollywood in 1939 to remake *Intermezzo* in English. At her own insistence, Bergman came to do just the one film rather than on the then traditional seven-year contract. She was already married to Peter Lindström, a Swedish doctor who, at 34, could not be expected to throw up his career, and she had a one-year-old daughter, Pia.

Only when *Intermezzo* (1939) proved to be a great success did Bergman agree to stay in Hollywood. Her husband re-arranged his affairs to work in Los Angeles, but their marriage fell victim to the different commitments that kept them apart.

Prime years

Under her Selznick contract, Bergman made 11 pictures, all but two of them on loan to other companies. These were her prime years. She won her first Oscar for *Gaslight* (1944), then worked for Hitchcock, appearing in *Spellbound* (1945) and *Notorious* (1946).

In 1946, at the age of 30 and with her contract running out, Bergman's life reached the crossroads. Only Bing Crosby still topped her at the box office. In loaning her to RKO to appear with Crosby in *The Bells of St Mary's* (1945), Selznick commanded cash and rights terms worth $½ million. Bergman now had other plans; she had seen in New York a film that was to change her life, Roberto Rossellini's *Roma Città Aperta*.

Fired with new enthusiasm and encouraged by a more settled period in her marriage, she went freelance and launched into three movies that Selznick would never have sanctioned. In *Arch of Triumph* (1948), she played a prostitute and received bad notices, a double blow because she and Lindström had invested capital in the film. *Joan of Arc* (1948), was as resounding a flop as the Maxwell Anderson play on which it was based had been a hit. *Under Capricorn* (1949) was a minor Hitchcock movie and failed at the box office.

But Bergman had now seen *Paisan*, like *Roma* directed by Rossellini. Beset by failure, Bergman saw the Italian neo-realist school as a beacon of hope and she wrote to

Below: *International acclaim opposite Leslie Howard in* **Intermezzo** *(1939).*

Rossellini: "I am ready to come and make a film with you for the sheer pleasure of the experience." Rossellini met the Lindströms and together they planned *Stromboli* (1950), a movie to be written and directed by Rossellini, in Italy, starring Bergman, and exciting intense speculation.

Disgrace

It is not known at what point Bergman and Rossellini became lovers but, within a year of her March 1949 arrival in Rome, their son Robertino was born. Lindström filed for divorce and Rossellini's own marriage was annulled on the grounds that he had been drugged at his wedding.

There was a tremendous outcry. In the US Senate, Bergman was denounced as "Hollywood's apostle of degradation", and Prime Minister Nehru of India called Rossellini "a scoundrel". As if that were not enough, the five other movies she made with her second husband were disasters, virtually unshown in America.

The Rossellini period came to an end in 1956, by which time Bergman had produced twin daughters.

Triumphant return

She returned to English language movies in *Anastasia* (1956) and won her second Oscar, more for her return—which was as triumphant as her earlier exile had been ignominious—than for her performance.

Bergman divorced Rossellini and, in 1958, married the Swedish impresario Lars Schmidt. She also renewed acquaintance with her estranged daughter Pia.

Bergman divided her last 25 years between theater, television and films made in a number of countries. Her output was enlivened by *The Inn of the Sixth Happiness* (1958), her supporting Oscar for *Murder on the Orient Express* (1974) and her one movie with her countryman Ingmar Bergman, *Autumn Sonata* (1978). But when she died in August 1982, after a courageous and long battle against cancer, it was *Casablanca* that television stations the world over reached for as a tribute to her consummate art and appeal.

Humphrey Bogart

Humphrey Bogart was a turn-of-the-century Christmas present for upper-middle-class parents who didn't really deserve one. "Got gypped out of a proper birthday, goddammit," was his long running protest about entering the world on December 25, 1899 but, in fact, he had more cause for complaint than that. His father, a Manhattan surgeon, and his bossy, artist mother were both critical and cold, and Bogart responded by setting up a veil of insolence to protect himself from them.

In the long term, that anti-authoritarian veneer became his screen stock in trade but it did not impress his parents. He continued to disappoint them, failing to pass the entrance examination for Yale University.

Scarred in a scuffle

To escape their rage he joined the US Navy, where a scuffle with a prisoner he was escorting resulted in a wound to his lip that left him with the lopsided smile and inimitable lisp that even now, nearly 30 years after his death, contribute to the charm of the world's most popular film actor.

After an honorable discharge in 1918 and a spell as a runner for a Wall Street broker, Bogart took to the boards in a play called *Drifting* (1922). The critics were not impressed, but his first line, "Tennis anyone?" set the tone for his early stage career as an upper crust, sophisticated juvenile lead.

Whisky galore

To Bogart this establishment image was an anathema and he set about counteracting it with long drinks and short marriages. He formed a life-long bond with Scotch whisky which he drank heavily, and at times excessively, without ever letting it affect his work. "I don't trust any bastard who doesn't drink," was one of his creeds, and he repeated it often.

As for women, he found them at work. The first was Helen Menken, a former child star whom he met in *Drifting* and married when he was 25. As she was a sophisticated, intelligent woman of the theatrical world while he

Top right: *The classic gangster at the peak of his career in the mid-1940s.*
Right: *Dressed to fight the night away with third wife Mayo Methot in 1942.*

was an ignorant and frequently unemployed hick, the union never put down roots.

Helen was replaced in 1928 by Mary Philips, a stabilizing influence through 10 long years of struggle as Bogart tried to establish himself. "Mary was exactly right for him during the time he required more comfort than inspiration," observed Louise Brooks. That time ran out when his portrayal of Duke Mantee in *The Petrified Forest* (1936) finally proved his potential.

Battling Bogarts

Wife number three was Mayo Methot, a sub-Mae West with a deep cleavage and a ferocious jealousy of any woman her husband met. As Bogart was to churn out more than 20 carbon copies of Duke Mantee in four years, he came into close contact with every starlet who could play a gangster's moll. So began the era of "The Battling Bogarts", with Mayo not only keeping a vengeful eye on his progress with the ladies, but matching him refill for refill, although she had nothing like his resistance to alcohol.

A surprisingly diminutive screen tough guy, Bogart was familiar with the occupational hazard of large drunks towering over him with intent to pulp him just to prove they could. With Mayo around to back him up in the bar-room brawls, he sometimes gave in to the stirrer's temptation to go too far. On other occasions, he became

With Lauren Bacall and their boxer dog Harvey (below); *heading the march on Washington in protest against the House of Un-American Activities investigations in 1947* (bottom).

the focus of her violence, once even getting a carving knife in the back. "Only went in a little way," he commented to the doctor.

One of Bogie's many good qualities was his loyalty. Even when Mayo became a confirmed alcoholic, losing her looks and career in the process, she could count on his support. "She's an actress, a damned good one, but she's not working much at the moment, which is tough for her. Understand?" And anyone who really valued his friendship did.

The fourth Mrs Humphrey Bogart presented no such problems. He met and fell in love with Lauren Bacall, commonly known as Betty, when they worked together on the set of *To Have and Have Not* (1944).

A perfect marriage

It was a marriage made in heaven, although she was 20 and he 45. He never looked at another woman. He loved her honesty, spirit, common sense and the way she never nagged, as well as her spectacular looks. He even cut back on Scotch, "Because Betty doesn't go for it too much."

When Bacall and Bogart met the actor was approaching the pinnacle of his career. His association with John Huston, in *High Sierra* and *The Maltese Falcon* (both in 1941) triggered off a run of triumphs that included *Casablanca* (1943) for Michael Curtiz and *To Have and Have Not* and *The Big Sleep* (1946) for Howard Hawks. Another Huston trio, *The Treasure of the Sierra Madre* and *Key Largo* (both in 1948), and *The African Queen* (1951) set the seal on the creation of a cult hero, the last named winning him Best Actor's Oscar. Sadly, *The Caine Mutiny* (1954), was the only one of his remaining films to make much of a reputation—and by then he was a sick man.

Bogart died of cancer in January, 1957, almost a year after an eight-hour operation had failed to halt the disease. John Huston said in his funeral address, "No one who sat in his presence during the final weeks would ever forget. It was a unique display of sheer animal courage. After the first visit—it took that to get over the initial shock of his appearance—one quickened to the grandeur of it, expanded and felt strangely elated, proud to be there, proud to be his friend, the friend of such a brave man."

Clara Bow

In 1960, Clara Bow told gossip columnist Hedda Hopper, "I slip my old crown of 'It Girl' not to Taylor or Bardot but Monroe." In *The Plastic Age* (1925), Bow had been billed as "The Hottest Jazz Baby in Films", a wild party girl bursting with boop-boop-a-doop. Now, she was a 55-year-old recluse suffering from chronic insomnia and moving restlessly from one sanatorium to another, consoling herself with whisky.

Bow's choice of Monroe as her successor was doubly poignant, for her own career was a rehearsal for Marilyn's unhappy stardom. Like Marilyn, she was a child of the cinema, with great natural talent.

Escape from poverty

Clara was the model for all the aspiring young actresses who have escaped from poverty-stricken homes to the bright, empty glamor of Hollywood. There was a miserable childhood in Brooklyn and a mentally disturbed mother who threatened teenage Clara with a meat cleaver.

She was 17 when first prize in a beauty competition run by *Motion Picture Classic* magazine bought a ticket out of Brooklyn and a small part in *Beyond the Rainbow* (1922). Clara ended up on the cutting-room floor but later, when she was famous, the scenes were restored and the film re-issued.

A part in *Down to the Sea in Ships* (1923) led to a contract with independent producer B.P. Schulberg.

Beestung lips

When Schulberg went to Paramount in 1926, he took Bow with him as part of the deal. Within a year she was a star.

Paramount built *It* (1927) around her ebullient personality, casting her as Betty Lou, the shopgirl who sets her cap at her boss. Betty Lou embodied the 1920s belief that a girl with pep and bounce could always get on, provided that she had plenty of that mysterious quality "It".

Bow had "It" in abundance—in her beestung lips, expectantly pursed for a kiss, in her ripe body and tumbling mass of hennaed hair. Whenever a likely looking man appeared on the horizon, she moved into action, hips thrust provocatively forward in unabashed invitation.

Her sexiness was underlined by the skimpy costumes she often wore in her films. In *My Lady of Whims* (1926), her nipples were clearly visible, pressing against a clinging dress. In *The Wild Party* (1929), her first talkie, she arrived at a roadhouse wearing a mink coat over a sketchy swimsuit.

"The Brooklyn Bonfire"

Off the set, "The Brooklyn Bonfire" indulged a lifestyle which was an extension of her racy screen image. She was regularly seen driving down Wilshire Boulevard in a Kissel convertible, painted red to match her

Above: *A 1920s publicity shot of the "It Girl", with bee-sting lips and a lifestyle as racy off screen as on.*

hair, and accompanied by a pair of yapping chows whose coats had been dyed the same shade.

On a whim, she invited the whole USC football squad— famous as "The Thundering Herd"— to scrimmage with her on her lawn, at midnight. One of the Herd was a brawny young athlete called Marion Morrison, later to change his name to John Wayne.

Bow survived the arrival of sound, although her habit of dashing

impulsively all over the set posed a few problems for the primitive recording apparatus of the day. In a national USA poll of 1929, she was voted number 1 female star, but her days at the top were also numbered.

In 1930, the tabloid newspapers broke the story of "Clara's Love Balm Romance", the "Balm" in question being the intimate treatment provided by society doctor William Earl Pearson for a "nervous condition". Mrs Pearson successfully sued the star for "alienation of affections". No sooner had that scandal died down than Bow ran up a $14 000 gambling debt in a Nevada casino. She refused to pay up, claiming that she had not grasped the value of the IOUs she had scribbled.

Drink, gigolos and lovers
Then, she sued her former secretary Daisy DeVoe for embezzling $15 000. DeVoe hit back in the pages of a sleazy magazine, revealing many graphic details of Bow's penchant for drink, gigolos and famous lovers— including comedian Eddie Cantor, Gary Cooper and Bela Lugosi in his pre-Dracula days. Warming to her task, DeVoe described wild weekends in which the accommodating star was gangbanged by entire football teams, who were rewarded with crates of drink.

DeVoe went to prison, but Bow had won a hollow victory. The studio tried to make the best of a bad job by casting her as a saloon bar floozie in *No Limit* (1931), but the public stayed away. In the same year she collapsed while making *The Secret Call*, and was replaced. She suffered the same fate in *City Streets* (1931). In her last film, Fox's *Hoopla* (1933), she was reduced to playing a pale echo of the great Mae West.

In retirement, she put on weight so alarmingly that it prevented a comeback in the 1936 *Under Two Flags*. In 1939 it was reported that she weighed 200 lb. She was a forgotten figure when, in 1947, she appeared as the mystery guest in a TV panel game.

When Bow died of a heart attack in 1965, Hedda Hopper recalled that in her later years Bow would send her a card at Christmas, asking in a spidery hand, "Do you still remember me?"

Marlon Brando

Brando is a celebrity who has transcended myth and passed straight into history. He can command $1 million for a week's work and is the man responsible for changing the style of movies, in the process influencing many actors.

Right from his first appearance, as Stanley Kowalski in Tennessee Williams' play *A Streetcar Named Desire*, on stage and then in Elia Kazan's film in 1951, Brando created characters that were painfully realistic and his then unusual style of acting, his unsmiling face, mumbling diction and belligerent attitude caused a furore.

Once described as having "the build of a gladiator, the face of a poet", Brando was born in Omaha, Nebraska on April 3, 1924. His mother was involved in the theater, but his businessman father hoped his offspring would make it in the business world. It was not to be.

Brando attended exclusive public schools including the Shattuck Military Academy in Minnesota which he left before graduating. He then went to New York, spending a year at drama school before a season in stock resulted in work on Broadway in *I Remember Mama* and other plays.

Left: *The charismatic young actor as he first hit the headlines, in* **A Streetcar Named Desire** *(1951).*

Below: *Hiding the ravages of time on his Tahitian atoll after being elected "Fat Boy of the Year", in 1977.*

Decade of successes

His appearance in *A Streetcar Named Desire* (1951) heralded a decade of glowing successes, and won him an Academy Award nomination. His next film *Viva Zapata!* (1952) brought a second. *Julius Caesar* (1953) and *The Wild One* (1954) preceded his first Oscar performance, as ex-boxer Terry Molloy in *On The Waterfront* (1954).

Throughout the 1950s he appeared in frequently controversial but always brilliant and versatile performances which veered from singing and dancing in *Guys and Dolls* (1955) to being an Oriental soothsayer in *Teahouse of the August Moon* (1956) and equally diverse parts in *Sayonara* (1957), *The Young Lions* (1958) and *The Fugitive Kind* (1959).

Brando made his directorial debut with *One-Eyed Jacks* (1961) which he also produced and starred in.

The start of a downward slide to some disappointing lows came in the 1960s when he was held partly responsible for the ill-fated and costly *Mutiny On The Bounty* (1962).

Human rights campaign

He halted his career's plummet, with a stunning comeback in Francis Ford Coppola's *The Godfather* (1972), which won him his second Oscar. By then Brando's social conscience had emerged and he sent an American Indian woman to the Academy to accept the award on his behalf, using the occasion as a mouthpiece for his personal *cause célèbre*, the plight of the American Indian.

Since then the still magnetic but now heavily overweight actor has appeared in *Last Tango in Paris* (1972), and *The Missouri Breaks* (1976) with Jack Nicholson. He also played Superman's father in *Superman* (1978), for which 10 minute cameo he earned $2¼ million plus sued-for damages which resulted in 11 per cent of the film's profits being paid to him.

The following year he was in Coppola's *Apocalypse Now* (1979), as the mad Green Beret commando who established his own empire deep in the Cambodian jungle. Then he played a Paul Getty type oil tycoon in *The Formula* (1980).

Between these recent films much of his time has been devoted to publicizing various human rights subjects. Brando worked for nothing in a 13-part TV series on Indians which

Above: *The start of something good – a gentle, first kiss for Tarita on the set of* **Mutiny On The Bounty** *(1962).*
Below: *Discretion's no longer the name of a game played with Maria Schneider in* **Last Tango in Paris** *(1972).*

he made after winning an Emmy for his TV debut as Rockwell in the series *Roots: The Next Generation*. He has also spent vast amounts on underwriting programs for the underprivileged.

Stormy relationships

Brando owns a mammoth mountaintop estate in Beverly Hills, and a 13-island atoll in Tahiti called Tetiaroa which he discovered while making *Mutiny*. Also while making *Mutiny* he met Tahitian actress Tarita Teripaim, with whom he now has a son and daughter.

His exotic and stormy relationships with women have always made front page news. He has been married and divorced twice, to actress Anna Kashfi from 1957 to 1959, who published a revealingly personal book called *Brando For Breakfast* and, in 1960, for eight years to actress Movita Castenada. He has a child from each marriage and for many years was in violent court clashes with Kashfi over the custody of their son. Latest reports claim that he plans to marry a Japanese multi-millionaire's daughter, 31 years his junior.

Now increasingly reclusive, Brando spends part of the year living on Tetiaroa.

"It's very elemental here. You have the sky, the sea, the trees, the crabs, the fish, the sun… the basics. I never run out of things to think about when I'm here," he says of his South Sea paradise.

His next film is *The Assassination of Frank Wilson* (1985) in which he will play Al Capone.

James Cagney

At his birth in July 1899, James Cagney put in an uncharacteristically frail appearance for the small but wiry human tornado who has swept through the next 85 years without impediment. It was lucky his weakness was so fleeting because turn-of-the-century New York, where his parents raised their brood, was no place for fools or those who couldn't defend themselves.

Cagney's Irish father was a gentle joker and gambler who drank his way into an early grave, so it was left to his mother, an indomitable Irish Norwegian, to hold the family together.

From her, the young Cagney inherited bright red hair and a temper to match. If survival meant fighting, and it usually did in Manhattan's teeming lower East Side, Cagney was ready and willing. He learned to box clever when he was six, and might have become a professional had not his mother had other ideas.

Chorus girl debut

Of course, these ideas did not include acting, an occupation so effete in the Cagneys' world as to be unthinkable. But when Cagney, ungainfully employed tying parcels in Wanamaker's store, heard that more than twice his salary was to be had for turning "chorus girl" in a revue called *Every Sailor*, he did not hesitate.

"We had a lot of fun and it never occurred to any of us to be ashamed of it," he said later. "I lost all consciousness of that fellow, Jim Cagney, when I put on skirts, wig, paint, powder, feathers and spangles!"

On the breadline

The hoofing skills Cagney acquired during his breadline years on and off Broadway were the ones that remained dearest to his heart. However, Hollywood had other ideas in the 1930s and it was as a gangster that he made his name in such classics as *The Public Enemy* (1931), *Angels With Dirty Faces* (1938) and *The Roaring Twenties* (1939), pictures that rocketed

Top right: *Public face of a private man after 10 years in Hollywood.*
Right: *Trial by grapefruit for Mae Clark in* **The Public Enemy** *(1931).*

him to the top of the earning lists by the end of the decade.

As he has always freely admitted, what mattered was cash in the bank. He worked "to put groceries on the table", and to provide for his family, especially his mother with whom he retained a strong bond until her death. Even she had to play second fiddle from 1920 to the only other woman in his life, Frances Willard Vernon, commonly known as "Bill", whom he met in a Broadway show.

The marriage is one of the wonders of Hollywood, more than 60 years of love and mutual devotion. "I can't conceive of how lucky a guy can get, but it's been joy all the way. My Bill and I hit it off from the beginning. Marrying her was certainly the smartest thing that I ever did."

Gun-toting maniacs
Cagney, always outspoken and obstinate, has never concealed the disdain he felt for the profession that made him rich. He bitterly resented the gun-toting maniacs and brutalizers of women it thrust upon him; he knew first hand that crime bred endless human tragedy. He hated the way that Warner Brothers systematically glamorized violence with his assistance and, on several occasions, walked out. One such absence lasted for two long years, but mogul power was still so strong in the mid-1930s that it proved impossible to work outside the system.

Above: *Spirited resistance to the cops in* **Angels with Dirty Faces** *(1938).*

However, Cagney extracted a better deal for himself and paved the way for other actors to break the studio stranglehold. Warner Brothers eventually paid all their debts to him by casting him as George M. Cohan, one of the greatest hoofers of them all, in *Yankee Doodle Dandy* (1942). The part won him his Best Actor's Oscar.

Country retreat
In films, Cagney was known for his rat-a-tat speech and rapid movement, but off the set he is a quiet, mild-mannered man. He might sip an occasional glass of champagne, but his father's experiences put him off serious drinking.

His love of the countryside began in childhood when the family spent two weeks at the house of a great-aunt in Flatbush, Brooklyn (now part of Kennedy Airport).

The Cagneys, and their two adopted children, spent their summers at their house in Martha's Vineyard, but it was only after his first retirement in 1961 that Cagney was able to indulge his countryman's instincts to the full. He bought land in Dutchess County, New York State, as a retreat. There he lived in an unpretentious stone house he helped to build.

He bred Western Highland cattle and Morgan horses, tough little

working animals that reflected his own short compact build, and frequently carried off prizes at local shows.

Today, Cagney divides his time between winter homes in Coldwater Canyon and Palm Springs and the Dutchess County farm. His re-appearance, after nearly two decades, in *Ragtime* (1981) proved that he is as alert as ever, though stoutness and stiffness have taken their toll of that electrifying hoofer's speed, and film offers still follow him to his pastoral and peaceful retreat.

Above: *Stern and poised as ever for his acclaimed comeback in* **Ragtime** *(1982).*

Charlie Chaplin

Few people would dispute that one of the greatest comic creations in the history of cinema is Charlie Chaplin's wistful, baggy trousered tramp. Everyone's favorite "little man" fighting against the odds, he not only survived the most desperate situations but made whole generations laugh and cry at the same time.

What audiences sometimes did not appreciate was that the character was the direct result of the circumstances of Chaplin's own early life.

Charles Spencer Chaplin was born over a shoe-repair shop in South London in April 1889. When he was a year old his drunken father deserted his family and, from that time on,

Mrs Chaplin—a music-hall singer—struggled alone to support her children. They just about survived until her over-strained voice began to falter. On one occasion, Chaplin, then aged five was thrust on to the stage to sing when his mother's voice failed in mid-song.

Eventually she was committed to an asylum, half-mad from malnutrition, and that night the 10-year-old Chaplin came home to "a half packet of tea,

Below left: In **Modern Times** *(1935), with third wife Paulette Goddard, whom he married two years earlier.*
Below: Re-living his own arrival in America in **The Immigrant** *(1917), with fellow silent star, Edna Purviance.*

three half-pence, some keys and several pawn tickets". He and his younger brother saved themselves from starving by earning money singing and dancing on street corners.

Charlie goes to Hollywood
His mother's music hall friends eventually got Chaplin a place with a team of child dancers and by the age of 12, still unable to read or write, he was touring the country playing a pageboy in *Sherlock Holmes*. In 1912 he went to New York with Fred Karno's comedy troup and was spotted by Mack Sennett, America's foremost producer of comedy films. Sennett took him to Hollywood.

Masterpieces

By his second film, *Kid Auto Races at Venice* (1914) Chaplin was already wearing his bowler hat and ill-fitting trousers, and carrying a cane as an essential prop. Masterpieces such as *The Tramp* (1915), *The Pawnshop* (1916) and *Easy Street* (1917) followed and he became one of the luminaries of silent Hollywood.

Although always an outsider from the glamorous and decadent movie colony, he began to live in style and founded the United Artists Corporation with D.W. Griffith, Mary Pickford and Douglas Fairbanks.

Weakness for teenagers

By then, however, Chaplin's weakness for pretty teenagers was leading him into trouble. He married his first wife, 16-year-old Mildred Harris, when he realized that she was pregnant; but the child only lived for a few days.

Following their divorce, Chaplin found himself forced into a shotgun wedding with Lita Grey, a teenage starlet who announced that she, too, was pregnant. Chaplin chose marriage rather than prison for unlawful sex with a minor. What was from all accounts a hellish marriage ended in a $625 000 divorce settlement. Even 50 years later Chaplin chose not to write about her in his autobiography on the grounds that he did not want to say anything bad about the mother of his two eldest sons.

Chaplin's reputation as a comic genius grew even greater with films like *The Kid* (1921), *City Lights* (1931) and *Modern Times* (1936), which starred Paulette Goddard, whom he had secretly married in 1933 when he was 44 and she 19.

By the time *Monsieur Verdoux* (1947) was released, however, the tide of popularity had long turned against him. In 1942, hard on the heels of his marriage to Oona O'Neil, his fourth teenage bride, Chaplin found himself named in a paternity suit brought by Joan Barry, who had once enjoyed a brief liaison with him.

Outcast

Blood tests proved that her daughter was *not* Chaplin's, but his enemies, who included some of Hollywood's most powerful gossip columnists, continued to portray him as a wicked seducer of innocent American girlhood.

More destructive, they denounced

Above: *Neither a broken ankle nor his wife Oona can prevent the veteran Chaplin from returning to work on* **A Countess From Hong Kong** *(1966).*

him as a wicked Communist seducer, because Chaplin, a life-long socialist, had actively campaigned for Russian war relief. They ignored the fact that, at the time, America and Russia were allies! Nevertheless, during the McCarthy years such accusations were enough to ruin a career and powerful pressure groups organized a boycott of the pacifist *Monsieur Verdoux*.

Horrified and upset, Chaplin struck back with an article which began: "I have made up my mind to declare war, for once and for all, on Hollywood and its inhabitants." He continued, "Before long I shall perhaps leave the US."

The prophecy was fulfilled in a harsher way than he had imagined. While Chaplin, still a British citizen, and Oona were sailing to Britain for the première of *Limelight* (1952) news came that the immigration authorities would not re-admit him to America unless he underwent an examination of his "moral worth".

Chaplin moved to Vevey in Switzerland with Oona and vowed he would never return to the United States: "I have no further use for America—I wouldn't go back there if Jesus Christ was President."

Knighthood

In fact, in 1972, Chaplin did go back to receive a special Oscar for "the incalculable effect he has had on making motion pictures, the art form of this century". "Beautiful people," he murmered as he collected the award. "This is my renaissance."

Even greater honour was to be bestowed upon him: early in 1975, two years before his death, he was knighted by the Queen. Thus, the little man in the baggy pants ended his days as Sir Charles Spencer Chaplin.

Maurice Chevalier

"Paris has two monuments—the Eiffel Tower and Maurice Chevalier," said the poet and film-maker Jean Cocteau. An apt comparison, since both of these enduring symbols of France made their appearance in the world in the same year, 1888. Chevalier's 70 years in showbusiness was probably the longest career of any great star and in that time he became the best-known Frenchman in the world. His straw hat, carefully preserved accent, jutting lip and boulevardier's carefree strut were as familiar as Charlie Chaplin's battered bowler, cane and waddling walk.

Effortless charm

Behind the seemingly effortless charm there was an immensely hard-working professional who contrived to turn even his limitations to advantage. He had a very light voice but, as he himself remarked, "I have always sung more with my heart than my throat."

The youngest of nine children, he was born into extreme poverty in Paris and made a precocious debut as a professional entertainer at the age of 12, singing obscene songs to café audiences of pimps and prostitutes.

His first film appearance was in *Trop Crédule* (1908), and in the following year he became the dancing partner of the great music-hall star Mistinguett, at the Folies Bergère. They were soon lovers, and the romance continued until 1920, ending in a row over billing.

Chevalier's film career was interrupted by World War One in which he served and was seriously wounded in the lung. He was captured by the Germans and spent the next two years in Alten Grabow prisoner-of-war camp, where a friendly British sergeant taught him to speak English.

Nervous breakdown

After the Armistice he quickly became a major star. His London debut was in a revue of 1919, *Hullo America*, in which he first adopted his distinctive outfit of straw hat and tuxedo.

In 1925 he took his act to America but, in rehearsals, suffered a serious

Top right: *Always a boulevardier to his fingertips, he cashed in handsomely on his image in* **Gigi** *(1958).*
Right: *With Josephine Baker, inspiring the French troops in December, 1939.*

nervous breakdown brought on by fear of "drying" in front of an audience. Returning to France he was nursed back to health by Yvonne Vallée, a young dancer he had discovered. They married in 1926 but were divorced six years later. Despite his immense fame and wealth, Chevalier was to remain an essentially lonely man. He once said, "My mother was the great passion in my life—apart from her, I don't think I know what love is."

Chevalier's second assault on the US came in 1929. He had already made a screen test in Paris for MGM's Irving Thalberg, but had been turned down. Cannily, Chevalier kept the print, showed it to Paramount's Adolph Zukor and was placed under contract.

His first film for Paramount was *Innocents of Paris* (1929), in which he sang *Every Little Breeze Seems to Whisper Louise*.

He found the ideal counterfoil for his cheerful bawdiness when cast opposite prim and proper Jeanette MacDonald in films like *The Love Parade* (1929), *One Hour With You* and *Love Me Tonight* (both in 1932) and *The Merry Widow* (1935).

Then came another squabble over billing. He refused to take second place in a new film with opera star Grace Moore and returned to Europe, declaring that he would rather top the bill at the Montparnasse Casino for 100 francs a week than be second at the Palace, New York, for $1000 a day. He kept himself busy on stage and made a string of films, the last of which, *Pièges* (1939), gave him his first dramatic role.

Traitor
The Second World War very nearly ended his career. After the fall of France, he had returned to his home in Cannes with his Rumanian-Jewish mistress Nita Raya and her mother. Under great pressure from the Germans, he finally agreed to give a concert at Alten.Grabow, the prisoner-of-war camp where he had been captive 25 years earlier. His fee was the release of 10 French soldiers.

The Germans kept the bargain, but made great propaganda out of the visit—claiming falsely that Chevalier had gone on to make a tour of Germany. He was denounced as a traitor on the BBC's French service, and in Algiers the singer Josephine Baker declared, "Chevalier is to the stage what Laval is to diplomacy."

After the liberation of France in 1944 he was arrested by the Maquis and narrowly escaped execution.

After the war, Chevalier was exonerated from all charges of collaboration and returned to films in René Clair's *Le Silence est D'Or* (1947). However, political controversy continued to dog him. In 1951 he was one of the signatories of the Stockholm Peace Petition against nuclear weapons, and three years later—at the height of the McCarthy frenzy in the United States—was refused a visa on ground of "Communist sympathies".

"The Woman in Black"
He finally received an invitation from Hollywood to play the young Audrey Hepburn's father in *Love in the Afternoon* (1957), filmed in Paris. Then *Gigi* (1958) gave him the chance to create a new screen image as an elderly mock-cynical roué. In the same

Above: *Towards the end of his seven decades in show business, the man who stood second only to de Gaulle in the French hall of fame, again starred with Leslie Caron in* **Fanny** *(1961).*

year he received a special Oscar.

He returned to Hollywood for *Count Your Blessings* (1959), and, after an absence of 30 years, was back on the Paramount lot for *A New Kind of Love* (1963).

In 1969 he gave up touring in his one-man show and fell prey to the depression which had afflicted him once before in the 1920s. When he died in 1972, the bulk of his $20 million fortune went to Madame Odette Meslier Junet, dubbed by the Paris newspapers "The Woman in Black", who—with her mute seven-year-old daughter—had been Chevalier's friend and companion in his last years.

Sean Connery

Life at the bottom as well as the top has taught Sean Connery the value of money. But, with a personal fortune of millions, he could afford to shrug off the improbability of his ever receiving the record damages he was awarded in 1984 when suing for misappropriation of funds. After the verdict, he said that it was the principle that mattered most. By bringing the issue out into the open he hoped to ensure that no one else would fall victim to the same kind of abuse.

Universally acknowledged as an actor of presence, authority and total commitment, Connery still maintains a healthy disregard for publicity directly relative to his acting career. Hardly surprising, in view of the snide suggestions that, as an ex-truck driver, milkman, bricklayer and coffin polisher, he was miscast as the impeccably bred Bond when he first received his "license to kill" in *Dr No* (1962). Audiences felt differently and Connery was to be so closely identified with the role that it was difficult to break away from it.

Musical break

Britain's only true post-war movie super-star was born in Edinburgh in August 1930, the son of a rubber mill laborer. As a youth, he served in the Royal Navy, before being discharged at the young age of 19 on account of a duodenal ulcer.

After drifting in and out of work, Connery successfully auditioned for a part in the 1951 London production of the hit musical *South Pacific*. While on tour, he fell for a pretty, young actress, Carol Sopel, also appearing in the show. They were inseparable for a time, but Carol came from a strictly orthodox Jewish family, who would not consider her marrying a gentile. The brief affair ended.

A time in repertory, some parts in TV—and small ones in films—followed. In 1957, Connery signed a contract with 20th Century-Fox, who loaned him out to star opposite Lana Turner in *Another Time, Another Place* (1958). Connery's rugged good looks aroused some anxiety in Johnny Stompanato, Lana Turner's lover, who tersely warned him to "keep away from the kid". Connery clearly did not take kindly to threats from a small-time hood and responded by punching Stompanato on the nose.

In 1962, Connery married Diane Cilento. She was already established as an actress—and one who played strong, self-willed women more than capable of holding their own—when Connery was cast as her lover in a TV production of Eugene O'Neill's *Anna Christie*.

Diane's first marriage was already more or less over but its demise may well have been hastened by the appearance of the virile Scot.

A challenge

Diane's background was very different from that of Connery. Both of her parents were doctors and her father received a knighthood for his services to medicine. Her childhood was definitely "upper crust" and sophisticated. She was also very much a liberated woman—and Connery seems to have found her both an emotional and a professional challenge.

His ever increasing value as news-material did not help their marriage, however. Both were essentially very private people and the stress of being constantly in the public eye resulted in the marriage being dissolved in 1974.

After the divorce, Connery said loudly and often that he never meant to marry again. But on a golf tournament in Morocco—he is a highly proficient golfer—he met and fell for the lively, beautiful and totally cosmopolitan Micheline Roquebrune—a fellow golfer. At 38, she was also an artist of considerable talent and a linguist.

Secret marriage

When she met Connery, she was already divorced and the mother of a teenage son. Clearly, like Cilento before her, she represented a new challenge—not least because she was equally wary of rushing into matrimony. Nevertheless, they set up house together in Connery's new property near Marbella and by Christmas 1975 had secretly married.

He has a totally professional

Right: The unveiling of a British superstar – James Bond as he was when he first became licensed to kill on the cinema screen in **Dr. No** *(1962).*

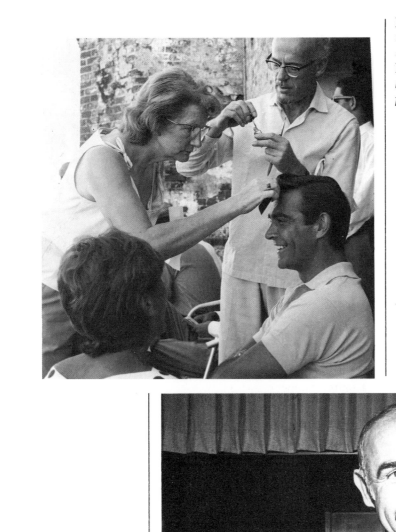

Left: *In the pre-toupee days of* **Dr. No,** *the Connery Bond image is in the hands of experts.*

Below: *With Micheline Roquebrune, his second wife whom he met while playing in a golf tournament in Morocco.*

approach to his acting career, exemplified by superb performances in diverse roles. For Hitchcock, he played the rich amateur psychiatrist, Mark Rutland, who marries a beautiful kleptomaniac in *Marnie* (1964). He was the dogged and determined soldier in *The Hill* (1965) and the tough—or not really so tough—police inspector in *The Offence* (1973). Such roles prove beyond any doubt that while Connery is and likely to remain the definitive James Bond—he was persuaded to make one last appearance in this role in 1983—Ian Fleming's impeccable embodiment of sophisticated fantasy is by no means the definitive Sean Connery.

Gary Cooper

To his adoring public he was the strong, silent, all-American hero. Off-screen Gary Cooper was also well known for his sexual appetite. To quote a friend : "Coop was probably the greatest cocksman that ever lived."

Born of English parents, in Montana, on May 7, 1901, Cooper began his film career with stunt work in early Westerns. A former would-be cartoonist, he "quit trying to draw when I started falling off horses for a living."

So good was he at riding (and falling off) horses, that he appeared in 50 Westerns in his first year-and-a-half in the business. His first important film was *The Winning of Barbara Worth* (1926), in which, rather unexpectedly, he won the lead.

Well bruised

Cooper seemed to embody the values of the mythical "West" and was soon identified with the deeply moral characters he played. But many who knew him, considered him opportunist for sleeping with girls at various levels in the hierarchy of film production.

Not surprisingly, he soon added "It" girl Clara Bow to his conquests. They starred in *Children of Divorce* (1927) and the vivacious actress was more than a match for him. It was often necessary to disguise Cooper's scratches and bruises after a night of their passionate love-making. He later declared that the relationship was a publicity stunt, but at the time he was clearly in love.

Cooper's sex appeal was apparent and though Paramount Studio's attempt to pair him and Fay Wray as "Paramount's glorious young lovers" never really worked, producers were shrewd enough to promote him as a sex object.

With the advent of the "talkies" his new love was the extrovert Mexican actress Lupe Velez. When they filmed *Wolf Song* (1929) together, rumors of an excised nude bathing scene abounded.

This very public affair was discouraged by Paramount. Velez was considered bad for Cooper's image and as her income was more than triple his at the time, it again seemed that he might have pursued her with a view to furthering his career.

Nudism

Whatever the gossips might say, Cooper liked and was kind to women—which probably partly accounted for his popularity. His shy, rather stumbling manner appealed to their maternal instincts. On the other hand, he practiced nudism in his dressing room, much to the embarrassment of friends who called in on him.

By the end of the 1920s he was exhausted by five years of work without a break. At times he was making two films at once. When he went on a long rest cure to Europe, even his departure sparked off a rumor—that Velez had attempted to shoot him.

In Italy Cooper met the Countess Dorothy di Frasso, an American-born socialite who married into Italian nobility. The difference in their ages—he was 30 and she 43—provoked more talk of Cooper's cynical social aspirations.

Marrying "Rocky"

Surprisingly, despite his many love-affairs, Cooper only married once—in December 1933. His young wife Veronica Balfe—"Rocky"—was a minor actress from a wealthy society background. She sensibly made light of his continuing flirtations and, within two years, the most fertile period of his career was underway. With Frank Capra's *Mr Deeds Goes to Town* (1936) he established his screen image as the man of the people. "To get folks to like you," Cooper reasoned, "I figured you had to sort of be their ideal. I don't mean a handsome knight riding a white horse, but a fellow who answered the description of a 'right guy'."

Turning down the part of Rhett Butler in *Gone With the Wind* (1939) may not have been smart, but the title role in *Sergeant York* (1941), top money-maker of the year, won him the Best Actor Oscar.

Meanwhile, Cooper's romantic life flourished. An affair with Marlene Dietrich was kept quiet but Ingrid Bergman who co-starred in *For Whom the Bell Tolls* (1943) was seen with him in public, thus delaying the film's release.

Continuing the tradition of dating

Top: *Riding the range flanked by Susan Hayward and Richard Widmark in* **Garden of Evil** *(1954).*
Above: *A portrait of a man who loved leading ladies, particularly his own.*

his leading ladies, Cooper started a liaison with the young Patricia Neal on location for *The Fountainhead* (1949). His marriage was threatened for the first time. Criticism of the lovers drew them even more closely together but over two years later, still nothing had been resolved.

He was under other pressures, too. As one of the right-wing "friendly" witnesses to the House Un-American Activities Committee, Cooper was now ironically suffering from the censorious attitudes of others. He was indecisive—mainly on account of his daughter, raised in her mother's Catholic faith—and Neal finally despaired of the situation and left him late in 1951.

Final honour

Cooper and his wife were reconciled after a four year separation, by which time he had won another Best Actor Oscar for *High Noon* (1952). He was the top box office star of 1953, but his health was failing. Even so, he made 14 more films and was awarded an honorary Oscar in April 1961. This was accepted on his behalf by a tearful James Stewart, who had just learned of Cooper's incurable cancer. A month later, on May 13, the much-loved "Coop" was dead.

Left: *Suavely handsome in a naval uniform in* **Souls at Sea** *(1937).*
Above: *With his one and only wife, society beauty Veronica Balfe, who made light of his countless affairs.*

Joan Crawford

Named "First Queen of the Movies" in her lifetime, Joan Crawford has acquired a posthumous reputation for being a ruthlessly competitive woman, driven by phobias and an obsession with cleanliness.

Her film career spanned 45 years, during which time she made 81 films and married four times. The shopgirl who became "The Shopgirl's Dream", she never really felt accepted by Hollywood, although her international popularity was immense. Her shapely legs, huge eyes and somewhat imperious manner conformed to the ideal of a Hollywood star. She courted publicity and always had friendly relations with the press, her fans and the film crews.

"Billie" and "Dodo"

Born on March 23, 1906, and christened Lucille Le Sueur, Crawford always wanted to dance. After a spell on Broadway she was placed under contract to MGM in 1925, and her first big success was *Our Dancing Daughters* (1928).

After an affair with wealthy heir Mike Cudahy, Crawford married the highly eligible Douglas Fairbanks Jnr in June 1929. A very intimate couple, they spoke a private language and called each other "Billie" and "Dodo". But already the domineering personality that was to blight her future affairs began to assert itself.

Possessed

As her career flourished and her income exceeded his, the tension between them grew. A diversion came in the shape of Clark Gable. Crawford co-starred with him in *Possessed* (1931) and they fell in love. MGM studio boss Louis B. Mayer intervened and Crawford did not divorce until 1933. She and Gable never did marry but they remained friends and occasional lovers until his death from a heart attack in 1960.

Throughout the 1930s Crawford became increasingly eccentric; she suffered from claustrophobia and a

Right: *Texan-born Lucille Le Sueur, ex-laundress, waitress and shopgirl, realises her girlhood dream of stepping out for the cameras as Joan Crawford in* **Taxi Dancer** *(1926).*

Above: *No hint of what's to come from "Mommie Dearest" for adopted Cindy and Cathy, on their eighth birthday.*

fear of flying, was fanatical about hygiene (she scrubbed her own floors even as a star) and at one time was fixated on gardenias. She could be very generous but was intolerant of friends who did not meet her extremely high standard of loyalty.

Husband number 2

She met second husband Franchot Tone on the set of *Today We Live* (1933), and he used his theatrical experience to help her professionally. They married in secret in October 1935, living in Crawford's house. By this time, she was one of Hollywood's 10 top money earners. She eased off her relentless pursuit of publicity in deference to Tone, but the marriage was beginning to falter by the time she made *Mannequin* (1938) with Spencer Tracy. An involvement with Tracy ended because he wanted no further complications to his marriage.

In 1938 an article appeared naming Crawford, among other stars, as "box-office poison". MGM exploited the situation by offering her unfavorable terms when her contract came up for renewal. In addition, Tone was becoming moody, had affairs, drank a lot and even hit her. They were divorced in April 1939.

Her third marriage to little-known actor Phillip Terry, in July 1942, also lasted only four years. The couple were demonstrative in public but there was

no real affection and Terry chafed at her dominance.

When she dated handsome attorney Greg Bautzer after her divorce in April 1946, she liked him to walk two paces behind her and once demanded that he kneel in front of her to apologize, as Franchot Tone had done. Bautzer was not as compliant and their relationship ended after a party at which he talked briefly to another woman.

Meanwhile, her failing career had revived with the release of *Mildred Pierce* (1945), in which she played the sacrificing mother. She received excellent reviews and won an Oscar.

Cult hit

Unable to have children of her own, Crawford adopted four and they often featured in publicity material that showed her to be a loving and generous mother. However, her harsh and punitive treatment of them in private has been highly publicized since her death and was the subject of *Mommie Dearest*, her eldest daughter Christina's account of their relationship. The film version (1981), became a cult hit.

As she grew older, she became jealous of young actresses. There was a controversial attack on Monroe's blatant sexuality in 1953 and, while filming *Johnny Guitar* (1954), she started a feud with co-star Mercedes McCambridge. There was also animosity between her and Bette Davis on the set of *Whatever Happened to*

Right: *An Oscar winner's sleep after her triumph in* **Mildred Pierce** *(1945).*

Baby Jane? (1962), her last important film, made when both women were 54.

Estranged

Her fourth and last marriage, in May 1955 – to the president of Pepsi-Cola, Alfred Steele – marked a break from Hollywood and from her run of ineffectual husbands. Crawford helped to publicize Pepsi-Cola before Steele's death in May 1959, when she was elected to the board of directors.

Her last film was *Trog* (1970). She was estranged from her two eldest children, was beginning to drink heavily and eventually became a recluse in her New York apartment. She had been a Christian Scientist since the 1930s and when she fell ill, refused treatment. Thus she died of "acute coronary occlusion" on May 10, 1977, a lonely and ignominious death.

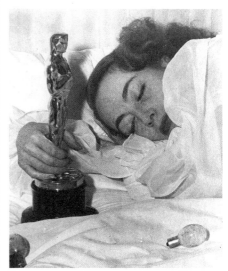

Bing Crosby

"Once or twice I've been described as a light comedian … the most accurate description of my abilities I've seen. That's just about all I am. I'm not a very funny fellow and I'm not a very serious fellow. Nor do I give off a terribly romantic aura."

Bing's characteristically modest self-portrait was part and parcel of his relaxed and amiable image—as an ordinary guy who somehow managed to become one of the world's most popular entertainers. His singing sounded so effortless that every amateur crooner imagined that he could reproduce that distinctive lazy tone—and, of course, failed.

Jailhouse blues

The young Crosby was vastly different from the pipe-smoking, golfing, family man of later years. In 1921, fresh out of college and aged 20, he put together an act with Al Rinker, "Two Boys and a Piano—Singing Songs Their Own Way". Later they were signed by bandleader Paul Whiteman and, with Harry Barris, became Paul Whiteman's Rhythm Boys.

Bing quickly gained a reputation as a hard-drinking hell-raiser and his carousing nearly wrecked his feature debut in *King of Jazz* (1930). When shooting began, Crosby was in jail on a drunken driving charge. The authorities obligingly allowed him out every day for his scenes with the Rhythm Boys. But he lost the big solo, *Song of the Dawn*; the number went to John Boles instead.

Marriage, in 1930, to starlet Dixie Lee eventually calmed Crosby down, although not before Dixie had threatened divorce if he didn't reform.

Most bankable star

He got another chance to sing solo in *Reaching for the Moon* (1930). A year later a radio show brought him national fame and a three-year contract for five films with Paramount. He moved up to second lead in the *Big Broadcast* (1932), stealing the show. For the rest of his career he never relinquished top billing and until the early 1950s remained Paramount's most bankable star.

By all accounts, he remained utterly unconcerned about his appearance. His receding hairline soon required the help of a toupee, which he dutifully wore. But personally, Crosby didn't give a hang about the "scalp doily".

Flapping ears

The studio had problems too, with his prominent ears. At first Crosby reluctantly allowed them to be glued back with spirit gum. On set, however, the heat from the lights quickly softened the fixative, and those jug-ears would flap back into their natural position. Eventually Paramount conceded that the world would just have to get used to them.

In the 1930s, Bing glided through a series of tailor-made vehicles, ranging from light musicals to a dramatic role in *Sing You Sinners* (1938), and sentimental comedy with Joan Blondell in Universal's *East Side of Heaven* (1939).

In the following year he joined Bob Hope and Dorothy Lamour on *The Road to Singapore*, the first of the highly popular "Road" films.

In *Holiday Inn* (1942), a huge hit, he sang *White Christmas*, and two years later won an Oscar for his performance as Father O'Malley, the singing priest in *Going My Way* (1944).

Thrashings

Crosby was by now a national institution, and to criticize him would have been considered distinctly un-American. Fan magazines poured

Below: *Waiting for action with 'Road' movies co-star, Dorothy Lamour.*

out treacly stories about his all-American family life—four sturdy sons and the devoted Dixie Lee—but the truth was more complicated. In private life, Crosby was an aloof figure. "Bing" was just a character he could switch on and off at will. His son Gary has recalled long, silent drives to Paramount studios, at the end of which his father would "suddenly change into Bing Crosby".

He was also a harsh disciplinarian, using a belt dotted with metal studs to beat his sons until the blood ran. His remoteness was in part behind Dixie's descent into alcoholism after her retirement from the screen in 1935.

Dixie died of cancer in 1953, at a time when Crosby's career had run into the doldrums. It was rescued by *White Christmas* (1954) and a moving performance as a broken-down singer in *The Country Girl* (1954). *High Society* (1956) was his last screen hit.

His film career ended with a disastrous remake of the John Ford classic, *Stagecoach* (1966).

Since 1957, however, he had been happily married to the much younger, former actress, Kathryn Grant, and a second chance at family life proved happier than the first.

Crosby died in 1977, on the golf course. He had just won a game and, as he turned to acknowledge the applause, suffered a massive heart attack; death was instantaneous.

Left: *Alone in the wide open spaces of the set for* **The Emperor's Waltz** *(1948).*
Below left: *A normal home, but Dixie Lee Crosby found Bing cold.*
Below: *Displaying an appetite for golf that would only end with his death.*

Bette Davis

Throughout a career that spans more than half a century, two Oscars, one hundred films and four marriages, Bette Davis has shown again and again that talent is far more enduring than a pretty face. Her perpetual hallmarks are a pair of saucer eyes, a red gash of a mouth and a raspy voice that delivers cutting candor with inimitable style.

Born in Massachusetts in 1908 of good solid New England stock, and christened Ruth Elizabeth, she says that as long as she still has legs and her make-up box she will not retire.

She who dares
A wonderfully "wicked lady" since the 1940s, when she played an endless string of such roles, Davis's career has veered from once being the highest paid actress in the world to an all-time low when she took a full-page advertisement in *The Hollywood Reporter* which read: "Experienced actress wants work" and featured her name and telephone number. Nobody had ever done that before. For Davis it worked!

When she first arrived in Hollywood in 1930, fresh from Broadway and with an offer from Universal, nobody could quite see why she had been hired. She didn't look like the conventional beauties of the time and her early roles—in terrible films—were instantly forgettable.

Warners, however, took her up after Universal's contract expired and by the time she appeared in *Ex-Lady* (1933), she had star status. When she turned "dramatic" in *Of Human Bondage* (1934), opposite Leslie Howard, people began to take her seriously.

Battling Bette
Davis won her first Oscar for *Dangerous* (1935), and a second for *Jezebel* (1938). Her other classics include *Dark Victory* (1939), *The Little Foxes* (1941), *Now, Voyager* (1942) and *All About Eve* (1950).

She also took up the issue of the slavery of the star contract system and fought a legal battle with Jack Warner against it. Although she lost the case, she did not lose face. The move established her as an actress with determination to match her talent.

The Star (1952) won her one of her 10 Academy Award nominations. After

Top: *The opulently fur-framed face of stardom in the early 1940s.*

Above: *Percy Westmore creates a very different image for* **Little Foxes** *(1941).*

Above: *A truce for Jack Warner in his Crawford and Davis star wars.*

Below: *A heavy hand with the lipstick maintains the image in later years.*

returning to Broadway to do a musical, *Two's Company*, she underwent an operation for osteomyelitis of the jaw, and for the remainder of the 1950s there was a lull in her career.

It was *What Ever Happened to Baby Jane?* (1962), co-starring Joan Crawford, that started a new Bette Davis boom.

A run of intense and eccentric roles in films like *Hush...Hush Sweet Charlotte* (1964), *The Nanny* (1965), *The Anniversary* (1967) and *Madame Sin* (1971) followed—and her first TV special, *Strangers* (1979), which won her an Emmy.

One-woman show

"Films are hard to find at my age," says Davis, who Hollywood honored with the American Film Institute's Life Achievement Award in 1977. "I don't want to end up playing little old grandmothers."

She elected to take her one-woman show around America rather than endure such a fate, commenting: "I guess audiences may be surprised I still can walk across a stage at 74!"

Early in 1983 she released an album called *Miss Bette Davis Sings*, mainly of songs from her films. She has also written two candid autobiographies entitled *The Lonely Life* (1962) and *Mother Goddam* (1974).

Veteran

A veteran of four marriages, in 1932 Davis wed her childhood sweetheart, orchestra leader Ham Nelson, to whom she credits her early success. After their divorce she married aircraft engineer Arthur Farnsworth, who died three years later. Her third husband was artist William Sherry, by whom she had a daughter. Her final marriage, to actor Gary Merrill, lasted 10 years. She has never considered a fifth, saying: "You live by yourself for more than two decades and there is no way to share any more." It is also said that in her early days she had an affair with Howard Hughes.

Her last film for the big screen was *Watcher In The Woods* (1980), made for Disney. Since then she has appeared in several TV films including *White Mama* (1980), *Skyward* and *Family Reunion* (both in 1981).

In 1983 she suffered a mastectomy and a stroke which temporarily slowed her down to a septuagenarian pace, but she lives in style in one of the oldest apartment buildings in the film city.

45

Doris Day

Hollywood wit Oscar Levant once joked, "I knew Doris Day before she was a virgin." And that is how most people remember her—squeaky clean and so pure it could not be true.

In fact, the girl who was christened Doris von Kappelhoff was nothing like the sunny, naïve blonde conjured up by the Hollywood publicity machine. The real Day survived a tempestuous private life which would have destroyed weaker women. Always a fighter, she made it to the top by hard work and professionalism.

She always took her public image with a pinch of salt. "Doris Day, Miss Chastity Belt, America's Happy Virgin," she once mocked, and then continued in a more serious vein: "When men call you 'a professional virgin' it usually means that you won't sleep with them and I'm happy to be regarded as a someone who is strong enough to resist all that."

Life in danger
Born in April 1924, Day's grueling life as a performer began at the age of 12, when she became a professional dancer. The following year, however, her plans were abruptly halted when a car in which she was a passenger was trapped between gates at a level crossing and struck by a train. For a time her life was in danger; after that it seemed doubtful whether she would ever walk, never mind dance, again.

On her release from hospital 14 months later, Day switched her ambitions to singing and persuaded a local radio station to let her gain microphone experience by performing for nothing. Bandleader Barney Rapp was impressed by the teenager's rendition of *Day By Day* and offered her a job. She changed her name to Day after the song that had brought her luck and toured with Rapp's band.

Disastrous move
The routine of nightclubs, speakeasies and cheap hotels was broken when Day, now 16, married Al Jorden, a trombonist with the Jimmy Dorsey orchestra. It was a disastrous move.

Above right: *Stripped for action, at 40 plus, in* **The Glass-Bottomed Boat** *(1966)*
Right: *With regular screen mate, Rock Hudson, in* **Send Me No Flowers** *(1964).*

interested directors of the caliber of Hitchcock who used her in his *The Man Who Knew Too Much* (1956). Day was pleased: "It is good to see a picture of myself without a smile. I'm always smiling in films—and you can't go on smiling forever. Life isn't one long smile anyway."

Mismanagement

By then Day's career was being handled by Marty Melcher and they eventually married. Melcher's management amounted to almost puritan over-protectiveness of her image. Pictures in the *Love Me or Leave Me* mold were turned down as being too complex. Interviews became joint affairs, with Melcher vetoing the question that could be asked. Despite this, Day achieved some happiness with him and was distraught when he died suddenly in 1968. Other shocks followed. It became clear that Melcher was either guilty of gross financial mismanagement, or else had systematically embezzled her money. Instead of the millionairess she should have been, Day was almost broke.

She picked herself up and continued working, just as she had done after past crises. And she initiated a lawsuit against Jerome Rosenthal, a lawyer who had worked closely with Melcher. He was found guilty of fraud and she was awarded $22 million in damages.

Slightly eccentric

She established a self-reliant, if slightly eccentric, life for herself as the chief worker for the Doris Day Pet Foundation which rescues and cares for neglected animals. Even this created problems when restaurant host Barry Comden began to woo her with bags of scraps for her 14 dogs. She married him, but after only a year the relationship began to flounder. A.E. Hotchner, who collaborated with Day on her autobiography, told the press: "Doris took Comden into her heart like she does a stray dog, but he broke her heart."

Once again, the Day resilience triumphed and she went back to looking after her animals on her own. "I'm a whole person already," she told an interviewer, "not a half-person looking for the other half. I'm complete and when people are complete there is no real need for marriage. I've learnt something from all my marriages, but you know—it's lovely being on my own."

Jorden, in Day's own words, was a "psychopathic beast". Just two days after their wedding the obsessively jealous musician saw his wife speak to another man. "He hit me again and again," she recalled in her autobiography.

Death threats

Later, when Jorden learned that Day was pregnant he tried first to insist that she had an illegal abortion, then threatened to kill her and her unborn child. She left him immediately after her son Terry was born.

A 19-year-old single parent with no money and her only skill in her voice, Day was forced to leave Terry with her mother and go back on the road with another danceband. But she began to have national hit songs and Al Levy, a Hollywood agent, took an interest in her career.

At this time Day was living in a trailer with her second husband

Top: *Under Hitchcock's eagle eye in* **The Man Who Knew Too Much** *(1956).* Above: *With Marty Melcher, a dubious business manager who become the third of her four husbands.*

saxophonist George Weidler. Once again things were not working out and she cried throughout an audition with Hollywood producer Michael Curtiz. Despite this Curtiz gave her a part in *Romance on the High Seas* (1948), and Day's recording of one of the songs, *It's Magic*, was a big hit. Well pleased, Warners rushed her into a series of light comedy musicals which, by 1952, had made her the biggest female box office attraction.

Films like *Calamity Jane* (1953), a rumbustious Wild West musical which is Day's favorite, and *Love Me or Leave Me* (1955)—a close-to-home biography of a nightclub singer involved with a violent, small-time hoodlum, increased her range and

James Dean

Since his premature death in a car crash in 1955 at the age of 24, James Dean has epitomized the "live fast, die young" image for subsequent generations of teenagers. He has been described as "the perfect mythological hero" and his much-copied, casual style of dress has never dated.

Behind the surface bravado however, was a troubled and insecure soul. Born in Indiana on February 8, 1931, he was profoundly affected by his mother's death in 1939, after which he was raised by an aunt and uncle in Iowa. Drama was to provide an early outlet for his sadness and in 1950 he enrolled at UCLA in California.

Moodiness

A part in a Pepsi-Cola commercial soon led to more taxing television work but he suffered depression and moodiness that descended on him without warning and were to plague him for the rest of his short working life. Part of the problem lay in his complete identification with the characters he played; he could not "switch off" once work was over. Dean was inclined to be aggressive, especially when drunk, and carried a switchblade.

Tired of California and the formalities of college, Dean left for New York in 1952. He was signed to the Louis Schurr agency who got him a few bit parts. At 21, he was accepted into Lee Strasberg's Actors' Studio.

New York suited Dean's way of life; dancer Dizzy Sheridan was one of a loose circle of friends and he lived with her for a time. There is speculation that he was bisexual and, certainly, he did not yet commit himself to anyone, male or female, drifting in and out of people's lives.

Live television dramas in which he was usually cast as a "problem youth" were his main source of work, beating Steve McQueen and Paul Newman to parts, and receiving much fan mail.

Rejected

Of his many girlfriends, Dean only became seriously involved with one: Italian actress Pier Angeli whom he met while making his first important film, *East of Eden* (1955). He wanted to marry her and was willing to convert to Catholicism but her mother persuaded her to wed singer Vic Damone instead.

Dean sat outside the church on a motorcycle during the ceremony then disappeared for ten days, distrustful and withdrawn once again. Shortly before Angeli's own early death she wrote to a friend: "I was only in love once in my life and that was with Jimmy Dean."

Director Elia Kazan had seen Dean perform in *The Immoralist* (1954), a stage role which won him a Tony award for most promising newcomer. Kazan was impressed and offered him a part in *East of Eden* (1955), but there was growing antipathy between the two men, as Kazan became irritated by the young actor's self-absorption. Dean was unpredictable: he was often late, had temper tantrums, fussed interminably over direction and had a disconcerting habit of falling asleep without warning—due in part to the fact that he was also an insomniac.

When his photograph appeared in the studio canteen, he tore it down saying, "I told them I didn't want this stuff. I told them no pictures on the wall. No pictures of me in any place. Can't they understand? I don't want it." But such behaviour attracted the very publicity he wanted to avoid. The gossip columnists found Dean insufferable; they claimed he was dirty, surly and bad tempered, possibly because he refused to defer to them.

Even so, *East of Eden* generated an overwhelmingly enthusiastic public response. It was the only one of Dean's three major films to be released in his tragically short lifetime.

"Mad for speed"

After this success he bought a Porsche Speedster, took up racing and became "mad for speed". In the same year, shooting began on *Rebel Without a Cause* (1955), which provided Dean with his most demanding role. He died a month before the film's release and the critics were unanimous in their praise of his performance and regret at his loss.

Dean had badly wanted the part of Jett Rink in *Giant* (1956), but his glamorous co-star Elizabeth Taylor

Right: *Unaware that he's making his last film, the star of* **Giant** *(1955) strikes a pose for Elizabeth Taylor.*

made him nervous and Dennis Hopper recalls that before Dean played his first scene with her, he suddenly walked towards the four-thousand spectators and urinated in front of them. Asked what made him do such a thing, he replied that if he could do that in front of so many people, he could do anything with Taylor in front of the camera!

Like his earlier co-stars, Taylor built up a close rapport with Dean.

Giant was completed on September 22, 1955. On September 30, Dean was dead, killed in a car crash on his way to compete in a race meeting.

Death-wish

He had been obsessed with death. Asked what he respected most, he replied, "That's easy. Death. It's the only thing left to respect. It's the one inevitable, undeniable truth."

But theories about a death-wish are implausible. Dean's future was bright, with several excellent film and television roles lined up.

However, dying in his prime assured him legendary status. He received a posthumous Oscar nomination for his part in *Giant*, which was a big financial success. In the year after his death, fan letters addressed to Dean still outnumbered those to any living star. Many devotees refused to believe he was dead and a vast industry cashed in on the fervent interest in him.

Even now the cult surrounds him and for many people who have not even seen his films, he remains the perfect, untouchable star.

The moody anti-hero who epitomized the 1950s beat generation (left) in **East of Eden** *and* **Rebel Without A Cause** *(both in 1955) surrounded himself with the trappings of his culture (above). All too soon he would become a legend (below), victim of his twin obsessions – racing cars and death.*

Robert De Niro

Hollywood superstar Robert De Niro can still walk down Sunset Boulevard unmolested by autograph hunters. The secret? A chameleon-like ability to change his appearance. From film to film he is unrecognizable, greasing his hair back for *The Godfather, Part II* (1974), growing a beard for *The Deer Hunter* (1978) and putting on 60 pounds for his role in *Raging Bull* (1980), which reportedly brought his sex life to new heights as he later recalled, "Some women like heavier men. That's something I learned. They treat you like a teddy bear. And no it wasn't because of who I am. Because they didn't *know* who I was!"

Like most of his screen characters, De Niro is a product of the tough Lower East Side of New York City. Born in Greenwich Village in 1943, the only son of two artists, the young De Niro enrolled as a drama student at 16 and immersed himself in his studies for the next two-and-a-half years.

On completing his course he appeared in off-Broadway plays, including Shelley Winters' under-rated *One Night Stands with a Noisy Passenger*. He made his film debut in

Left: *Ready and willing to take on the Viet Cong in* **The Deer Hunter** *(1978).* Below: *Showing his range, with Liza Minnelli in* **New York, New York** *(1977).*

50

Greetings (1968), and went on to acquit himself well in several more character roles. But stardom only came with films like *Mean Streets* (1973), in which he played a small hood; *Taxi Driver* (1976), as the well-intentioned but psychotic cabbie, Travis Bickle, and *New York, New York* (1977).

Neurotic

In Hollywood this enigmatic superstar, described by the Italian director Bernardo Bertolucci as "a very sensitive, and probably neurotic person", is very much an actor's actor. He feels a sense of responsibility towards his public, apparent in his almost fanatical attention to detail. For his role as young Vito Corleone in *The Godfather, Part II* (1974), De Niro disappeared to Sicily armed with cassette recorder and script and asked the locals to read his lines. The result of this enterprise was an Oscar-winning performance in a role that required less than a page of English dialogue.

Big build-up

De Niro's most remarkable absorption in a role was as champion boxer Jake La Motta in *Raging Bull* (1980). He worked by day on a road gang and trained by night in a gymnasium to build up the physique of a boxer. To play La Motta in decline, he had to add 60 pounds to his natural 160 pound frame. He tackled the challenge with characteristic dedication, cramming himself with carbohydrates and fats.

And to accomplish the weight increase in record time he got up early each morning to allow sufficient time to recover from his first huge intake of food at breakfast, before being further bloated by enormous lunches and dinners. His reward was a well deserved Academy Award for best actor of 1980.

De Niro blamed the pressures which fame brought with it for the break-up of his marriage to black actress Diahnne Abbot. "I would probably have gone on being an ordinary guy, living a simple life and nothing would have changed my marriage," he later said. The couple married in 1976, the year in which De Niro reached superstar-status with his starring role in *Taxi Driver*.

While in Rome in 1981 De Niro's desire to remain incognito led to his arrest as a suspected terrorist. For 90 minutes he was kept under lock and key while his identity was checked. Needless to say, a number of policemen had red faces after discovering who they had locked up!

Ready to kill

De Niro has no delusions about stardom. After filming *King of Comedy* (1983), he qualified the film's rather cynical view of showbusiness by remarking that, "If it is bleak, that is because I see show business that way."

Below: *60lbs heavier to play boxer, Jack La Motta in* **Raging Bull** *(1980).*

He even refused to lunch with his co-star Jerry Lewis, saying, "How could I, when in the film I am supposed to be at his throat and ready to kill him for my chance?"

The star's sometimes over-serious approach to his roles is not always appreciated by fellow actors. Jerry Lewis commented that "De Niro has obviously never heard Noel Coward's advice to actors—that their job was to say their lines and not bump into furniture. He just could not forget the part at the end of a day's work." But then Robert De Niro doesn't play by ordinary rules and he's certainly no ordinary actor.

Below: *Red faces for the Italian police after they arrested this "terrorist".*

Marlene Dietrich

Marlene Dietrich was literally an overnight sensation when her first major film *The Blue Angel* (1930) was released. She was a completely sensual being—"sex without gender" according to critic Kenneth Tynan— legendary for her legs and the insolent sexual challenge she issued to men and women alike. Her lovers included some of the biggest names in the film industry in America and Europe and she was also the darling of the intellectuals.

Dietrich was born in Berlin on December 27, 1901. Working in the theater in the 1920s she enjoyed the wild hedonism of her native city with its bisexual nightclubs and all-night champagne parties.

In 1924, she married Czechoslovakian production assistant Rudolf Sieber and though an early affair with her leading man Willi Forst marked the end of conventional married life, she never divorced.

Discovered

Dietrich made several films but preferred live stage work—until she was discovered by Josef von Sternberg who cast her in *The Blue Angel*. Von Sternberg had a love-hate relationship with her and was infuriated by her lack of response to his infatuation, but under his direction the film made her an international star.

Hollywood producer Joe Pasternak urged Paramount to sign her. She had, he said, "... the one essential ingredient of international stardom: millions of guys would want to make love to her."

Vampish seductress

The screen image Von Sternberg had created for her was that of a vampish seductress, a siren who lured men to their doom. On screen and off they went willingly.

When *The Blue Angel* was premièred in Berlin, the audience went wild and enthusiastically mobbed Dietrich. She left Germany for Hollywood just in time. She was to become a symbol of freedom for other exiles and disdainfully refused Hitler's invitation to return as his mistress.

Hollywood daringly exploited her unusual, androgynous appeal. When she refused to change out of slacks for publicity photos, the pictures were captioned "the woman even women can adore".

Her first Hollywood film *Morocco* (1930) repeated her earlier success and introduced her to Gary Cooper, soon to be her lover. The professional coupling with Von Sternberg however, was not always happy and his wife served Dietrich a writ during divorce proceedings. This was later dropped but Von Sternberg's obsession with Dietrich was not.

Passionate love affairs

Her own friendships and love affairs were passionate. Always, she was open and generous—as with lesbian author Mercedes d'Acosta whom she met in 1931.

By 1934 she was reputedly the third highest paid person in the United States (after William Randolph Hearst and Mae West), earning $350 000 a year. She spent most of it, owed back taxes and refused to invest.

Her collaboration with Von Sternberg over, Dietrich traveled a lot in Europe although one of her most serious affairs to date occurred back in Hollywood.

She fell in love with John Gilbert, former star of the silent era who had become a casualty of the "talkies". Ill, from the effects of excessive alcohol, he appealed to her protective feelings and she persuaded Paramount to feature him with her in *Desire* (1936). He lost the part through ill-health and Dietrich walked out on him when she saw him with his former love Greta Garbo. She found consolation with Gary Cooper, who was announced the male lead in *Desire*, just as Gilbert died, heartbroken, in January 1936. Dietrich was devastated and continued to burn candles by a photo of Gilbert

Top right: *Presenting the androgynous image that shocked the world, as she arrives in Paris with Rudolf Seiber.*
Far top right: *The woman millions of men wanted to make love to, as she appeared in* **Shanghai Express** *(1932).*
Far right: *In her 50s, she tours with her one-woman show.*
Right: *As Catherine The Great in* **The Scarlet Empress** *(1934) with Joseph von Sternberg, her friend and mentor.*

for some time after his premature death.

Labeled "box office poison" later in 1936, Dietrich treated this as a joke and continued to enjoy an extravagant lifestyle. She often attended costume parties dressed as a man and danced with other women, as she had done when she lived in Berlin.

War-time hero

Her next big involvement was with the writer and intellectual Erich Maria Remarque, to whom she was devoted. He drank too much and suffered depressions—a complete contrast with French film star Jean Gabin, perhaps her greatest love. Very physical and a war-time hero, he impressed Dietrich and eclipsed Remarque.

Gabin eventually walked out on her to join the Free French in North Africa, but, in truth, she never really stopped loving him.

Her affairs were not always so intense. After her career had declined she made a surprise comeback with *Destry Rides Again* (1939), and was instantly attracted to co-star James Stewart.

John Wayne was another lover. When she first saw him she reportedly commanded "Daddy buy me that!" although she was still with Gabin at the time.

Perhaps Dietrich's greatest personal triumph was the reaction by United States troops to her grueling 18-month tour of the war fronts. Probably the most desired woman in the world, she reveled in the adulation and obligingly displayed her famous legs.

Disenchanted

After the war she became disenchanted with the technical demands of film-making, telling a journalist: "If you'd ever tried making love to someone in a scene and cast a soulful glance outward to see that damned microphone … you'd realize how maddening it could be."

Work on Hitchcock's *Stage Fright* (1950) however, brought about an affair with Michael Wilding who was said to be "emotionally torn" between her and Elizabeth Taylor.

Throughout the 1960s, she toured internationally presenting a one-woman show, her popularity undiminished. The woman "millions of guys would want to make love to" had not lost her extraordinary touch, or her glamor.

Faye Dunaway

Anyone taking Faye Dunaway for a dumb blonde couldn't be more mistaken. Her style combines Southern sensuality and Fifth Avenue elegance; her method of acting is based on a ferocious attention to detail, often accompanied by between-take combustibility; and in relationships with men she demands equal power.

Consequently, it's hardly surprising that she commands unflagging, million-dollar star treatment.

Born in Florida in 1941, she was christened Dorothy Faye and, as the daughter of a sergeant, spent her childhood in army camps in America and Europe. It wasn't until her parents divorced when she was 13 years old that she settled down with her mother in Talahassee. Determined to succeed, Faye waitressed at night to pay her way through a drama degree at Florida University. Later, a scholarship took her to Boston to study Fine and Applied Arts. She was spotted in a production of *Medea* by Elia Kazan and went to New York to work in his Lincoln Center Repertory Company, a move which forced her to turn down a Fullbright scholarship to study at London's highly prestigious Royal Academy of Dramatic Art.

Multi-film contract

Dunaway's great break came while appearing in an off-Broadway play called *Hogan's Goat* – which required her to break her neck nightly – film producer Sam Spiegel signed her up for her first film, *The Happening* (1967). This was followed by an offer of a multi-film contract with Otto Preminger which she took up but dropped after only one movie, *Hurry Sundown* (1967).

"Actors are artists, they are not pieces of meat although a lot of moviemakers like to think so," she remarked at the time, having spent a fortune buying herself out so that she could take the cigar-chomping Bonnie role in *Bonnie and Clyde* (1967).

Oscar nominations

Dunaway knew it would become her landmark film. It brought her brilliant recognition, a Best Actress nomination and a leap in fee to $500 000 a film.

Seven years later came her second Academy nomination for her performance in *Chinatown* (1974).

Between the two awards she made a dozen films, including her first major venture into comedy – as Milady de Winter in Richard Lester's *The Three Musketeers* (1973). She also had several colorful affairs, one with *A Place for Lovers* (1969) co-star Marcello Mastroianni ("I wanted a child by him but he gave it to Catherine Deneuve instead"), with Jerry Schatzberg who directed her in *A Puzzle Of A Downfall Child* (1970), and reportedly also with the American stand-up comedian and satirist, the highly controversial Lenny Bruce.

Period of self-doubt

At 34 she met and married rock musician Peter Wolf, six years her junior. The marriage lasted three years, after which the actress retreated into the sanctuary of work and what appears to have been a period of self-doubt and psychoanalysis.

The turning point was in 1976, when she won an Oscar for *Network* and fell in love with Terry O'Neill, the British photographer who took pictures of her with her award. She had first met him in Spain while making *Doc* (1971). Their second meeting marked her renaissance. They set up home together, opened an *objets* shop in Los Angeles and formed a film production company.

Below: *Triumphant in* **Network** *(1976), she won her first Oscar.*

54

Left: *It's bedtime with Robert Redford in* **Three Days of the Condor** *(1975).*

For a time she gave very few interviews and took on virtually no work, devoting every minute to *Mommie Dearest* (1981), the film of the Joan Crawford story which O'Neill produced and she acted in. Hated and loved, the film made a fortune. The husband and wife team moved to a mansion in Connecticut where she secretly had their son, Liam, before decamping to London. Here they married (also in secret) having been turned down by New York's St Patrick's Catholic Cathedral because both had been married previously.

They lived in Belgravia, renting the home of sporting baronet William Pigott-Brown, and Dunaway returned to comedy in the role of the wicked Lady Barbara Skelton in a remake of the film *The Wicked Lady* (1983).

Formidable business woman
Continuing in her comedy vein she raised many eyebrows by playing a sorceress in *Supergirl* (1984). She also took violin lessons at London's Royal College of Music in order to play the lead in *Duet For One* (1985) under the direction of her husband. With *Duet For One* she has proved herself to be a formidable businesswoman, concerning herself with production, scripts, budgets and casting. It looks as though the lissom, green-eyed actress has only just begun to realize her full dramatic potential.

Below: *With her husband, the photographer Terry O'Neill.*

Clint Eastwood

Since 1971 the laconic, slow talking "Man With No Name" has been the number one box-office star in the world. Women are attracted by his good looks and lean, masculine body, while men identify with the tough, cool loners he portrays.

Now reputedly the richest actor in the world, Eastwood can afford to make the films *he* wants to make and has started to play against type in films like *Broncho Billy* (1980) and *Honky Tonk Man* (1983), in both of which his characters were losers. Judging by the phenomenal success of his fourth Dirty Harry film, *Sudden Impact* (1983), however, it seems his fans prefer him in the more familiar macho roles.

Child of the depression
Eastwood was a child of the Great Depression, born in San Francisco in 1930.

His early childhood was unsettled, his family constantly up-rooted as his father traveled the West Coast in search of work. As a schoolboy, he found it difficult to mix with the kids at the many schools he attended. Like the characters he later played on the big screen, he was an outsider.

As a teenager, Eastwood was scared of girls, later recalling "I don't think there was a class I was ever in where I didn't have a crush on some girl. But I was so much of a loner that I couldn't express myself."

After graduation, he drifted through several manual jobs, including

firefighter, logger, steel furnace stoker, gas pumper and lumberjack. Then he served in the US Army as a swimming instructor.

After that, Eastwood made his way to Hollywood, where his clean-cut good looks won him a contract with Universal. But he was only offered walk-on roles in low budget movies like *Revenge of the Creature* and *Tarantula* (both in 1955). The studio dropped Eastwood in 1956, having decided that he was not the stuff of which leading men were made: his adam's apple protruded, he had a chipped tooth and delivered his lines too slowly.

He was not unemployed for long however, before signing to play the good guy cowboy Rowdy Yates in the long running TV series *Rawhide*.

Spaghetti stardom
Eastwood married in 1953, and it was his wife Maggie who talked him into going to Europe to play the cheroot-smoking, poncho-clad, unshaven "Man With No Name" in the spaghetti Western *A Fistful of Dollars* (1964). With the success of this film and its two sequels—*For a Few Dollars More* (1965) and *The Good the Bad and the Ugly* (1966)—Eastwood returned to Hollywood, to become the most sought after actor in town.

Left: *Shooting it out as Harry Callahan, the sadistic, trigger happy San Francisco cop he played in* **Dirty Harry** *(1971) and three more films.*

Million-dollar split

For many years Eastwood's private life was a closed book. He was rarely seen in Hollywood, unless making a film, and chose instead to live with his wife and two children in the seclusion of his luxurious beach house on the Northern Californian coast. This all changed in 1979 when it was announced that Eastwood had left his wife for actress Sondra Locke. The news took Hollywood by surprise; the Eastwoods had been married for 26 years.

Sondra Locke was cast as the wide-eyed, innocent East Coast settler in Eastwood's Western *The Outlaw Josey Wales* (1976). Since then she has co-starred in most of his films, most notably in *The Gauntlet* (1977).

Divorce

After a multi-million dollar settlement, Eastwood divorced his wife in what appears to have been an amicable split. He said afterwards, "Everybody has problems within marriage. Some people manage to resolve them and others don't. We have a good relationship. Neither of us is unhappy about it."

With the success of *Sudden Impact* (1983), Eastwood's career received another enormous boost.

Age has been kind to him. His lined face becomes more interesting as he grows older. But his ability to play the roles he has played for the past 20 years will inevitably diminish.

Eastwood will know better than anyone when that time arrives: "One of these days I'll look up at the screen and say, 'I'm tired of that guy looking back at me,' and I'll quit."

Top right: *Tense moments with Sondra Locke in* **The Gauntlet** *(1977)*.
Right: *Putting a director's eye to the viewfinder on* **The Beguiled** *(1971)*.

W. C. Fields

"There's no one quite like Bill … thank God," said Mae West, who co-starred with Fields in *My Little Chickadee* (1940). He was unique, an impossible man and eccentric genius who turned his paranoid view of the world into great comedy.

The characters he played were invariably cheats, cowardly braggarts or drunks, sometimes all three. Bombastic con-men and chiseling, henpecked shopkeepers were his stock in trade—suspiciously picking their way through the minefields of life with baleful, bloodshot eyes wary of impending disaster. In *It's a Gift* (1934), Fields' store is wrecked by the flailing white stick of a blind customer; in *The Man on the Flying Trapeze* (1935), he contrives to commit several driving offences while remaining parked at the kerbside.

Women and children were the principal butts of his humour. Once, when asked if he liked children, he replied, "I do, if they are properly cooked." In *My Little Chickadee*, he launched into the tale of how, singlehanded, he beat up Waterfront Nell. Interrupted by a barman who claimed credit for the deed, he replied, "Well, I started kicking her first."

Living rough

It is almost impossible to separate the real Fields from the characters he played with such relish. Like all great comedians, his art sprang from experience. He was born in Philadelphia in 1879 and ran away from home at the age of 12. Living rough, he acquired his famous bottle nose—later reddened by drink—in countless street fights.

He went into showbusiness as a novelty juggler and by the time he was

A tough time for the man who hated women and kids; will he burn when Baby Leroy lights the fuse (above) *in* **David Copperfield** *(1935) or will the 1930s starlets get him first* (left)?

25 had become an international star. In 1913 he shared a bill with the great Sarah Bernhardt, who paid him the compliment of breaking a lifetime vow that she would *never* appear in a show with a juggler.

By 1915 he had incorporated comedy routines into his act, and

appeared in his first film, *Pool Sharks* (1915), a record of his famous pool hall routine. In the 1920s he signed with Paramount, but proved so difficult that when the talkies came in he was dropped.

Ironically, it was Fields' rasping voice which fully rounded out his comic character, although it was not until he signed with Mack Sennett in 1932 that he regained a foothold in Hollywood. The results were four classic shorts—*The Dentist* (1932), *The Fatal Glass of Beer*, *The*

Above: *Checking through the magazines at Universal in 1942.*

Pharmacist and *The Barber Shop* (all in 1933) Fields' terms of pay were characteristically eccentric. He was to be paid his weekly salary in two equal installments—on Mondays and Wednesdays.

Bank accounts worldwide
His miserliness was legendary; he was said to have over 700 bank accounts throughout the world. It is tempting to imagine that many were opened in the outlandish names he created for his screen characters: Eustace McGargle, Larson E. Whipsnade or Harold Bissonette.

After the success of *International House* (1933), he returned to Paramount on a long-term contract. The studio never knew quite what to do with his undisciplined genius, attempting at first to make him a star turn in other people's films. He came into his own in *The Old-Fashioned Way* and *It's a Gift* (both in 1934), in which he tangled with the child star Baby LeRoy. Fields found his little co-star so tiresome that he spiked LeRoy's orange juice with gin.

Drunk again
His Micawber, in MGM's *David Copperfield* (1935), was inspired casting. But Fields' drinking was rapidly undermining his health, and after *Poppy* (1936) he was off the screen for two years.

Martini was his consuming passion and by 1935 he was on two quarts a day. It was said that when he traveled, he needed three trunks—one for clothes and two for liquor. Wherever

he went, whatever he did, there was always a drink in his hand. At home, if the Martini shaker ran dry, he would summon replenishments by blowing on a hunting horn.

Finally, he was persuaded to give up drinking for most of 1937, which proved just how ill he was. While he was in hospital, Carole Lombard presented him with a pig and bicycle, a reference to a long rambling joke he had once told. Perking up, Fields cycled down the hospital's corridors, the pig trotting behind.

Last and wildest
He returned to the screen in *The Big Broadcast of 1938* (1938), then moved to Universal, where he made a series of films which defied virtually every law of the film industry. He was paid $125 000 a picture, plus $25 000 for the story, which was usually little more than random jottings on scraps of paper. He also peppered the films with slyly obscene jokes calculated to escape the attention of the censors.

The last, and wildest, of the Universal features was *Never Give a Sucker an Even Break* (1941). At one point he suggested that the billing be changed to *"Fields: Sucker"*. The plot concerns the adventures which befall Fields after he drops a bottle of whisky from an aircraft and dives after it.

His alcoholism was now completely out of control and complicated by polyneuritis. There were no more features, although he managed three appearances as himself, looking like a man pickled in gin, in low-budget musicals. He died on Christmas Day 1946, with a typical sense of timing— he had always professed to hate the Yuletide season.

Errol Flynn

Like the swashbuckling rogues he portrayed, Errol Flynn lived life to the hilt—giving rise to suggestions that he was a Nazi spy, IRA sympathizer, a bi-sexual junkie and chronic alcoholic. The real truth will never be known because Flynn hugely enjoyed his wild reputation, fabricating much of his life story for the "autobiography" *My Wicked, Wicked Ways*, published in 1959. And throughout his career he laid elaborate traps for future researchers and biographers.

Illustrious relative

What *is* known is that Errol Leslie Thomas Flynn was born in Hobart, Tasmania on June 20, 1909, the son of a marine biologist father, whom he worshiped, and a strict mother, whom he hated. She was a descendant of the famous mutineer Fletcher Christian and it is, perhaps, from this illustrious distant relative that Flynn acquired his love of the sea.

He got off to "a bad start" with expulsion from schools in Australia and Britain. On leaving school he had an unusual assortment of jobs—ship's cook, pearl diver, boxer and colonial official in New Guinea—which, he later claimed, gave him his only real education.

Around this time, fact and fantasy begin to merge into an intricate web.

His first acting role, believe it or not, was as Fletcher Christian in a semi-documentary called *In The Wake Of The Bounty* (1933). He then traveled to Britain, gained acting experience at the Northampton Repertory Company, and next appeared in low-budget British pictures.

The gates of Hollywood finally opened in 1935 and, during the Atlantic crossing, he met and married the actress Lili Damita.

Pin-up

Flynn became an instant pin-up through *Captain Blood* (1935), the first of his many pirate movies, with the dashing swordplay that was in effect to typecast him for life. As the fearless hero he led the Charge of the Light Brigade, plundered Spanish gold for Elizabeth I, rescued Maid Marian from the Sheriff of Nottingham's evil clutches and, of course, won and broke many a female heart.

Not that Flynn's appeal was restricted solely to women. The fantasies he lived out on screen were those of many a Walter Mitty on both sides of the Atlantic.

His off-screen antics made newspaper headlines around the world: bar room brawls, assaulting policemen, minor indiscretions with some of the many women in his life. In 1942, he was divorced from Lili Damita and landed himself in a serious court case on a false charge of statutory rape. Acquitted, he emerged from the

Below: *Newly arrived in Hollywood, the Australian swashbuckler rides high in* **The Charge of the Light Brigade** *(1936).*

Above: *Consultations with lawyer Jerry Giesler; the girl who accused him of rape walks by unnoticed.*

episode with his popularity intact and a new phrase was coined for a successful sexual liaison: "in like Flynn".

During his trial, he met the unknown Nora Eddington who became the second Mrs Flynn in 1943.

Rejected by the Forces
Tongue-in-cheek Flynn once commented that he could not understand why "a quiet, reserved fellow like me should be involved in the news so much".

But his hell-raising took its toll in other ways, too. He volunteered for every branch of the armed forces after Pearl Harbor, but was rejected on account of a heart defect, recurrent malaria and tuberculosis. Deprived of the opportunity for active service, he spent the war years making propaganda movies, one of which—*Objective Burma* (1943)—showed him beating back the Japanese single-handed.

In 1949 he obtained his second divorce and married actress Patrice Wymore the following year.

In 1952, broke through high taxation, alimony and the bottle, Flynn left Hollywood for Britain. He once said that he was disinterested in money so long as his net income was reconciled to his gross habits, but as one of the highest paid actors in the world he had managed to squander an extremely large fortune.

From Britain, he went to Jamaica, where he indulged in his second favorite pastime of sailing. His favorite pastime?—"a prolonged bout in the bedroom with a woman".

The lure of Hollywood proved too strong however, and Flynn returned in 1956. After the critical acclaim of his performance as an alcoholic in *The Sun Also Rises* (1957) he played drunks in his next two movies.

Ravaged
By now overweight and out of condition, his swashbuckling days were over but, before his death in 1959, Flynn did apparently become involved in some real action. After befriending Che Guevara, he joined Castro's fight against the Cuban dictator Batista during the final throes of the revolution.

The years of high living, a growing dependence on various drugs and a liking for vodka, finally proved to much—even for Flynn, the cinema's greatest swashbuckler. When he died of a heart attack in October 1959 in Vancouver, Canada, the post mortem revealed that his body was also ravaged by many other afflictions.

Below: *Shortly before his death in 1959, a love for vodka took its toll of his magnificent physique.*

Henry Fonda

When still a gawky lad, Henry Fonda had acting thrust upon him by no less a person than Dorothy "Do" Brando. At the time Do's own son, Marlon, was just one year old, so she begged her neighbors, William and Herberta Fonda, for the loan of their only son, Hank, for the juvenile lead in a production of *You and I* (1925) at the Omaha Community Playhouse. Young Fonda was then 20 years old—he was born in 1905—and just right for the part.

"I was too self-conscious to say I didn't want to do it or that I didn't know how to do it," he recalled. "I was so painfully introverted that I tucked the book under my arm, mumbled a few words, went home and memorized the part."

Magic

The acting bug bit deeply. "I discovered the magic of theater that I had never known anything about. I liked the feeling of being up there... I lost most of my shyness and began to relax. It took me three years to decide that maybe this was what I really wanted to do."

Fonda's assets were $100, a lean, handsome face with huge honest eyes, a rough-hewn physique and a resonant mid-western drawl. He needed all of them, plus a talent for designing and painting sets, to survive until his rise to star status on Broadway in *The Farmer Takes a Wife* (1935). This success transported him to Hollywood for the film version the next year.

Disastrous marriages

Long before this, he'd married his first wife, Margaret Sullavan, but lived with her for just four months before moving back to his flat mates, James Stewart, Joshua Logan and Myron McCormick. The quartet sowed their wild oats from a run-down apartment in Manhattan. Only in their company could Fonda relax and be himself. His relations with

all of his first four wives were disastrous, betraying an emotional immaturity that ran and ran.

The second Mrs Henry Fonda, the beautiful and wealthy widow Frances Seymour Brokaw, bore him his two famous children—Jane in 1937 and Peter two years later— before falling victim to mental illness and committing suicide in 1950. In December of that year, the 45-year-old actor married Susan Blanchard, 23 years his junior, an autumn-spring romance he repeated, more briefly, with Contessa Afdera Franchetti in 1957.

Ashamed

"I was ashamed as hell that a guy with a solid background like mine kept screwing up his personal life," Fonda admitted, but the barriers he had

Left: *An Oscar-winning performance in* On Golden Pond *(1982).*
Top: *With Jack Lemmon and William Powell in* Mr Roberts *(1955).*
Above: *With fifth wife, Shirlee, the woman who tamed the aging actor.*

erected between himself and his family remained, while his career went from strength to strength.

Among the screen roles that made him rich and famous before he signed on as a seaman for the Second World War in 1942, were *Young Mr Lincoln* (1939), Tom Joad in *The Grapes of Wrath* (1940) and the cowboy hero of *The Oxbow Incident* (1943). Post-war, his star continued to

rise, especially with *Mister Roberts* (1955), a title role he immortalized on Broadway before repeating it in Hollywood, and *12 Angry Men* (1957), which he was also responsible for co-producing.

Indifferent father

Some of the Fonda millions went into a luxurious Bel Air mansion. It had the statutory swimming pool, and stables to house donkeys for Jane and Peter— but that was about the extent of his care for his offspring.

Fonda took the garden more seriously than his duties as a parent, and his children had to endure his indifference as well as the loss of their mother. Later he attempted to rationalize his behaviour: "I didn't help or discourage them or lead them by the hand... I think I knew instinctively that if they made it, they'd like to know they did it on their own." He was lucky that both of them stood by him and that all the rifts were healed before he died, after a decade of ill health, in 1982.

Most of the credit for the softening of the aging actor belongs to Shirlee Adams, the airline hostess who became the fifth Mrs Fonda in 1965. Again, many years his junior, she yet managed to quiet his restless spirit.

In the 1970s Fonda pursued his hobbies between roles that included television and commercials.

Later in the decade, the movie world woke up to the fact that he had made over 100 films and given dozens of stage performances, with barely an award to show for it. Faced with his failing health, the moguls heaped recognition on him. The Tony Award for Achievement in Drama, the Golden Globe, the Cecil B. DeMille Award and the American Film Institute's Life Achievement Award, all were quickly accorded to him.

One more tribute

The best—the Oscar for his performance as the dying octogenarian, Norman Thayer, in *On Golden Pond* (1981)—came last. Too ill to attend the ceremony, he watched on television as Jane received the trophy on his behalf. However, there was one more tribute that he never knew about, that would have pleased him even more: the founding of the Henry Fonda Memorial Theater as an addition to the Omaha Community Playhouse where his career began all those years before.

Jane Fonda

Jane Fonda is not just one of the world's most popular actresses, she is one of America's most determined women. Her svelte figure is evident proof of her life-style—a lot of muscle and no fat. It is a style that sent shivers down the spines of congressmen in the late 1960s and early 1970s when she pulled just about every punch in her opposition to the United States' involvement in the war in Vietnam.

The daughter of Henry Fonda and his second wife Margaret Seymour Brokaw, Jane was born in 1937. As a child, she saw little of her father, who was on active service with the navy in the South Pacific. He later admitted that he felt alienated from his children and found it difficult to settle back into family life. He filed for divorce in 1949.

Jane's mother sank into a deep depression, eventually committing suicide in a mental institution. The truth about her death was kept from Jane who only stumbled on the fact by chance.

At Vassar, she dabbled with acting, and although her father was at first reluctant to encourage her pursuit of an acting career, he soon realized that she had a very real talent as an actress. She appeared with him in summer stock productions of *The Country Girl* and *The Male Animal*.

By her first film *Tall Story* (1960), Fonda had lost every vestige of chubbiness and acquired a new shapeliness more in keeping with that of "La BB Américaine", as the French press was later to dub her.

Three days in bed
Her first real romance was with a struggling young actor, Timmy Everett, a fellow pupil at Lee Strasberg's acting school. The story goes that, while rehearsing a scene together in her New York apartment, Fonda and Everett clicked and spent much of the next three days in bed together. Their liaison was short-lived, however. Fonda soon fell for the Hellenic charm of director Andreas Voutsinas, a much older man. They were inseparable for the next two years.

In 1963, during her stay in France, Roger Vadim, Bardot's ex-husband,

Left: *The 1980s Fonda, a woman of style, intelligence and humanity.*

offered her a part in his film *La Ronde* (1964). She not only agreed to play the part, but fell in love with Vadim.

Sex kitten
The so-American Fonda blossomed in the sophisticated milieu of the French. In 1965, she married Vadim, who was quick to mold his new wife into a sex-kitten for *Barbarella* (1967), in which she appeared complete with futuristic see-through bra. But the projected image of vacant sexiness was untrue to the real Fonda.

Her daughter, Vanessa, was born in 1968, after her return to America, where a proud Henry Fonda declared motherhood had stabilized his daughter's life.

By 1969 the marriage to Vadim was over. She could no longer cope with his admitted liaisons with other women and moved out of their Malibu beach house. Throughout the filming of *Klute* (1971) for which she won an Oscar, Fonda lived with her co-star, Canadian actor, Donald Sutherland. With an Oscar to her name, she was no longer simply "Henry Fonda's daughter". She was recognized as an accomplished actress in her own right.

Vietnam
Fonda's considerable energies began to turn towards the American involvement in Vietnam. Her father was a Democrat who had served on various committees, but he was never so vociferous as she in proclaiming political beliefs. He feared that her acting career would suffer, particularly after her broadcast from Hanoi and denouncing Nixon as "a liar, a cynic and a murderer". It was even mooted that her US citizenship might be revoked.

Through her political activities, however, Fonda met Tom Hayden, a fellow activist whom she married in 1973.

Now in her late forties, still a picture of health and beauty, and with a highly successful chain of exercise studios and interests in the fashion trade to occupy her seemingly inexhaustible energies, Fonda lives modestly and quietly with a husband who shares her political convictions. Assiduously avoiding the Hollywood social scene, she can now make the films *she* wants to make and play the parts *she* wants to play. A little more mellowed by time, she remains a fine actress and a woman of powerful conviction.

Top: *Speaking out with characteristic forcefulness against the Vietnam War during a march in 1970.*

Above: *Putting in an Oscar winning performance as the prostitute in* **Klute** *(1971), opposite Donald Sutherland.*

65

Clark Gable

When eager autograph hunters besieged the set of MGM's *Test Pilot* (1938), Clark Gable signed their books in his customary scrupulous fashion. Co-star Spencer Tracy, eyeing the mêlée, bawled "Hail to the King". Later, he jokingly crowned Gable with a cardboard coronet and dubbed him "King of the Lot". Columnist Ed Sullivan promptly launched a nationwide poll to choose Hollywood's King and Queen and Gable was overwhelmingly elected, with his *Test Pilot* leading lady Myrna Loy easily winning the title of Queen.

Animal magnetism
As Joan Blondell succinctly put it: "Gable affected all females, unless they were dead." Of the new, working class "ordinary guys" launched as stars in the 1930s, he was the sexiest. And his image was sealed by a typically

Above: *Turning on the magnetism as Rhett Butler to Vivien Leigh's Scarlett in* Gone With the Wind *(1939).*
Right: *With Kay Spreckels, the last of his wives, just before he died in 1961.*

Tight-fisted

In fact, Gable the man was in several ways quite unlike the virile, careless rogue he played with such conviction on screen. He was tight-fisted — perhaps in response to his father's feckless example — and this despite the $¾ million MGM paid him between *Gone With The Wind* and his departure for active service in 1942.

He was obsessively clean, showering practically on the hour and keeping his chest and armpits free of hair. He was shy of fellow stars, terrified of risk, and remained obedient to Metro for 23 years, making pictures he cordially loathed because the bosses told him to. Embarrassed by all the adulation and publicity, he nevertheless remained dutiful to the fans. But he squirmed when Judy Garland sang *Dear Mr Gable: You Made Me Love You* on the screen and again when his first post-war movie, *Adventure* (1945), in which he starred with Greer Garson, was sold with the line "Gable's back and Garson's got him".

Haunted by tragedy

Gable never fully recovered from the shock of his wife Carole Lombard's death in a 1942 plane crash while selling war bonds. Her last cable — "Pappy, you'd better join this man's Army" — haunted him, and he joined up even though officially over-age.

His two later wives were both plainly in her image. The last, Kay Spreckels, bore him his only child but he died before his son was born.

Monroe, risks and alcohol

Gable's MGM contract expired in 1954 and, to his surprise and anger, was not renewed. Gable-type movies were out of fashion. As a freelance, he still topped the salary scale but a growing alcohol problem made him a bad risk.

His last movie, however, *The Misfits* (1961) ensured his legend would live. Gable's initial wooing of Marilyn Monroe was an excruciating evocation of the style of his youth but in the later scenes with her and with the rest of a great cast, now virtually all deceased, he gave the performance of his career. However, his insistence on performing in all the takes for the movie's climax — a terrifying battle of wills between man and wild horse — was to prove fatal. Twelve days after filming was completed, his heart gave out: "The King" was dead.

Hollywood twist of fortune.

Gable's seventh film, *A Free Soul* (1931), had him vying with the pale and not always interesting Leslie Howard for rich bitch Norma Shearer. Head of production Irving Thalberg, viewing the rushes, saw Gable's emergent animal magnetism running away with the picture. Thalberg plotted to stop this — Shearer was his wife — and wrote in a scene where Gable slapped her about. His intention was to lose Gable the audience's sympathy but instead he became the idol of macho men everywhere and every woman's idea of "rough trade". His Oscar-winning bare chest in *It Happened One Night* (1934), confirmed his appeal and almost destroyed the singlet industry.

When presented with the Oscar, he muttered, "I'm still gonna wear the same size hat." And he did.

Gable appealed to women of all ages, and he had a natural empathy with older women — his first two wives were respectively 14 and 17 years his senior. This might be traced to the unwavering support he received from

Above: **The Misfits** (1961) *was Gable's and Monroe's last film.*

his stepmother in the face of his father's ferocious opposition to his career. His natural mother died shortly after his birth in February 1901.

Sexual appetite

Gable's affairs with stars such as Jean Harlow and Ava Gardner made gossip column copy throughout his career, but the most celebrated liaison was with Joan Crawford, eight times his co-star in the 1930s. MGM insisted their ardor be cooled: after all, Gable had just begun his second marriage and Crawford was married to Douglas Fairbanks Jnr. Amusingly, Gable married Fairbanks' stepmother in 1949.

In a later interview, Crawford said she liked Gable because "he had balls". and the legend was underscored by his movies. Who can forget the relish with which Vivien Leigh's Scarlett greets the morning after the night when Gable's Rhett Butler bore her up the stairs in *Gone with the Wind* (1939)?

Greta Garbo

Greta Garbo was still only 35 when she retired after making *Two-Faced Woman* (1941). Although she had been the dominant star at MGM for more than a decade and still had a powerful contract, she chose to abandon all further claim to fame and fortune and has shunned public life ever since. If Hollywood mimicked dreams, cultivated myths and built a pantheon for those they raised on high, no screen goddess has cloaked herself in more mystery than the divine, elusive Garbo.

Since the much publicized Cecil Beaton photographs of the late 1940s, there have only been those rare, blurred snaps caught in flurries of excitement on city streets.

Legend
That the Garbo legend survives is tribute to the potency of movie-making. Her mystery was perhaps best used and explained by Rouben Mamoulian when directing her last shot for *Queen Christina* (1933): "I want your face to be a blank sheet of paper. I want the writing to be done by every member of the audience. I'd like it if you could avoid blinking your eyes, so that you're nothing but a beautiful mask."

Garbo's career comprised only 31 movies, 6 of them now lost. She mostly

Left: *At 14 she modelled hats in a Stockholm store but made even better use of them in Hollywood in the 1930s*
Below: *Elegant romance with John Gilbert in* **Flesh and The Devil** *(1926).*

worked with second-rate leading men, third-rate directors and bargain basement stories, but these unpromising materials were off-set by Cedric Gibbons' designs, Adrian's gowns, Salka Viertel's sympathetic dialog and William Daniels' cinematography, which patiently explored her beauty. For the rest, Garbo intrigues, mystifies, haunts, bewitches, tantalizes. Who is that behind the mask?

Always sad
Born in Stockholm, September 18, 1905, she was christened Greta Louisa Gustafsson and formally became Greta Garbo on December 4, 1923, appearing in her second film, *The Saga of Gösta Berling* (1924), with that identity. There have been many theories as to the origin of her professional name but Garbo herself would only say, "Anything is possible."

That her early years were spent in poverty is well established. Garbo described her childhood in a 1931 interview: "I was always sad, for as long as I can think back. I hated crowds of people and used to sit in a corner by myself, just thinking. I was 14 when my father died after a long, lingering illness. He was only 48."

Two months after his death, Garbo began work unpacking hats at PUB, Stockholm's biggest department store. Soon she began to model the hats and this led to publicity films for the store.

Her first important film role came when director Erik A. Petschler spotted her in the street. Thereafter she was taken up by the great Mauritz Stiller who told his Svensk film bosses: "You only get a face like that in front of a camera once in a century." It was he who directed her in *The Saga of Gösta Berling*.

While in Berlin for the making of Pabst's *Joyless Street* (1925), Garbo and Stiller met Louis B. Mayer of MGM. But Mayer was impressed only by Stiller. Speaking of Garbo, he told his interpreter, "American men don't like fat women." Only because Stiller insisted on Garbo being contracted did Mayer buy her services.

In July 1925 they arrived in New York, only to be ignored by MGM. After languishing on the east coast until September, they were actually booking their passage home when some photographs of Garbo appeared in *Vanity Fair* magazine and a humbled Mayer rushed the pair to Los Angeles.

The wicked innocent
There were more delays before a screen-test won her the lead in *The Torrent* (1926) and her second film, *The Temptress* (1926) sealed her type-casting, much to her chagrin. "I am not vamp," she was to complain in 1928. "In Germany, I play sweet, innocent girls. Never am I wicked type. Here they say yes, I am. I do not like." Her former champion, Stiller, was no longer alive to support her. Soon after work started on *The Temptress*, he died.

Flesh and the Devil (1926) teamed Garbo with John Gilbert. None of her leading men was a bigger star than Gilbert in his day and with no other did she have a romance. MGM were delighted and announced their next

Below: *Capturing her elusive, haunting beauty on the set of* **Romance** *(1930).*
Bottom: *A rare sighting of the older Garbo as she arrived in New York in 1949, after her early retirement.*

movie as "Gilbert and Garbo in *Love*". But twice she fled virtually from the altar and, after two years, Gilbert abandoned the chase.

The final enigma
Garbo formed other liaisons—with conductor Leopold Stokowski, 23 years her senior; with director Mamoulian; with photographer Beaton; with dietitian Gaylord Hauser; with fashion millionare George Schlee. But she remained true to her line in *Queen Christina* (1933): "I shall die a bachelor."

No-one knows the real nature of her relationships. Reputedly some of her closest men friends were exclusively or predominantly homosexual.

Probably we shall never know the whole or even half of the truth about Garbo's life, for she will never tell us. In this way, mystery remains mystery, and that, surely, is the secret of her enduring appeal as a star. The woman, perhaps, couldn't care less.

Judy Garland

Of all the victims of Hollywood's studio system, Judy Garland was perhaps the most tragic. Her life and career were run almost entirely by others and when she died at 47, she had been dependent on pills since the early days of stardom.

Born Frances Gumm in Minnesota on June 10, 1922, Garland made her first stage appearance before she was three. At 12, she acquired her first Hollywood agent and an MGM contract. And when her beloved father died suddenly, the all-powerful studio boss Louis B. Mayer became the dominant male in her life, controlling her personal and professional affairs.

Life-time debt

There was speculation about Mayer's intentions to Garland when she was only 14. In any event, no financial safeguards were made for her future and she was in debt for most of her life. Her losing battle with narcotics also began at 14. When she developed unbecoming puppy fat, she was given slimming and sleeping pills, and her diet was strictly regulated.

In later years she told a reporter: "Lana Turner, Elizabeth Taylor, Mickey Rooney and me—we all came out of there a little ticky and kooky."

Garland was teamed with Rooney in nine films. But, to cinema audiences, she was the main draw and as Dorothy in *The Wizard of Oz* (1939) touched their hearts. She later said: "I think the American people put their arms around me when I was a child performer and they've kept them there—even when I was in trouble."

Even her dates were arranged by the studio. When she started seeing Tyrone Power, Mayer stepped in—such a romance was bad for her image. They made a brief fight of it, Power risking arrest (she was still a minor), but were forced to separate and he turned to Lana Turner.

Garland's insomnia started about then. She needed more and more pills to help her sleep, followed by as many "uppers" to revive her.

Her first marriage was to orchestra

Beginning and end: with Mickey Rooney, in **Nine Juveniles** *(above right) and Dirk Bogarde* (right) *in* **I Could Go On Singing** *(1963).*

70

conductor David Rose, with whom she eloped in July 1941. When she became pregnant, her mother and husband sided with the studio over an abortion and, lacking support, Garland reluctantly agreed.

By the age of 21 she was one of the top 10 box office stars in the United States. She was also having secret sessions with a psychiatrist and her marriage was failing. She was divorced in February 1943.

For the next few years there was a pattern of breakdowns, hospitalization and a too-early return to work. After her first suicide attempt she saw an analyst daily for five years.

While filming *Meet Me in St Louis* (1944), one of MGM's most lavish and successful musicals, Garland fell in love with the director, Vincente Minnelli. They married in June 1945. Desperate for someone to protect her, she was disappointed again by the studio's demands on Minnelli.

Afraid of sex

After the birth of Liza Minnelli, Garland was addicted, depressed, exhausted and afraid of sex. She also became very thin. Having forced her to slim in the past, the studio now tried to fatten her up but eating made her nauseous. At 25 she suffered a complete breakdown.

The marriage to Minnelli floundered and Garland refused to work with him again after making *The Pirate* (1948). They divorced in March 1951, by which time MGM had fired her for failure to work. There had been several more suicide attempts.

Two-year collapse

Garland's business manager and new love, Sidney Luft, encouraged her to do stage work. Concerts in London and New York won excellent reviews but, again, no money came her way and her health continued to deteriorate.

Garland and Luft married in June 1952 but after her mother's death a few months later, she suffered a two-year collapse. After filming *A Star is Born* (1954) she became antagonistic to Luft—like her previous husbands he seemed to put her career before her personal happiness. They finally divorced in May 1965.

Garland meanwhile survived a string of brilliant "comebacks" and abrupt reversals. Dirk Bogarde co-starred in her last film *I Could Go On Singing* (1963), and said: "Judy is a schizo; Judy is a mess; Judy is a genius."

Garland was lost without a man in her life but her fourth marriage, to aspiring actor Mark Herron, lasted only six months.

Whether her fifth, to 34-year-old discotheque manager, Mickey Deans, would have fared any better it is hard to say. She collapsed and died on June 22, 1969 after a final, triumphant concert tour. They had been married for only three months. As daughter Liza Minnelli said at the time: "Mama was just like a beautiful flower that withered and died."

Below: *With Mickey Deans, her fifth husband-to-be, in London in 1968.*
Bottom: *Like mother, like daugther: Liza Minnelli visits Judy on the set of* **Summer Stock** *(1950).*

Lillian Gish

With a certain beauty, even in her eighties, gracious in an old fashioned way, but also tough and incredibly hard working, Lillian Gish has been described as the "First Lady of the Silent Screen" and "Lady" is an apt word for her.

Her father, a ne'er do well, died before he was 30 and part of a dedication in one of her books reads: "To my father who gave me insecurity". Penniless, Gish's mother overcame her deep shame at the very prospect and went on stage, her daughters Dorothy and Lillian following her—as Baby Dorothy and Baby Lillian. But always they were in plays that their mother deemed to be of a sufficiently high moral tone.

"We were good children," Gish later said. "Mother taught us good manners, to think of others before ourselves. We never learnt to play, we got into the habit of work."

Shameful profession

The Gish girls made friends with the Smiths, another hard-up theatrical family, but when Gladys Smith made her screen debut Mrs Gish was appalled: to her mind appearing in films was even more shameful than going on stage. "What terrible misfortune can have befallen Mrs Smith that Gladys should be in the movies?"

However, Gladys's new film name was Mary Pickford, and not only was she destined to become a superstar herself, she introduced the Gish family to the same possibility. It was while waiting for her in the Biograph Studios that they were spotted by D.W. Griffith, who put Mrs Gish, Lillian and Dorothy into *An Unseen Enemy* (1912), labeling the girls with red and blue ribbons so that he could tell them apart.

From there, he took Dorothy and Lillian to Hollywood, making them stars in films like *Birth of a Nation* (1915), *Broken Blossoms* (1919) and *Way Down East* (1920) which stand among the greatest achievements of silent Hollywood. Over the next decade Lillian Gish went on to feature in over fifty D.W. Griffith films.

Exciting footage

"It was hard work, working for Mr Griffith," Gish has said with her characteristic mixture of

Below: Being chosen by D.W. Griffith was a mixed blessing.
Right: With her seducer, Lowell Sherman, in **Way Down East** *(1920).*

understatement and politeness. Five of the cast died of exposure when they were making *Way Down East*. "Mr Griffith kept shouting 'Look into the camera' but I couldn't —I had icicles on my eyelids."

Gish herself was nearly killed when an ice-floe she was standing on unexpectedly broke away and sped down-river towards a waterfall, but she was rescued by Richard Barthelmess, the leading man. Griffith, typically, stood by—making sure that the cameras were still turning so that he could use the exciting footage.

Spaghetti with Valentino

The same rigorous standards applied on other films too. "Once, when I was filming in the desert sun, I went to a studio car to change. I touched the door handle—and left half the skin of my hand on it. It was dangerous. But we never questioned it. We would never use stand-ins," Gish later said.

In Hollywood Gish was surrounded

by admirers but kept herself aloof from the sordid scandal-mongering that was all around. She was friendly with Rudolph Valentino, the man for whom women killed themselves or spent their lives in mourning. "Rudi was a nice boy," she once said. "He used to come up and cook spaghetti for Dorothy and me."

She worked 12 hours a day, seven days a week and has said that that is why she never married. "Somehow marriage seemed like a full time job and I never had that kind of time. I had a lot of good men friends, but I thought why ruin their lives by marrying them? I never wanted to possess anybody."

Unlike some other silent performers whose voices proved unsuitable for the "talkies", Gish was driven out of Hollywood by changing styles. Her almost ethereal beauty was too subtle for an age ready for the more overt sex appeal of heroines like Garbo and Dietrich.

Lesser spirits might have given up,

but the complex, stubborn and intelligent Gish returned to Broadway, in classic plays like *Hamlet* and *Uncle Vanya*. Broadway critic George Jean Nathan tried hard to persuade her to marry him, but she claimed that she was too busy for such a commitment.

Fighting back
She continued to work at a furious pace, touring the world with retrospectives of her work, writing (her book on Griffith is acknowledged as the best description of his methods and influence), and making films—notably *Duel in the Sun* (1947) and *Night of the Hunter* (1955). At 80 she appeared in a cameo role in Robert Altman's *A Wedding* (1978).

"I've never known what to do except work; if you start acting when you are five there isn't a lot of point in trying to do something else when you're 84," she told an interviewer. "I expect I'll still have a couple of days shooting to do when they bury me."

Above: **Birth of a Nation** *reunion with Donald Crisp and Mae Marsh.*
Below: *Proving she has lost none of her skill in Altman's* **A Wedding** *(1978).*

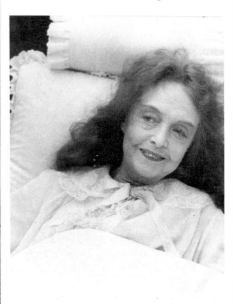

Betty Grable

"I've got two reasons for success," Betty Grable once quipped in a typically self-effacing way "and I'm standing on both of them." Those famous legs were insured with Lloyds of London for half a million dollars, but she had other assets too, not least of which were her straight-forward humor and her generosity.

Funny, good natured and just a little bit brash, she was the undisputed pin-up girl of American GIs throughout the Second World War. Yet, despite her huge appeal—she was said to be the highest paid woman in the world in 1949—she never displayed the phoney self-importance which marred so many lesser stars.

She once told an interviewer, "People who take themselves too seriously in this business cause themselves a lot of unhappiness. As a dancer I couldn't outdance Ginger Rogers. As a singer I'm no Doris Day. As an actress I don't take myself seriously… I don't think I've ever had a good review. My films don't get them either. Yet, they all did well at the box-office."

When the *Harvard Lampoon* decided that she was the worst actress of the year she sent them a telegram saying, "You are so right!"

Hard grind to stardom

One reason for her down-to-earth attitude to fame is that it was not Grable who courted success, but her mother, Lillian—ambitious for her daughter from her birth in December 1916. "I had the stage mother to end all stage mothers," Grable said. "I had every kind of lesson. Tap, toe, ballet, acrobatic tumbling, ice skating, roller skating. I can even play a saxophone."

When Grable was 13, Lillian decided to move both of them to Hollywood, breaking up her own marriage in the process. By lying about her age Grable got into the blacked-up chorus of *Let's Go Places* (1930).

She was noticed and Fox gave her an option on a contract, but later dropped it. This pattern would be repeated many times but Lillian was always there to push and prod, whenever the starlet felt like quitting.

Right: *The legs that inspired that legendary $500 000 insurance policy.*

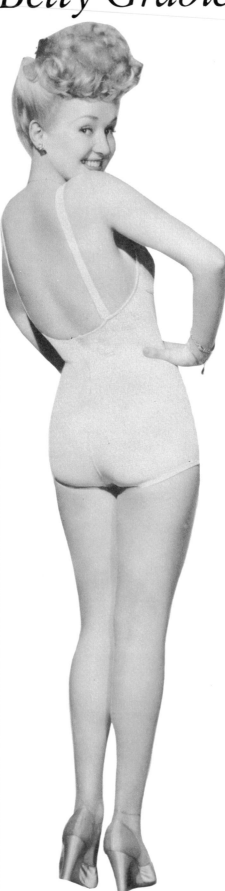

By 1937 Grable had been contracted then dropped by nearly every major studio in Hollywood. She went on vaudeville tour with ex-child star Jackie Coogan and they married in the same year. When they divorced just two years later Grable moved to Broadway to star in *Du Barry was a Lady*—a smash hit show which revived 20th Century-Fox's interest in her.

At the time the studio was planning *Down Argentine Way* (1940) an early technicolor film with Alice Faye—then *the* blonde bombshell. Faye became seriously ill and Grable stepped into the part, scoring a huge box-office success and delighting the studio.

Forces pin-up

The war years made her into the forces sweetheart, and her pictures were just as popular with civilians. No one, least of all Grable, pretended that they were masterpieces, but they had the right combination of sex, sentiment and fun to place her firmly at the top of the list of most popular female stars. And it wasn't just men who liked Grable: fan letters by the sackful came from

women as well. "Women feel no competition because I look ordinary," she said.

Grable's marriage to band-leader Harry James in 1943 put the seal on her popularity, and she held on to her position for another eight years after the war. Fox tried to present her in serious, dramatic parts, but Grable always resisted, even at the price of suspension. "They paid me for raising my skirt, not playing Sarah Bernhardt," she said.

Declining star
How to Marry a Millionaire (1953) was the beginning of the end. About three gold-diggers in search of rich husbands, the films was a hit, but one of her co-stars was a new beautiful, blonde actress who would eventually replace her at the top—Marilyn Monroe. Typically, Grable went out of her way to encourage the young actress. Finally, when Monroe was moved into Grable's dressing room, Grable told her, "Honey, I've had it. It's your turn now. Go and get it."

Grable made two more films, *Three for the Show* and *How to be Very,*

One of Hollywood's nicest stars: with a glum George Raft (right) *and taking a break from the razzmatazz* (below).

Very Popular (both in 1955), but she realized that her peak had passed and retired for several years. When, to general surprise, her 20-year marriage to James broke up, Grable made a stage comeback. Her Broadway shows were successful, but an attempt at a show of her own in London closed after only 16 days. "Life's like that," she laughed. "Sometimes you win. Sometimes you lose."

Resigned and courageous
In 1972, Grable—always a heavy smoker—contracted lung cancer. She took the news with her usual good-natured resignation and until her death, a year later, remained always a courageous and undemanding patient.

At her funeral there was a capacity crowd, with both of her husbands and former friends and co-stars like Mitzi Gaynor and Dorothy Lamour present to pay their last respects. And all for the girl who said, looking back at her career, "You know, I used to wake up in the middle of the night wondernig how long it would be before they found me out and ran me off the lot!"

Above: *The brashness that made her a GI pin-up in* **Moon Over Miami** *(1941).*

Cary Grant

Cary Grant's screen image as an engaging and witty charmer remained constant throughout his 34-year film career and his reputation was unshaken by revelations about his unconventional personal life.

Eventful childhood

Grant was born in Bristol, England on January 18, 1904, and christened Archibald Alexander Leach. His childhood was not a happy one. His mother had a breakdown when he was 12 and the following year he ran away from home to work in a theater. Then he joined a traveling troupe of acrobats with whom he went to the United States when he was 16.

His early film career attracted no critical acclaim until *Blonde Venus* (1932), one of seven films he made that year. He was spotted by Mae West who wanted him for *She Done Him Wrong* (1933). She thought he had "class" as well as good looks. "If he can talk I'll take him," she said.

In 1934 he married the first of his five wives, actress Virginia Cherrill. She left him after a few stormy months and Grant made the headlines a week later when he was found unconscious, with a tablet bottle marked "Poison" close by. A stomach pump was used, but Grant later said that he had been drunk and the tablets were planted as a joke by friends.

The couple were divorced in March 1935. For Cherrill it was claimed that Grant "used liquor excessively, choked her, beat her, threatened her life..."

No fortune hunter

His second marriage fared no better, though it lasted longer. In 1938 he met the fabulously wealthy Woolworth heiress Barbara Hutton. They married in July 1942, by which time he had become an American citizen. In the period leading up to the wedding Grant was attacked by the press for being a social climber. He and Hutton were referred to as "Cash and Cary", though he was hardly a fortune hunter: he signed away all claims to Hutton's wealth—the only one of her seven husbands to do so.

Left: *Beefcake on the beach – the English immigrant tones up during his early days in Hollywood.*

Above: *Party time for Grant, first wife Virginia Cherrill and Randolph Scott.*
Below: *A less happy occasion as Raymond Massey and Peter Lorre go to work with a vengeance in Frank Capra's* Arsenic and Old Lace *(1944).*

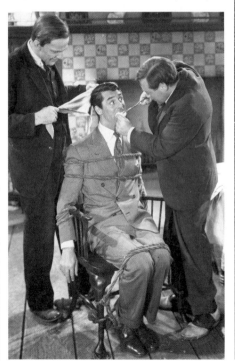

Meanwhile, his career was taking off. *Sylvia Scarlett* (1936), co-starring Katharine Hepburn, established him in the kind of comic/romantic role which best suited him. The 1930s generally were peak years; throughout, he worked with important directors such as Howard Hawks, George Cukor and Leo McCarey.

Hawks' *His Girl Friday* (1940) was another big success, with a part tailor-made for him, and for a time he dated co-star Rosalind Russell. Other romances had been with Mary Brian, Ginger Rogers and Phyllis Brooks. But Grant had something more serious on his mind: whether he should return to England to aid the war effort. In the end he stayed in Hollywood and did the best he could from there, donating money and services to various war-time causes.

Although they had little else in common, one of Grant's joint ventures with Barbara Hutton was to finance a clinic in San Francisco for wounded servicemen. The *Daily Mail* called Grant "probably the most generous man in Hollywood", but his second marriage ended in the divorce courts in August 1945.

Experiments with LSD

Two years later Grant met actress Betsy Drake, 20 years his junior. They married on Christmas Day 1949—flown to their wedding by their best man, the eccentric tycoon Howard Hughes. It was Drake who introduced Grant to hypnosis and LSD. He apparently became adept at self-hypnosis, able to anesthetize any part of his body. His experiments with LSD were carried out under scientific control and he reportedly commented "My intention in taking LSD was to make myself happy. A man would be a fool to take something that *didn't* make him happy."

The marriage lasted 12 years, even surviving a crisis in the mid-1950s when Grant met Sophia Loren in Europe on the set of *The Pride and The Passion* (1957). Rumors of their affair were confirmed by Loren: "I knew he loved me and that, if I chose to, I could marry him." But recent plans to film a reconstruction of their romance did not meet with Grant's approval. "I cannot believe that anyone would exploit an old friendship like this," he said.

Drake divorced him in August 1962 on grounds of mental cruelty but they remained on good terms. Grant was always deferential to his ex-wives, and only his fourth marriage, to actress Dyan Cannon, ended acrimoniously. She was 35 years his junior (confirming his preference for younger women) and they married in July 1965. Almost from the start the much-publicized age gap brought problems and they had nothing in common. A child—Grant's only one—was born in February 1966 but the couple separated in the following December.

Grant always kept close links with England, making frequent visits to relatives in Bristol. After his retirement from the cinema with *Walk, Don't Run* (1966), he became an executive of a cosmetics company. It was on a trip to England in this capacity that he met Barbara Harris, 47 years his junior. They married in April 1981.

Threat to sue

As for the untarnished reputation—in 1980 Grant threatened to sue American comedian Chevy Chase for alluding to him as a homosexual. The $10 million suit was dropped but, in any case, the remarks have in no way affected Grant's status as one of the most endearing and enduring screen heart-throbs of all time.

Gene Hackman

When Gene Hackman was a young hopeful at Los Angeles' famed Pasadena Playhouse he was considered the least likely of the aspiring actors there to succeed. He was stocky, ordinary-looking, an introvert to the point of being antisocial, with a personality that not only unsettled him but the others, too.

As an actor, he was hardly noticed at all until he was 37, but then it was in a role that brought an Academy Award nomination, as Warren Beatty's older brother in *Bonnie and Clyde* (1967).

Accolades

Now, the curly-headed actor is a great character actor who has won a string of international accolades, three Oscar nominations and an Oscar for *The French Connection* (1971).

His acceptance speech for that award revealed more about the man than any number of articles. It consisted of one line: "I want to thank Fay Maltese for bringing me uptown." The "uptown" reference dated back to when they met in his early New York days, living in "cold water flats" grubbing a living on Off-Broadway.

Born in California in 1930, he first wanted to follow his father and grandfather into journalism but quickly discovered that he lacked writing talent. He turned his attentions elsewhere, joining the US Marine Corps, at 16, by lying about his age.

Discharged from the service he worked in television as a floor manager. Then he went into summer stock before heading to New York. There he studied with a drama coach, a move that paid off with small parts in television and stage productions. One in particular, Irwin Shaw's *Children At Their Games*, though it closed after one performance, amazingly, brought him a Clarence Derwent Award.

His first starring role on Broadway was with Sandy Dennis in the hit comedy *Any Wednesday* and he made his screen debut, aged 34, in *Lilith* (1964), starring Jean Seberg and Warren Beatty. Three years later when Beatty was casting *Bonnie and Clyde* he recommended Hackman to director Arthur Penn.

Right: *In bed with Elizabeth Hubbard in* **I Never Sang for My Father** *(1970).*

Below left: *The rough diamond with Burt Reynolds and Liza Minnelli in* **Lucky Lady** *(1975).*

Below: *A touch of uneasy chic as he limps into a glittering occasion, the premiere of* **The Godfather** *(1972).*

In the same year, 1967, Hackman was fired from rehearsals of *The Graduate*, from the part of Mr Robinson—which friend Dustin Hoffman had secured for him—on grounds of "not being capable of giving the director what he wanted".

Improvization

"My training is improvization. I believe it takes 10 years to become an actor—there's no substitute for experience," said Hackman in retrospect. At that stage he considered films to be simply a means to make quick money so that he could return to New York and the theater.

However, once accepted into the film world, he went on to acquire another Oscar nomination, for *I Never Sang For My Father* (1970), before hitting the top with the dogged detective Doyle in *The French Connection*.

From then he became one of Hollywood's hardest working stars. Between 1971 and 1978 he made a staggering 15 films, among the most impressive being *Scarecrow* (1973); also *The Conversation* and *Young Frankenstein* (both in 1974), and another for Arthur Penn, *Night Moves* (1975).

Then Hackman's apparently secure life started to fall apart. He split up with his wife and decided to stop acting before he was forced to stop after making four bad films in a row: *Lucky Lady* (1975), *The Domino Principle* (1977), *A Bridge Too Far* and *March or Die* (both in 1977).

"I should have stopped after the first one and gone back to taking parts for what they were and not what they paid," he said.

Two year break

He took a two year break and spent the time painting, sculpting and flying—he owns three planes, one of which is a Pitts biplane—with his three sons, back home in Santa Barbara.

Interestingly diverse roles marked his return to the screen: Superman's arch enemy Lex Luthor in *Superman* (1978) and *Superman II* (1980), Barbra Streisand's partner in *All Night Long* (1981) and a cameo in Beatty's *Reds* (1981) because "I owed him one". A darker and more serious side of the actor was seen in *Eureka* (1983) in the role of Jack McCann, a man who has used his power to get where he is and doesn't know what to do with it any more.

Arguably the best performance he has turned in since *The French Connection* is *Under Fire* (1983), as Alex the foreign correspondent involved in a civil war in Nicaragua, a part for which he learned to play the piano and melodica.

Hackman is now determined to make new inroads in filming and he has bought a screenplay called *Open and Shut*, about a rape case, which he intends to direct before returning to the stage to "stretch" in some of the American classics.

Jean Harlow

Platinum blonde Jean Harlow made her mark on the big screen by deliberately cultivating a blatant sexuality while, all around her, other would-be female stars strived their utmost to be ladies. And if her life was shockingly short—she was only 26 when she died—she packed those years with enough experience to last most of us a much longer lifespan.

Born March 3, 1911 and christened Harlean Carpenter, she was sent to boarding school in Illinois after her parents divorced and her mother married Marino Bello, who was thought to have mob connections. At 16, young Harlow eloped with 21-year-old Charles McGrew, son of one of Chicago's wealthiest and most prominent families. The McGrews intervened at once.

Returned to her mother's care, Harlean moved with the family to Hollywood where she worked as an extra at Paramount. She landed a part in a Laurel and Hardy short, *Double Whoopee* (1929), in which Laurel, as a hotel flunkey, managed to tear off most of her frock. By the time of this prophetic appearance, she was already platinum blonde and using her mother's maiden name of Jean Harlow.

Hell's Angel

Harlow was divorced from McGrew by the time she was taken up by the millionaire Howard Hughes, whose interest in her was not only sexual. His ambitious and expensive movie about Great War pilots, *Hell's Angels* (1930), had been overtaken by the "talkies" revolution and Hughes was re-shooting dialog scenes with voices. The film's love interest, Greta Nissen, sounded impenetrably Swedish so Harlow was substituted. Despite the competition of the superb aerial sequences, she drew attention and Hughes put her under long-term contract, loaning her out to other leading studios.

Platinum blonde

The parts started coming her way but the critics gave her a rough ride, finding her a touch too blatant. Harlow had never worn a bra and reputedly iced her nipples before any shot other than a close-up. Her gowns ran the gamut from low-cut to skimpy. Moreover, the primitive sound recording equipment

of the day made her brash voice ring even more shrill. What she lacked in subtlety and refinement, however, Harlow made up for in honesty: she called herself "the worst actress in Hollywood".

And the public liked her, particularly as gangster's moll to James Cagney's *Public Enemy* (1931). Her peroxided hair and high arcs of eyebrow pencil set a pervasive fashion—even Bette Davis followed suit for a time. Her image was fixed when she starred as the *Platinum Blonde* (1931).

MGM then bought her contract from Hughes, "cleaned up her act" and launched her as a glamorous but sexy comedy actress worthy of leading men such as Charles Boyer, John Barrymore and Franchot Tone. But her loose-living image was never far away, as in the exchange Donald Ogden Stewart

Above: *When it comes to creating a sex goddess, artifice stands in for art.*

wrote for the end of *Dinner at Eight* (1933)—Harlow: "I was reading... that machinery is going to take the place of every profession." Marie Dressler: "Oh my dear, that's something *you* need never worry about."

And the story is told of a swish Hollywood party attended by visiting English upper crust. To her intense irritation, Margot, Lady Asquith found Harlow introducing her to everyone as "Margotte" instead of "Margo". "My name is pronounced 'Margo'," she firmly informed the star. "The 't' is silent. As in 'Harlo'."

Nevertheless, Harlow was happy at MGM and, on July 2, 1932, she married Paul Bern, a former writer and

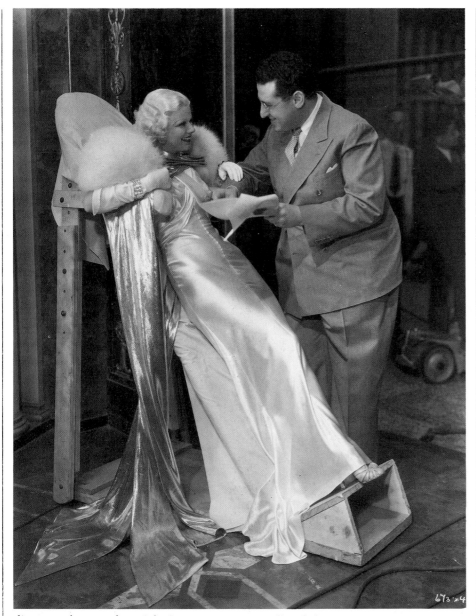

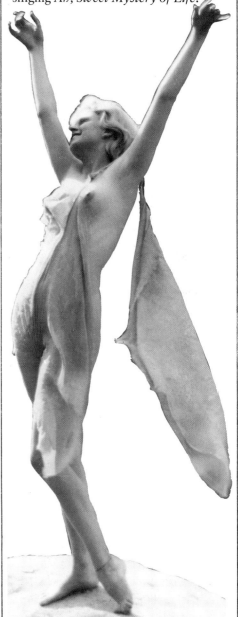

Left: *The girl with the iced nipples discusses her part with director, George Cukor on* **Dinner at Eight** *(1934).* Below: *No ordinary nude; photographed by Edwin Bower Hesser.*

shooting *Saratoga* (1937), Harlow collapsed and was rushed to hospital. Gossip suggested she was suffering all manner of outlandish illnesses, even peroxide poisoning, but both hospital and studio announced that the condition was uremic poisoning. When she died, on June 7, 1937, it was put about that her mother, a Christian Scientist, had opposed medical treatment.

Hollywood grieved. MGM gave her a royal Forest Lawn send-off with Nelson Eddy and Jeanette Macdonald singing *Ah, Sweet Mystery of Life.*

director who was then right-hand man to production head Irving Thalberg. At 42, he was twice Harlow's age and a sympathetic, avuncular figure, known to all as Father Confessor.

The marriage began badly. Harlow spent most of the wedding night at her agent's home, proclaiming that Bern had thrashed her with a stick. She also began an affair with Clark Gable, her co-star on the current *Red Dust* (1932).

The marriage quickly became a public farce and on the night of September 5, Harlow's butler found Bern shot dead. His naked body, doused with Mitsouko perfume, was stretched out before a full-length mirror with a .38 pistol by his side. A "suicide" note was found nearby. Rumor had it that the source of the "humiliation" mentioned in the note

was Bern's impotence.

Gossip was rife: one theory suggested that Bern was murdered by a mobster pal of Harlow's stepfather, another that the murderer was Bern's former mistress, Dorothy Millette, whose drowned body was discovered next day. Harlow's own alibi was provided by her mother.

Reckless

Nothing daunted, Harlow filmed *Reckless* (1935), whose plot-line veered excruciatingly close to the Bern debacle. She was also married for just eight months to cameraman Hal Rosson but they were, as Harlow announced, "uncongenial". Perhaps her happiest romance was with actor William Powell to whom she was engaged at the time of her death.

A few days before the end of

Rita Hayworth

Hailed as the "Love Goddess" of Hollywood, Rita Hayworth turned fantasy into fact by marrying a prince while at the height of her fame. But, like so many others, she found it hard to cope with the pressures of stardom. "I haven't had everything from life," she said, "I've had too much."

Margarita Cansino, as she was christened, was born on October 17, 1918 in Brooklyn. Her parents—a Ziegfeld Follies girl and a Spanish-born dancer—encouraged her natural talent and she was dancing in Mexican nightclubs by the age of 13. At 16 she took her first screen role in *Dante's Inferno* (1935), for Fox.

At 18 she married a wealthy promoter, Edward Judson—22 years her senior—and he took her career in hand. Under his guidance her appearance and name were changed, and she was given a part in Howard Hawks' *Only Angels Have Wings* (1939).

Hayworth was suddenly in demand as a glamor girl, and not only by the public. It was alleged that she had a short-lived affair with Anthony Quinn as she continued to rise in star status.

Cover girl
Hayworth and Judson separated in 1941, by which time she was being billed as "The most exciting girl on screen". So exciting was she that the newly-married Victor Mature fell for her and it was generally assumed they would marry as soon as they were free to do so. Then Judson demanded $30 000 to agree to a divorce. As Hayworth said: "He helped *me* with my career and helped *himself*—to my money."

After her divorce Hayworth did *not* marry Mature. Before he had even met her, the dynamic Orson Welles, filming in South America, declared: "I'm coming back to America to marry Rita Hayworth." And so he did—in September 1943.

Dubbed "Beauty and the Brain", they enjoyed an extravagant lifestyle

Above left: *Double vision of a strawberry blonde love goddess at the height of her powers in 1943.*
Above: *Nor had her act lost its allure when the femme fatale appeared in* **Miss Sadie Thompson** *(1953).*

and, inevitably, crowds hounded them. Hayworth soon tired of this and in vain tried to persuade the mercurial Welles to lead a quiet life. He reluctantly agreed to a separation.

Femme fatale
Meanwhile, Hayworth's screen image had crystallized. *Cover Girl* (1944) set the pace and after her most famous film ever, *Gilda* (1946), she was to remain permanently identified as a *femme fatale*. This was a problem for Hayworth, who was not at all like the bold and sensual Gilda. As she later said: "They fell in love with Gilda—and woke up with me."

Gilda made Hayworth *the* star of the moment, however. Her one unsuccessful venture during this

winning period was *The Lady from Shanghai* (1948), directed by Welles with whom she was briefly reconciled. Her long auburn hair was her trademark and Welles had cropped and bleached it for the film—a move unpopular with both the studio and her public.

Hayworth divorced Welles and took more control of her own career, negotiating a then unique deal whereby she received a percentage of the profits from every film she made.

Muslim leader Prince Aly Khan, the "playboy prince", seemed genuinely to fall in love with her when they met on the French Riviera. Both were still married and tried to keep their affair secret, but this proved to be impossible. They received unwelcome publicity, even after their wedding in May 1949.

"Illicit" marriage
Raised as a Catholic, Hayworth—now a princess—was condemned by the Vatican and her marriage declared "illicit". Khan continued to philander

and their personalities inevitably clashed. They separated in 1951, and Hayworth resumed her film career.

Her comeback film was *Affair in Trinidad* (1952), which reunited her with Glenn Ford, who had previously co-starred with her in *Gilda*.

Heavy drinker
By the time her divorce from Khan became final in January 1953 she was on the way to her fourth, disastrous marriage, to the 1940s singing idol Dick Haymes. She began to drink heavily, possibly to fortify herself against the numerous court hearings in connection with Haymes' financial and deportation problems and her own battle for the custody of her children. The marriage to Haymes was dissolved after two years.

Her fifth, to independent producer James Hill, in 1958, got off to a more promising start. He gave her a good role in *Separate Tables* (1958) which highlighted her qualities as an actress, not just as a sex symbol.

Top: *After her controversial marriage to Aly Khan in 1949 the Brooklyn girl became a princess – but it didn't last.* Above: *Still beautiful in her declining years.*

Drink was now a big problem, however, causing the couple to row fiercely. They separated and after her divorce, Hayworth appeared in several more (mostly European) films. Plans for stage work never materialized, although she made a number of television appearances in the last years of her extraordinary career.

"Goddess" in decline
In 1981 Hayworth was revealed to be suffering from Alzheimer's Disease, a form of pre-senility that left her unable to look after herself. This sad diagnosis came when the former "Love Goddess" was still only 62. Her daughter by Khan, the Princess Yasmin, eventually had to take legal steps to safeguard her physical and financial welfare.

Audrey Hepburn

With her elfin face, innocent, captivating eyes and swanlike neck, Audrey Hepburn was one of the most beautiful women to grace the screen in the 1950s. No one who saw *Roman Holiday* (1953) could easily forget her.

She was born in Arnhem in May 1929, the daughter of a Dutch baroness and an Anglo-Irish financier. Christened Edda Hepburn van Heemstra, she lived the life of a princess on her family's estate, until the German invasion of Holland in 1940. Then, in common with her fellow countrymen, she suffered the deprivations of war—though this did not stop her from taking an active role in the Dutch resistance, risking her life by carrying messages in her shoes.

Career takes off
After the war, her mother took her to England to study at the Ballet Rambert School in London. Here she was spotted by two Dutch film-makers who cast her as an air-stewardess in

Above: *Simplicity is the keynote for her wedding to first husband Mel Ferrer.*
Left: *The elfin, Dutch-born actress when she made* **Roman Holiday** *(1953), the film that won her an Oscar.*

Nederland in 7 Lessen (1948). This was the inauspicious start from which followed a meteoric rise to stardom, with an Oscar for *Roman Holiday* only four years away.

Gigi—and after
It was during the filming of *Monte Carlo Baby* (1952), in France, that the novelist Colette saw Hepburn and immediately wanted her for the title role of the Broadway production of *Gigi*.

With the overwhelming success of that production, Hepburn became a celebrity; and during the show's summer recess she flew to Italy to co-star with Gregory Peck in *Roman Holiday*, the film which made her an international star. Movie mogul Sam Goldwyn, a difficult man to please, declared that she was "The most exciting thing since Garbo and our own Hepburn—Katharine."

Sabrina (1954), *Funny Face* and *Love in the Afternoon* (both in 1957) and *The Nun's Story* (1959), all did extremely well, very quickly becoming box-office successes.

Unhappy marriages
In 1954, Hepburn had met and married the playwright, director and actor Mel Ferrer, 12 years her senior and married three times before. He played Prince Andrei to her Natasha in *War and Peace* (1956), and directed her in the fey *Green Mansions* (1959) and *Wait Until Dark* (1967) in which she played a terrorized blind girl—this role won her a fifth Oscar nomination. However, the marriage was not a happy one and ended in divorce in 1968.

Her screen career peaked with one of the most coveted female roles of the 1960s, that of Eliza Doolittle in *My Fair Lady* (1964), the musical adaptation of Bernard Shaw's *Pygmalion*. Though she received $1 million, Hepburn was not allowed to sing in the film; her songs were sung by Marni Nixon.

In 1969, she unexpectedly married an Italian psychiatrist, Dr Andrea Dotti, whom she met on a Mediterranean cruise, while recovering from her divorce. Dotti was 9 years her junior and had first met her during the shooting of *Roman Holiday*; he was a mere schoolboy on the occasion of that first meeting.

This time, Hepburn did not let her work interfere with her personal

happiness. She retired, announcing that she would only consider another film if it were made on her doorstep. The couple lived in Rome and Switzerland and, at 40, Audrey gave birth to her second child.

In a rare interview during that period, she said, "I think it's divine waiting for your husband to come home for lunch or sending your child off to school. Such things are not trivial to me."

Unfortunately, the couple were still newsworthy and pursued by reporters wherever they went. The strain proved too great and they divorced in 1980, and the press were soon linking her name romantically with the actor Ben Gazzara and then with the director Peter Bogdanovich.

Beautiful as ever
Audrey Hepburn did return to the screen, in *Robin And Marian* (1976). In her mid-forties, she was as beautiful as ever, playing Maid Marian to Sean Connery's Robin Hood. She has since made *Bloodline* (1979) and *They All Laughed* (1981).

Since her divorce from Andrea Dotti, Hepburn has lived happily with the Dutch actor and producer Robert Wohders.

Dressed to kill, (above) *in* **Bloodline** *(1979) and as Eliza Doolittle* (below), *the ingenue who stopped Royal Ascot in its tracks in the blockbusting* **My Fair Lady** *(1964).*

Katharine Hepburn

A steely-eyed independent, Katharine Hepburn was born with a Bostonian silver spoon in a mouth that became loud as soon as she could talk. Her parents set the pattern: Dr Thomas Hepburn, a surgeon and urologist, made it his mission to educate the public about venereal disease, while his wife, Katharine, picketed the White House on behalf of suffragettes and campaigned for birth control.

The Hepburns trained their six children to follow in their socially conscious footsteps, and Kate—born on November 8, 1909—was a good pupil, rarely winning friends but often influencing people in argument. Her privileged but isolated childhood, which included private tutors rather than schools, made her outwardly aggressive and self-confident, traits that alienated her peers when she went to the upmarket Bryn Mawr College at 16. It was here that she decided to become an actress.

The start of her chosen career was

Above: *Showing signs of that celebrated spirit early in her career.*
Above right: *Tackling a crusty John Wayne in* **Rooster Cogburn** *(1976).*

inauspicious. She was hampered by a shrill voice that could turn to a gabble under stress, as happened in *The Big Pond* (1928), her first New York play, in which she understudied the lead. When the star was fired, Hepburn took over, then fell apart. She arrived late for the first night, mixed up her lines, fell over her feet and talked so rapidly that even the rest of the cast couldn't understand her. She followed the first lead into the street.

"Terrified"
The incident set another pattern, which she later described: "I was always getting fired. I could always get a part quickly. But I couldn't keep it. The sight of people out there just terrified me."

Part of the problem was that the fiery

Hepburn, even at 21, was no sweet young *ingénue*, but a dominant woman who needed parts to match. When she got one as Queen of the Amazons in *The Warrior's Husband* (1932), her performance was greeted as a *tour de force*.

The Hepburn heroine was born and Hollywood was the next stop, thanks to George Cukor who recognized the talent behind the non-conformist exterior. He directed Hepburn in *A Bill of Divorcement* (1932), the picture that made her a star. Nor did her first Oscar winner, *Morning Glory*, and *Little Women* (both in 1933), do her any harm, but she was then cast in a string of failures that earned her the label "box office poison". The positive side of this apparent kiss of death was a switch from drama to comedy that led to some of her finest hours.

Howard Hawks was her mentor for the new genre in *Bringing Up Baby* (1938), and she could hardly have had a more satisfactory leading man than

Top: *With Spencer Tracy:* **Adam's Rib**.
Above: *Rehearsing for* **The Lion in Winter** *(1968)*.

Cary Grant, though her tendency to over-act was a hindrance at first.

But once she caught on, she was terrific, as she showed twice more with Grant in *Holiday* (1938) and *The Philadelphia Story* (1940), before she met Spencer Tracy, on the set of *Woman of the Year* (1942).

Enduring love
The chemistry between Hepburn and Tracy produced some of the greatest films in her career, among them *Adam's Rib* (1949), *Pat and Mike* (1952) and *Guess Who's Coming to Dinner* (1967). It also resulted in one of the longest running and most discreetly handled romances Hollywood has known.

The love affair showed the other side of Hepburn, who had always claimed the bonds of marriage and motherhood were not for her. Although she had had one husband, an old family friend called Ogden Ludlow Smith, whom she married in 1928, she only lived

with him for three months. Her affair with Howard Hughes also was made to play second fiddle to her career.

With Tracy it was different. He got top billing in their nine films together ("this is a movie, not a lifeboat", was how he saw it) and first call on Hepburn's time in that she shopped, cooked and cared for him. Marriage was never possible because the actor already had a wife, but Hepburn nursed him through his long drinking bouts and his final illness as lovingly as any spouse.

Model of independence
With the exception of this interlude, her life has been a model of independence through six decades of career decisions. Her portrayals of spinsters isolated by circumstances who learn to love in middle age, opposite Humphrey Bogart in *The African Queen* (1951), Burt Lancaster in *The Rainmaker* (1956) and John Wayne in *Rooster Cogburn* (1975)

have made her unique in an industry that usually prefers its radiant emotion under thirty.

Nor has age dimmed her athleticism. Although "she can't ride worth a damn", according to John Wayne, she insisted on doing all her own stunts in *Rooster Cogburn*. "I haven't waited all these years to do a cowboy picture with John to give up a single minute of it now," she stated with a conviction no one could deny.

Nine years later it was the same story on *The Ultimate Solution of Grace Quigley* (1984) opposite Nick Nolte. The picture has her walking fully clothed into the ocean, a scene she did herself in the autumn on the Eastern Seaboard some half a dozen times before she was fully satisfied. The fiery and perfectionist Kate is still one very determined lady.

Charlton Heston

Charlton Heston's aquiline features, piercing blue eyes and majestic torso have always marked him out as a warrior hero in the epic mold. He looks uncomfortable in a suit, but perfectly at home in a Roman breastplate or medieval chain mail.

Monolithic

Heston's monolithic presence has prompted some critics to suggest that he is not a fully rounded actor. But his career began with the classics, and he has regularly returned to the theater—particularly to his great love, Shakespeare.

Intelligent, dedicated and disarmingly modest, it was typical of him that, when he was already a father figure of cinema, he should record his pleasure and excitement at appearing with Henry Fonda in *Midway* (1976).

His introduction to screen acting came in two enterprising amateur productions directed by David Bradley, *Peer Gynt* (1941) and *Julius Caesar* (1949).

In the late 1940s he turned professional, and a performance as Rochester in a 1948 TV production *Jane Eyre* led to a contract with producer, Hal Wallis.

Fierce critic

His first film for Wallis was William Dieterle's *Dark City* (1950), a hardboiled urban thriller. Always his own fiercest critic, Heston later remarked of his performance, "I'm too fat, callow and trying too hard."

Then Cecil B. De Mille set him on course as the tough circus owner in *The Greatest Show on Earth* (1952). A string of rugged action roles followed: as an Indian in *The Savage* (1952); Buffalo Bill in *Pony Express* (1953); and an explorer on the trail of hidden treasure in *Secret of the Incas* (1954).

These were run of the mill efforts, but two films of the period hinted at his greater potential. In *The President's Lady* (1953) he played General Andrew Jackson with such nobility of bearing that Anthony Quinn persuaded him to repeat the role in *The Buccaneer* (1958). In *The Naked Jungle* (1954), he was an Amazonian planter battling against an invasion of soldier ants.

Then he also gave a towering performance as Moses in Cecil B. De Mille's biblical epic, *The Ten Commandments* (1956).

After *Three Violent People* (1957), Heston's self-improving urge drove him to take on relatively uninteresting roles in Orson Welles' *Touch of Evil* (1958) and William Wyler's *The Big Country* (1958), so that he could gain experience with these two distinguished directors.

Wyler directed Heston's Oscar-winning performance in *Ben Hur* (1959), the supreme test of the star's application and stamina. Learning to drive a chariot in the climactic race was only one of the daunting physical obstacles which he overcame.

Below: *A moment of reflection for the bearded Michelangelo in Carol Reed's* **The Agony and The Ecstasy** *(1965).*

Dealing with temperamental co-stars could sometimes be as difficult as handling a bucketing chariot. In *El Cid* (1961) playing the legendary Spanish warrior Rodrigo Diaz de Bivar, Heston had to age 20 years during the course of the film. But Sophia Loren, playing his wife, refused to submit to the aging make-up and ends the film looking not a day older than at the beginning.

"Whipped, poked, shot"

The next decade provided him with several opportunities to display his versatility. He outpointed Laurence Olivier in *Khartoum* (1966), adopting a clipped English accent to play the doomed General Gordon. In *Will Penny* (1967) he gave a quietly moving performance as a middle-aged, illiterate cowboy.

But age and changing fashion were beginning to catch up with him. While making *Planet of the Apes* (1967) he wrote in his diary: "There's hardly been a scene in this bloody film in which I've not been dragged, choked, netted, chased, doused, whipped, poked, shot, gagged, stoned, leaped on and generally mistreated."

Disaster movies

By the 1970s the fashion for epics had passed and Heston gradually worked his way into the twentieth century via a series of disaster movies—*Earthquake* and *Airport* (both in 1974), and *Gray Lady Down* (1978). He looked as virile as ever but was badly served by superficial plots. In recent years, in films like *The Mountain Men* (1980) and *Mother Lode* (1982), he has returned to the kind of outdoor actioners with which he began his career. It remains to be seen if he will allow himself to grow old gracefully.

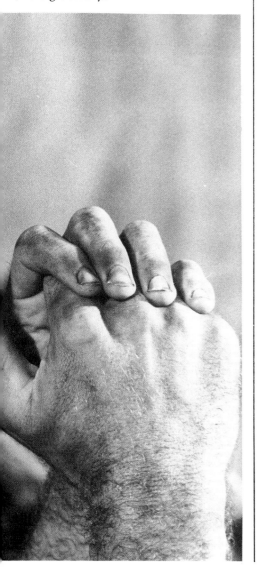

Top: *Caught in the eye of the camera by the "Monkey" king in the sci-fi thriller,* **Planet of the Apes** *(1965).*

Above: *Donating his methanol converted Corvette, to the Solar Lobby in front of the Capitol, 1983.*

Dustin Hoffman

Dustin Hoffman took the path of acting because he saw it as a way to meet pretty girls, something which, as a young man of diminutive height, with braces and a big nose, he had great difficulty in doing. "If you talk to a young actor and he says he wants to act so that he can meet girls, there's more of a chance that he will become a great actor than if he says he wants to be a serious artist," comments Hoffman.

Jazz to Broadway

Born in Los Angeles in 1937, he was a child of Hollywood but one that lived on the verge of poverty. His father was a set-dresser and prop man for Columbia pictures, his mother a failed dancer. She was a fervent film fan, to the extent of naming her younger son after silent-screen cowboy Dustin Farnum and her older son Ronald, after Ronald Colman.

Setting aside an earlier ambition to become a jazz pianist, young Hoffman studied drama at Santa Monica City College. Then, at the age of 22 he moved to New York, where he worked Off-Off Broadway, graduated to Off-Broadway and found tiny parts in TV series. He also joined the Theater Company of Boston.

To supplement his meager earnings he took jobs which ranged from emptying bedpans in a psychiatric clinic to stringing flowers on to Hawaiian leis and selling toys at Macy's.

Turning point

In 1965, *Harry, Noon and Night*, a play in which he played a homosexual, hunchback Nazi, was a turning point—leading to *Journey of the Fifth Horse* (1966), which brought him ecstatic notices for his portrayal of a crotchety Russian clerk. The successful comedy *Eh?* followed, also in 1966, and this prompted an invitation from director Mike Nichols to fly to California to audition for his film, *The Graduate* (1967). Hoffman fumbled his way through the screen-test with an acute, but timely, bout of nerves. Nichols felt the actor showed just the right amount of awkwardness for the part of the college graduate who has an affair with his girlfriend's mother and signed him up. By now, aged 30, Hoffman became an "overnight" star,

playing the 20-year-old graduate, and was nominated for an Oscar award.

His diffident screen manner seemed to suit the 1970s. He went from one film to another, revealing a remarkable versatility and a chameleon-like ability to play any age or character, except straight romantic leads, something he managed only partially to do in *John and Mary* (1969) with Mia Farrow.

His most notable triumphs have included two more Oscar nominations: for the pathetic Ratso Rizzo in *Midnight Cowboy* (1969) and *Lenny* (1974), the film of the life and times of American satirist Lenny Bruce. Other major films have been *Little Big Man* (1970), in which he ages to 121; *Straw*

Right: *A bravura performance as the stand-up comic* **Lenny** *(1974).*
Below: *Few laughs with Mia Farrow in* **John and Mary** *(1969), a comedy about a one night stand.*

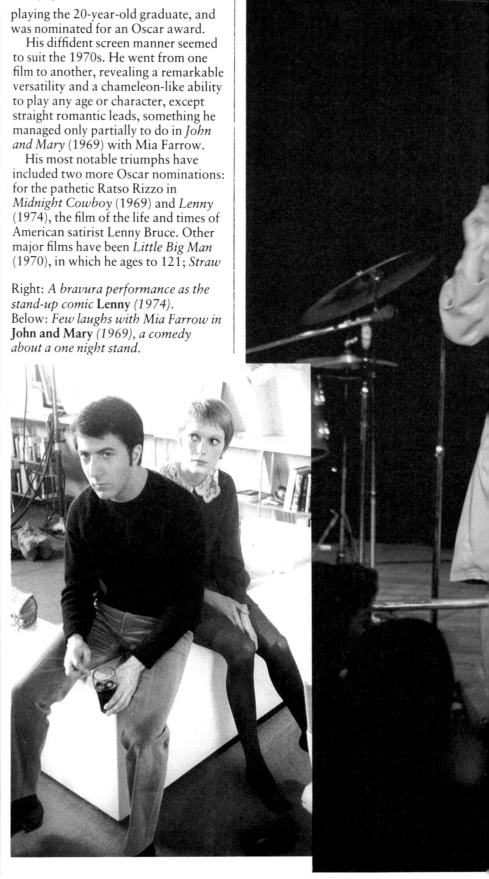

Above: *Aging ungraciously to play the 121-year-old survivor of Custer's Last Stand in* **Little Big Man** *(1970).*
Below: *Drag artist extraordinary, with Jessica Lange in* **Tootsie** *(1983).*

Dogs (1971); *Papillon* (1973); *All the President's Men* (1976), as newspaper reporter Carl Bernstein, and *Marathon Man* (1976).

Hoffman made his first attempt at directing, taking on *Straight Time* (1977) in the dual role of director and leading man but, finding himself overburdened, eventually asked Ulu Grosbard to take over the direction. The final version did not receive the critical acclaim anticipated, nor did his next independent project, *Agatha* (1979), which was produced in Britain by First Artists, a company founded by Hoffman with other acting friends.

Then came *Kramer Versus Kramer* (1979), a film about a broken marriage and a suit for child custody. The role of Ted Kramer came at a time when his own 10-year marriage to ballet dancer Anne Byrne was falling apart and although there was no child custody suit his wife moved out with daughters Karina (Byrne's child from a previous marriage whom Hoffman adopted) and Jenna. The couple's lengthy divorce coincided with the New York Film Critics' Circle choosing *Kramer Versus Kramer* as the best film of the year, followed by Hoffman being awarded a well-deserved Oscar.

Cradle snatcher
After winning the Oscar he stayed away from the screen for three years during which time he re-met and married his second wife, Lisa, a law graduate, 17 years his junior. He had formerly known her as the tot-next-door whom he babysat.

At their plush home in Manhattan, he has started a second family, become a tennis and jogging devotee and seems to have become much more relaxed. "Now I really enjoy every part of my life and home is just as important as work," says Hoffman.

Hoffman resumed acting for $4½ million in a role that challenged him to show the prettier side of his face—as a woman—in *Tootsie* (1982), a comedy that won him another Academy Award nomination. In this demanding dual role, he plays an out-of-work actor Michael Dorsey who resorts to changing gender, in order to win a role in a TV soap opera.

Since *Tootsie*, Hoffman has turned his attentions to seeking out a suitable play to stage in New York, where he intends to resume the stage career he dropped 17 years ago to pursue screen fame and fortune.

Bob Hope

The two most popular male performers to come out of the Second World War were Donald Duck and Bob Hope, according to director Frank Tashlin. Their screen characters were remarkably similar—they were both pushy, fast-talking smart-Alecks with an inbuilt cowardly streak. In the 1980s both are still with us.

Hope's heyday was the 1940s, when he was Mr Paramount. In *Road to Utopia* (1945), he and Bing Crosby trudge past an Alaskan peak which bears a resemblance to the studio's trademark, a snow-capped mountain. "Look at all that bread and butter," exclaims Hope. "You're losing your grip, that's a mountain," Bing observes—at which point the summit is ringed with glittering stars. "It may be a mountain to you, but it's bread and butter to me," replies Hope.

Soda-jerk

Leslie Townes Hope was born in 1903 in Eltham, a London suburb. In 1907 the Hope family emigrated to Cleveland, Ohio, where Hope quickly lost all trace of his English origins, and made his way as a soda-jerk, newsboy and prizefighter (boxing under the name of Packy East).

After he had won a few amateur contests, in which he imitated Charlie Chaplin, he moved into vaudeville and early in his new career was given a helping hand by the screen comic Fatty Arbuckle. It was he who introduced

Left: *Come Oscar time, Hope presented, but never received.*
Above: *Celtic overtones on* **The Road To Bali** *(1953).*

Hope to Fred Hurley, the producer of a touring revue, "Hurley's Jolly Follies".

In 1927, Hope arrived in New York where, initially, he had a tough time. The only work he could get was dancing with a pair of Siamese twins, Daisy and Violet Hilton.

His Broadway breakthrough came with a show called *Ballyhoo* and then a good part as the bandleader Huckleberry Hains in the 1933 musical *Roberta*. While playing in the show he met and married singer Dolores Reade, and their marriage has been one of the happiest in showbiz.

He made his film debut shortly afterwards, in comedy shorts for Educational Films and Warners. They were a complete disaster.

Striking gold
Hope was more successful in radio, and this led to his feature film debut in Paramount's *The Big Broadcast of 1938* (1938). With Shirley Ross he sang *Thanks for the Memory*, the number which was to become his signature tune.

After partnering Martha Raye in a string of snappy musicals, Hope struck gold in the comedy-thriller *The Cat and the Canary* (1939)—a remake of the old silent hit—taking the audience into his confidence with wisecracks like: "I'm so scared even my goose pimples have got goose pimples."

Road to Singapore (1940) launched him on his long partnership with Bing Crosby, cornering the market in the uncomplicated, reassuring humor demanded by wartime audiences. The films provided Hope with the perfect platform for his non-stop wisecracking, the jokes being provided by a small army of gagmen.

On the road
Sleek and self-assured, in the wartime years he became a one-man propaganda machine, undertaking arduous tours of Europe and the Far East to entertain the troops.

After the war, Hope's film career was less dynamic. There were still hits—*Monsieur Beaucaire* (1945), an hilarous remake of the Valentino classic, and an enjoyable spoof Western, *The Paleface* (1948), in which he played a cowardly dentist, who is mistaken for Wild Bill Hickock. But there were even more misses, and the running feud with Crosby was becoming a tired old joke.

Laughing to the bank
Undaunted, Hope became the first major motion picture star to work in television on a long-term contract, signing with CBS in 1950. In the 1950s his film work became increasingly erratic and his last film for Paramount was *Alias Jesse James* (1959), a reprise of the *Paleface* theme. After a lively marital comedy with Lucille Ball, *The Facts of Life* (1960), Hope's later films, failed to raise more than a smile from cinema audiences, but he was still laughing all the way to the bank. By the early 1970s he had become the richest man in showbusiness with assets of around $500 million, mostly from shrewd investments in real estate.

Charity
Despite his enormous wealth and status as a national institution, Hope was increasingly out of step with the times. When he went to entertain the troops in Vietnam, it was as if the Second World War had never ended—for Japs read Vietcong.

In 1970 he went to London to compère the Miss World competition and was rudely interrupted by heckling feminists. The mask slipped and for a moment the old pro became an anxious, elderly man hiding behind a barrage of reactionary bluster.

Eventually the Press turned against him and, in 1972, *Life* magazine alleged that in Vietnam he had turned a deaf ear to GIs who had criticized the conduct of the war and the jingoism of his show.

More recently he has been an innocent but aggrieved bystander in the financial collapse of the British professionals versus amateur charity golf tournament which bore his name.

Below: *With Gerald Ford and NBC's Jay Randolph, at the 1984 Bob Hope Desert Classic golf tournament.*

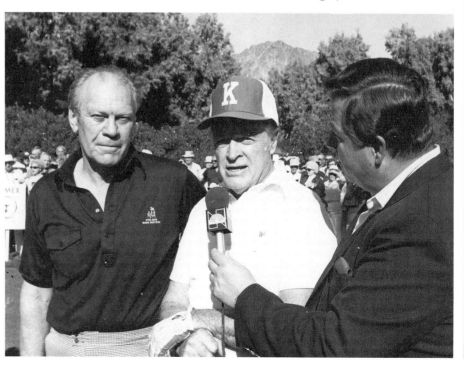

Boris Karloff

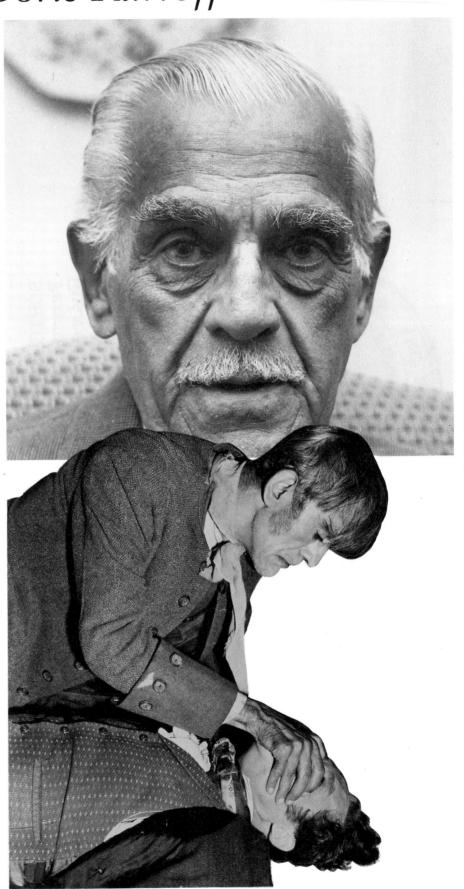

A mild-mannered and cultured Englishman, devoted to children and cricket, William Henry Pratt was never happier than when watching an afternoon's play at Lord's. But movie-goers knew him as Boris Karloff, King of Horror.

The movies rewarded Karloff with fame, but he was never a great star. Most of his work was in B features, and when he played in better films it was always as a supporting player, never the star. His long career was the extended aftermath to four superb performances in the early 1930s, in *Frankenstein* (1931), *The Mummy*, *The Old Dark House* and *The Mask of Fu Manchu* (all in 1932).

Traveling actor
He was born in the London suburb of Dulwich in November 1887, the son of a member of the Indian Civil Service. In 1909, when he was 22, he abandoned plans for a diplomatic career to emigrate to Canada and, after trying his hand at farming and real estate, became a traveling actor, adopting the name Boris Karloff

After 10 years with stock companies he arrived in Hollywood, first as an extra and then as a soldier in *His Majesty the American* (1919).

In the 1920s, the movies provided Karloff with a precarious living, his gaunt frame typecasting him as a Western desperado or Oriental villain. He finally made a breakthrough, repeating his stage role of the trusted convict turned killer in *The Criminal Code* (1931).

Creating a monster
His parts improved, particularly in *Five Star Final* and *The Mad Genius* (both in 1931), but he was still just a hard-working heavy. Then fate took a hand. After completing *The Mad Genius*, Karloff moved over to the Universal lot to play a murderer in *Graft* (1931). There, his lean and hungry features caught the attention of director James Whale, who was looking for an actor to play the

Above right: *The mild-mannered Englishman as he looked when he made* **Targets** *(1968)*.
Right: *Full of characteristic jut-jawed menace in* **The Body Snatcher** *(1945)*.

94

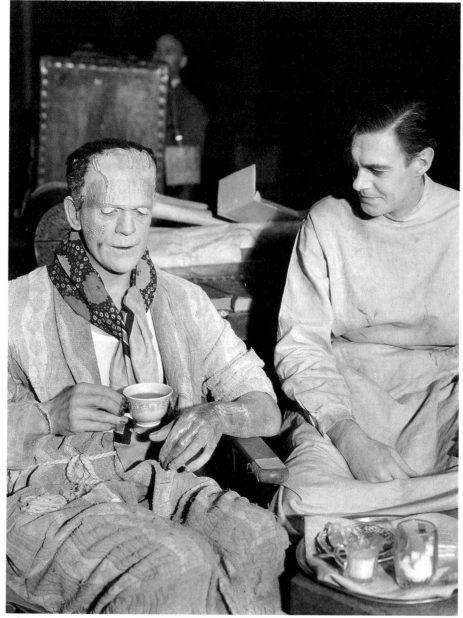

Above: *Tea with Colin Clive during the daily 4-hour change into the Monster for* **The Bride of Frankenstein** *(1935).*

Monster in *Frankenstein*, the studio's follow-up to *Dracula* (1931).

Later, Whale wrote: "Karloff's face fascinated me. I made drawings of his head, added bony ridges where I imagined the skull might have joined. His physique was weaker than I could wish, but that queer, penetrating personality of his ... was more important than his shape, which could be easily altered."

The alteration was accomplished by Universal's make-up wizard Jack P. Pierce. He built up the Monster's box-like head with layers of rubber and cotton. The two metal electrodes on Karloff's neck were fixed so tightly that he bore tiny scars there for a long time after filming was over.

Every day it took four hours to transform Karloff into the Monster and another two hours to remove the make-up—which weighed nearly 50lb—after shooting. To preserve secrecy, the entire film was shot in an enclosed studio, under lights in the heat of summer. In these conditions it is hardly surprising that the studio head, Carl Laemmlee, later reflected, "Karloff's eyes mirrored the suffering which we needed."

Great achievement

Frankenstein brought Karloff overnight fame which, with characteristic modesty, he later dismissed: "The part was what we call a 'natural'; any actor who played it was destined for success." But it was Karloff's achievement to create, underneath the make-up, a creature poignantly clutching at life.

After an impressive straight performance as a mobster in *Scarface* (1932), he disappeared under swathes of bandages to play the 3,700-year-old menace of *The Mummy*. He shambled menacingly through *The Old Dark House* as the sinister deaf-mute butler and in the title role of *The Mask of Fu Manchu* gave the definitive interpretation of Sax Rohmer's Oriental criminal mastermind. When he returned to England in 1933 to make *The Ghoul*, his name was synonymous with horror.

By 1936, with his second wife Dorothy Stine, he was living on a charming estate in Los Angeles's Coldwater Canyon. He was also a prominent member of the Hollywood Cricket Club, whose stalwarts included C. Aubrey Smith and Ronald Colman.

B films

He played Frankenstein's Monster twice more, in *The Bride of Frankenstein* (1935) and *Son of Frankenstein* (1939), and then slipped gently into starring roles in a string of undemanding B films—playing Mr Wong, the Chinese sleuth, in five films at Monogram, and an assortment of "mad doctors" at Columbia. To relieve the monotony of the B treadmill, he returned to the stage in 1941, playing the homicidal nephew in the Broadway run of *Arsenic and Old Lace*. Every night he brought the house down with the line, "I killed him because he said I looked like Boris Karloff."

In the mid-1940s, in a brief period at RKO, he produced three more memorable performances in *The Body Snatcher* and *Isle of the Dead* (both in 1945) and *Bedlam* (1946).

In the late 1950s he returned to live in England, and in the early 1960s producer/director Roger Corman gave him a new lease of life in an enjoyable series of spoof horror films—*The Raven*, *The Terror*, and *Comedy of Terrors* (all in 1963).

It was because Karloff still owed the parsimonious Corman a couple of days work that he appeared in Peter Bogdanovich's first film, *Targets* (1968), playing a thinly disguised version of himself—Byron Orlock, an elderly star of horror films. It was the swansong to nearly four decades of cultivated terror.

Buster Keaton

Dubbed "The Great Stone Face", Buster Keaton was perhaps the silent cinema's greatest comedian.

Born Joseph Frank Keaton, he was called Buster after he fell down a flight of stairs without injury at the age of six months and Harry Houdini exclaimed: "That's some buster your baby took!" to Keaton's parents Myra and Joe, fellow-performers on the vaudeville circuit.

Keaton entered into this world on October 4, 1895, practically between acts, in a boarding house next door to where his parents were appearing in the Mohawk Indian Medicine Company in Piqua, Kansas. From the age of two he took part in their shows, a family knockabout act.

When The Three Keatons broke up in 1917, he joined comedian Roscoe "Fatty" Arbuckle, the man who gave him his first chance in the movies. Together they made a long series of two-reelers, in which the Keaton persona was gradually formed, at a point when silent movies were becoming a major industry.

Soul-filled eyes

In 1920 the former Chaplin Studios were reopened as the Keaton Studios and the unsmiling little man with soul-filled eyes started directing (sometimes writing) and acting in his own features.

Over the next eight years he produced his most important features, at the rate of two a year. Costing on an average well under $200 000, they each grossed up to $2 million. *The Three Ages* (1923) was the first. A parody of D.W. Griffith's epic *Intolerance*, it came after a collection of 34 short films made between 1917 and 1923 and established Keaton as the master of silent comedy.

He went on to make *Our Hospitality* (1923) starring his wife Natalie, his father Joe and son Joseph; *Sherlock Junior* (1924), a surreal fantasy years ahead of its time; *The Navigator* (1924); *Seven Chances* and *Go West* (both in 1925). One of his personal favorites was *Battling Butler* (1926).

However, *The General* (1927), was considered to be his greatest masterpiece—set against a backdrop of the American Civil War.

By the age of 33, Keaton's creative period had practically ended. *The Cameraman* (1928) was his last great film made in Hollywood.

Battles with the moguls

His decline was accelerated by the birth of sound and worsened by his battles with the movie moguls. Although he produced and wrote more films, he worked mainly as a performer, controlled by the big studios.

During the 1930s he drifted into money problems, marriage problems and drinking problems. His films during this time included several unmemorable features made in Hollywood, two made in Europe, *Le Roi Des Champs-Elysées* (1934) and *An Old Spanish Custom* (1935),

Below: *Even masked by newsprint, the soulful eyes are unmistakable as Keaton awaits the next call to action.*

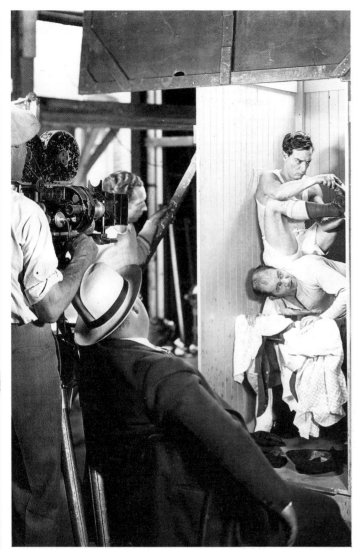

educational comedies and ten comedies which he made for Columbia studios between 1939 and 1941.

Come-back

During the 1940s, remarried—to actress Eleanor Norris—he acted as gagman to the Marx Brothers and to Abbott and Costello. In the 1950s he made a slow come-back with featured roles, a television show and a series of praised performances in the ring at the Cirque Medrano in Paris. Some of the old Keaton brilliance shone through his brief appearance in Chaplin's *Limelight* (1952) and he starred in *Around the World in Eighty Days* (1956).

The Buster Keaton Story (1957), starring Donald O'Connor as Keaton, helped to restore his former prominence and lost finances, and in 1959 he received a special Academy Award for his "unique talents which brought immortal comedies to the screen".

Above left: *Characteristic Keaton, solemn, purposeful – and hilarious.* Right: *Not a happy family occasion, it seems, for Buster, first wife, Natalie Talmadge and sons, Jimmy and Bob.*

His career took a distinct upturn in the 1960s, during which he made a dozen feature films, most notably *It's A Mad, Mad, Mad, Mad World* (1963) and *A Funny Thing Happened On The Way To The Forum* (1966).

Standing ovation

At the Venice Film Festival, where his silent-film *Film* (1965), written by Samuel Beckett for solo performance by Keaton, was presented as an entity, it and its star received a five minute standing ovation. "This is the first time I've been invited to a film festival," said Keaton, "but I hope it won't be the last."

Unfortunately it was: three months later he died of lung cancer at his Hollywood home.

Above: *The writer, director and actor working at home in the comeback years, before his death in late 1965.*

Gene Kelly

Above: *The pinnacle of a blameless life: the amiable Irish-American dancer co-directs himself in* **Singin' In The Rain** *(1952).*

The archetypal genial Irish-American, family man and hard-working pro, there is nothing remotely salacious to be reported about Eugene Curran Kelly.

The third of five children born to a Pittsburgh gramophone salesman and his wife, Harriet, he entered the world on August 23, 1912. The family was close, happy and comfortable. Though the Depression left Kelly senior redundant, they got by. The enterprising Harriet opened a dancing school in nearby Johnstown. It prospered—dance was very much in vogue—and Gene Kelly, after whom the school was named, took on tuition and choreography as well as devising many routines with his brother Fred.

He turned down the chance to become a ballet dancer when the Ballet Russe passed through Pittsburgh, and early attempts to break into Hollywood failed.

One-way ticket
The Gene Kelly Studio of the Dance was highly regarded however. Professionals trained there and sought the young man's help with choreography. But in August 1938 Kelly bought a one-way ticket to New York and joined the hundreds standing in line for auditions. The Johnstown years helped. Choreographer Robert Alton put him in Mary Martin's 1938 show *Leave It To Me* and fixed Kelly up with an agent.

Alton also cast Kelly in his next show, which led to a Theater Guild season and his first big success as Harry the Hoofer in Saroyan's *The Time of Your Life*.

Playing a louse
It was while choreographing for Alton that Kelly met 16-year-old dancer Betsy Blair and the pair started going out together.

Then, in 1940, Kelly landed one of the most sought-after roles on Broadway, the name part in Rodgers and Hart's *Pal Joey*. It made Kelly a Broadway star and won him a David O. Selznick movie contract. To celebrate, he and Betsy got married.

True to form, Selznick could never make up his mind what movie to put Kelly into and soon sold a half share in the contract to Louis B. Mayer. MGM

Above: *A doting father goes into his routine for 4-month-old Kerry, but his wife, Betsy Blair, enjoys it more.*

Below: *The two hoofing immortals of the twentieth century: Kelly and Astaire in* **That's Entertainment** *(1974).*

were already embarked on a program of musicals under producer Arthur Freed that would last 20 years, and Freed cast Kelly opposite Garland in *For Me and My Gal* (1942). Kelly had no qualms about playing a louse—Joey had been a louse, too—and, with his breezy manner, and ordinary-guy appearance Kelly appealed to a big, unsophisticated audience.

The Big Time
Mayer bought up the rest of his contract and signed him for seven years. Clearly the arrival of daughter Kerry that October would cause no financial worries.

Ironically, it was the first of only two movies Kelly made on loan during his time with MGM that really established him. *Cover Girl* (1944) with Columbia's Rita Hayworth proved him as a dancer and choreographer, not least in the famous "alter ego" dance which he devised with his protégé, Stanley Donen.

From then on, Kelly's movies were increasingly demanding and ambitious, notably *Anchors Aweigh* (1945), his first pairing with Frank Sinatra; *The Pirate* (1948) with Garland again; *On the Town* (1949), the first ever location-shot musical; *An American in Paris* (1951), a six-Oscar winner; and the apotheosis of the MGM musical, *Singin' in the Rain* (1952).

Gotta dance
Straining to top that pinnacle, Kelly could only go down. His notions of film-dance got more pretentious. To escape tax, he worked in Europe to less happy effect. The film musical had passed its peak. His 15-year marriage ended in 1957 and so did marriage to MGM. As a freelance, he continued to act, direct and occasionally dance in films, on stage, on television.

In 1960, Kelly married his old friend and assistant Jeannie Coyne, who had long adored him. They had 13 happy years and 2 children together before her death at 49 of leukemia.

Kelly's old age has seen a revival of interest in his work of the 1950s. The respect in which he is held has grown and grown. He has survived Hollywood and public scrutiny, his closet always open and no skeletons to be seen. Even his hair-pieces, written into his MGM contract, were scarcely a secret. No one has been less spoiled by success than the Irish-American with the compulsion "gotta dance".

Grace Kelly

Though not lacking a fairy tale element—she did, after all, marry a prince—Grace Kelly's story is far from being one of rags to riches. She was born in November 1928 into a wealthy Philadelphia family and had a privileged, if somewhat strict Catholic upbringing.

When she decided on an acting career, her family—led by her industrialist father—was not exactly pleased. Even so, as a student at the American Academy of Dramatic Art, she showed enough promise to be offered a film contract. This she turned down, to follow in her mother's footsteps and become a model.

In 1949, after several television appearances, she appeared on Broadway in *The Father*, opposite Raymond Massey. Her performance won her another offer from Hollywood which this time she accepted, making the first of her 11 films, *Fourteen Hours* (1951).

Working with Hitchcock

Her best performances were without doubt under the direction of Alfred Hitchcock, for whom she starred in: *Dial M for Murder* and *Rear Window* (both in 1954) and *To Catch a Thief* (1955). He cast her in roles to which she would lend a high moral and sophisticated tone, while appearing almost provocatively attractive.

In *To Catch a Thief*, as the haughty débutante on vacation in Monaco, she drives jewel thief Cary Grant recklessly round the hair pin bends of the Principality. Suddenly pulling off the road she produces a chicken picnic lunch and asks, apparently innocently, "leg or breast?"

Not that Kelly was ever a sex symbol. She was way above that. Her screen characters were all reflections of her off-screen persona—cool, calm and sophisticated. Hollywood did not really know what to make of her, with only rare mentions in the gossip columns, apart from a brief, but well publicized affair with designer Oleg Cassini in 1954. The Kelly family

Top: *The serene, sophisticated beauty who captivated the world.*
Right: *With Cary Grant in* **To Catch A Thief** *(1955), directed by Alfred Hitchcock. He made her a star.*

disapproved of the liaison because Cassini was divorced and not Catholic.

Kelly's first encounter with the Prince who was to change her life was set up as part of the publicity machine of the 1955 Cannes Film Festival. He was captivated by her beauty and sparkling conversation and she, in turn, by his suave yet direct manner. The happy couple married with the eyes of the world upon them and, to the delight of the Prince's subjects, Princess Grace gave birth to a son and heir, Prince Albert, in 1958.

The Princess was once tempted to return to the film world, in 1962, after reading the script of Hitchcock's *Marnie*. The Pope himself expressed the hope that she would set a good example to Catholic families everywhere by not leaving her children to return to work, and her 24 000 Monegasque subjects made it plain that it was their wish that she remain a princess. She acceded.

Not that Princess Grace forgot her past entirely. She maintained contact with Hollywood friends, and occasionally traveled abroad to meet them, but she remained first and foremost Her Serene Highness Princess Grace of Monaco.

Her Serene Highness
The conscientious but easy manner with which she carried out her duties, whether fund raising, organizing old people's homes or a flower show, consolidated the genuine rapport Princess Grace had established with her subjects.

Though discreet, her influence in matters of state was nonetheless real. At the time of trouble with France over the imposition of French tax laws in the Principality, she and Prince Rainier dined with General de Gaulle in Paris. The Prince allegedly found it very difficult to communicate with the lofty General. Not so the Princess, and the main points of the dispute were settled amicably and swiftly.

Own epitaph
Shortly before the fatal car crash in September 1982, Princess Grace unwittingly composed her own epitaph: "I'd like to be remembered as a decent human being and a caring one." Her unstinting charity work assures her of this, but it is above all as the radiant and dignified Princess that Grace Kelly will be most remembered: the role she seemed born to play.

Above: *High society wedding – the girl from Philadelphia marries her prince in Monaco's cathedral, April, 1956.*

Below: *A happy interlude out shopping with her children shortly before her tragically early death in 1982.*

Alan Ladd

On the screen Alan Ladd was cool and unsmiling, moving from stone-faced calm to violent action like a hawser that suddenly snaps under pressure. In real life, the pressure of being Alan Ladd—enduring the tired old jokes about his lack of height and inability to act—finally shattered his brittle confidence. He once told a friend, "I'm the most insecure guy in Hollywood."

Tough beginnings

His childhood was one of unrelieved misery. In 1917, when he was four, he saw his father die of a heart attack. His mother and stepfather moved from Arkansas to California in 1920, and his first home in the Sunshine State was a transient auto camp.

At high school—where he was nicknamed "Tiny"—he acted for the first time in a college production of *The Mikado*.

In 1932 he was taken on by Universal's school for young actors, but after a bit part in *Once in a Lifetime* (1932), he was dropped.

He ran a hot dog stand, tried the newspaper business and worked as a grip at Warner's Burbank studios before joining the Ben Bard school of acting. Times were hard for Ladd, his wife Midge—he married in 1936—and their son Alan Ladd Jnr. In 1937 his mother, an incurable alcoholic, killed herself by eating rat poison.

Discovered

For two years he persevered with radio work and stints as a bit player and extra in films until, in 1938, his luck changed when he was discovered by agent Sue Carol. Years later she recalled their first meeting, "He came into my office wearing a long white trench coat. His blond hair was bleached by the sun. He looked like a young Greek god."

Carol took over his career, and later his life—they married in 1942. She pitched him into a string of B films. In *Beast of Berlin* (1939), the budget was so tight that Ladd, after coming to a sticky end as a young anti-Nazi, can be

Right: *As the enigmatic killer in* **This Gun for Hire** *(1942), with Veronica Lake. Theirs was the perfect pairing because she was even shorter than he.*

pictures, although underneath the impassive exterior there was an actor struggling to get out. Howard da Silva, one of Ladd's co-stars in *Two Years Before the Mast* (1946), later recalled, "From the first I felt an aura of melancholy about him... There was enormous potential in that man, yet he was playing the same role every time."

The title role in *The Great Gatsby* (1949) was an attempt to break the mold, but the film was a flop. In the early 1950s, a simmering feud with Paramount finally came to the boil and Ladd signed with Warners. But there were still several Paramount films in the pipeline, including George Stevens' *Shane* (1953), a classic Western in which Ladd gave his finest performance.

All shrunken up
This personal triumph failed to arrest his decline in a sorry succession of limp actioners. In Columbia's *The Black Knight* (1954), he exchanged his customary trench coat for a preposterous suit of armour.

No one had bothered about Ladd's short stature in the 1940s, but now Shelley Winters, his co-star in *Saskatchewan* (1954), complained about having to act in a trench. Sophia Loren made the same protest when filming with him in *Boy on a Dolphin* (1957).

In 1959, Robert Mitchum, interviewed on location while making *The Angry Hills*, delivered the *coup de grâce* when he told gossip columnist Roderick Mann, "Originally they wanted Alan Ladd. But when they got to his desert home to see him, he'd just crawled out of his swimming pool and he was all shrunken up, like a dishwasher's hand..."

It was a savage blow for Ladd, who had long since lost his slim good looks. Heavy drinking had puffed up his face and a series of accidents and illnesses had undermined his health. His enormous wealth was no comfort. He was at the end of his tether.

In 1961 he arrived drunk and incoherent at the funeral of actress Gail Russell. A year later there was apparently a suicide attempt on his ranch. He survived to give a memorable performance as Nevada Smith—the aging cowboy film star—in *The Carpetbaggers* (1964). But by the time the film was released, he was dead—supposedly from a combination of alcohol and sedative poisoning.

---

spotted later in the film in a second role, when he is shown digging a grave for another victim.

First big role
His first big role came in RKO's *Joan of Paris* (1942), playing an airman shot down over occupied Europe, after which he was immediately cast by Paramount as the enigmatic hired killer Raven in *This Gun for Hire* (1942). The studio dyed his hair black for the part and provided him with the perfect foil in co-star Veronica Lake. She was 3 inches shorter than Ladd and together they enlivened two more classic thrillers of the 1940s—*The Glass Key* (1942) and *The Blue Dahlia* (1946).

Such was Ladd's overwhelming

Hollywood's most insecure actor hits the big time in **The Carpetbaggers** (1964) *with George Peppard* (top), *and proves it with the trappings of fame as he relaxes beside his pool* (above).

popularity that in 1943 *Modern Screen* magazine, which had a circulation of nearly two million, carried 16 features about him in 12 issues.

After a brief and somewhat inglorious spell in the Army Air Force—he was invalided out with a double hernia—he returned to the screen in *And Now Tomorrow* (1944), and stayed at the top for another 10 years, always more popular with cinema goers than the critics.

Paramount confined him to formula

Hedy Lamarr

Hedwig Kiesler, or Hedy Lamarr as she would become known, was just a rather naïve but ambitious and exceptionally beautiful 19-year-old actress when she met Gustav Machaty in 1933. He persuaded the Austrian teenager that his new film *Ecstasy* (1933) was just what her career needed.

According to Lamarr, she signed the contract without reading the small print and was horrified when Machaty expected her to take a nude dip in a woodside pool for the cameras and then run naked through the forest. Scared by Machaty's threat that she would be liable for the costs of the entire film, Lamarr complied, thereby giving both the film and herself a notoriety that endured for almost an entire decade.

Marriage to millionaire

Almost immediately after the Austrian release of the film Lamarr was wooed and won by Fritz Mandl, a middle-aged munitions millionaire. "He surrounded me with a luxury I never knew existed," Lamarr later explained. "Almost before I realized it we were married."

Mandl became intensely jealous of his stunning young bride and began locking her away from her many suitors, who included the brother of the King of Austria. He also spent huge sums in an attempt to buy up all the prints of *Ecstasy*. This somewhat futile venture gave the film more, rather than less, of a scandalous reputation, and he forgot to purchase the negative.

Escape to America

By this time, however, Lamarr was disillusioned with the marriage and ran away to London. From there she traveled on to the United States, managing to charm a seven-year contract out of co-passenger Louis B. Mayer *en route*.

Her first film for him was the glitteringly successful and sensuous *Algiers* (1938) and it seemed as though Lamarr, by now dubbed "the most beautiful woman in Hollywood" was made.

Her cool and mysterious dark-haired beauty became the model for European glamor and aroused the ardor of countless fans. But the studio bosses slowly became aware that she did not have either the personality or the acting ability of Dietrich or Garbo. Her successes, such as *White Cargo* (1942) were interspersed with middling to bad comedies and the Austrian beauty flopped at the box office.

Worse, Lamarr developed wildly inflated ideas of her own importance and consequently became almost impossible to deal with on, or off, set. She refused to do publicity tours and

Right: Bathing in Ecstasy *(1933), an act of nudity that made her notorious for years afterwards.*
Below: 1940s portrait, hinting at the arrogance that destroyed the career of the cool, mysterious Viennese beauty.

became convinced that only she could judge a good script. This led her to reject not only timeless *Casablanca* (1943), but also *Gaslight* (1944), both of which were enormous personal successes for Ingrid Bergman.

Lamarr's personal life was in almost as much disarray as her professional one. She left film-writer Gene Markey, who became her husband shortly after she arrived in Hollywood—claiming that he was "indifferent to her at home"—and quickly married British actor John Loder. They had two children doted upon by Lamarr, but within four years, this marriage was also on the rocks.

Biblical temptress
Then, her fortunes changed. Paramount cast her as the famous biblical temptress in *Samson and Delilah* (1949) and despite critical brickbats the film was a box-office success.

Lamarr decided to marry for the fourth time, this time nightclub owner Ernest Staffer. Ever dramatic, she announced an auction of her entire personal effects, including her three old wedding rings, 75 pairs of shoes and

480 dresses. "There are times when the past is dead and should be buried," Lamarr told reporters. "I have a new husband and a new life. I want to start afresh in Mexico. I'm through with Hollywood and I'm through with movies."

Seven months later she was planning a comeback in another (never filmed) biblical epic and announcing "Love is great. Men are great. It's marriage I'm a little disappointed in ... In a way my beauty has been a curse. Everywhere I attracted men who adored me for my beauty and wanted to be seen in my company. But none of them gave me the attention I wanted. And mostly that's why my marriages failed."

Arrested
Two more marriages came—and went—very quickly, while Lamarr starred in a number of unsuccessful historical films, hoping for the hit which would win back her place amongst the Hollywood stars. But her spell had been broken.

Lamarr, having squandered her way through both her own huge salary and the large divorce settlements made to her by several ex-husbands was suddenly very short of money. In 1965 she was arrested on a shop-lifting charge. "I was broke," she testified in the witness box. "The electricity was cut off because I couldn't pay the bills and I didn't have the money to buy food."

Although Lamarr was found not guilty, the publicity contributed to her being dropped from *Picture Mommy Dead* (1966).

Explicit revelations
She moved to a small apartment and devoted her time to planning her never-to-happen comeback and writing her explicit autobiography *Ecstasy and Me—My Life as a Woman*, which appeared in 1966. It was obviously a move that Lamarr regretted; three years later she attempted to sue her collaborators for $21 million damages for defrauding her of her good name and producing what she described as an "obscene, shocking, scandalous, naughty, wanton, fleshy, sensuous and scarlet edition".

Following this, Lamarr faded from the public eye, and only resurfaced briefly in 1975 when it was reported that she had applied for government social security in New York and was nearly blind.

Burt Lancaster

Burt Lancaster is no gentleman. Even his best friends admit that. Now in his seventies Mr Lancaster, as he expects to be called, has no time for fools or poseurs, or those who disagree with him. His legendary temper is more frequently held in check than it used to be, but when unleashed it is as sharp as ever.

This suppressed rage, effectively displayed in an impressive range of films over nearly 40 years, is the key to his film celebrity. It is the legacy of a stern but compassionate mother who struggled to raise four children in East Harlem through the first 30 years of the century.

"Ma was such a determined lady and she instilled concepts as strong as orthodox religion," her most famous son recalls. "However poor you were, you never lied, you never stole, and you always stuck by a promise."

His father, a New York Post Office clerk, earned $48 a week which made life bearable, but not easy. Burt was the baby of the family, then the runt. No one could have guessed that the child would develop into a strapping blue-eyed, blond athlete with a taste for basketball and the thrills of the high wire.

Arrogant front

Lancaster has emerged as a tough, self-disciplined character who consistently conceals his good qualities: generosity, loyalty to anyone who does him a good turn, and sympathy for the underdog, under an arrogant front. If his post-war career, following a decade of circus acrobatics and three years in the army, was meteoric, it was because he knew exactly how to seize opportunities with both hands.

A chance meeting in a New York elevator in 1945 put the jobless demob on Broadway in *A Sound of Hunting*. The play flopped but he had made an impression and was hot property, with seven Hollywood studios vying for his untested services.

Trapeze artist

Having scored with his first picture, *The Killers* (1946), Lancaster began to re-shape his alien environment to suit his requirements. Traditionally, actors tied into long contracts at fixed rates

Youth and age: the splendid physique of a circus acrobat displayed to its maximum advantage (above) *in the swashbuckling classic,* **The Crimson Pirate** *(1952) and, thirty years later, a much more cerebral actor* (inset).

had watched impotently while the moguls profited hugely from their labour. Not so Lancaster. Within a few years he had his own production company running in tandem with his two-picture-a-year deal with producer Hal Wallis.

Cashing in on his circus experience as a trapeze artist he appeared in *The Flame and The Arrow* (1950) and *The Crimson Pirate* (1952). At the same time he pressured Wallis into making him famous in risk productions with a touch of class, like *All My Sons* (1948), *From Here to Eternity* and *Come Back, Little Sheba* (both in 1953). Success did not do his character any good at all. He fought with his co-stars Katharine Hepburn, Gary Cooper and Kirk Douglas, and with most of the men he hired to direct him. But the pictures kept on coming, most notably *Sweet Smell of Success* (1957), *Separate Tables* (1958), his sole Oscar winner *Elmer Gantry* (1960), *Birdman of Alcatraz* (1962), and *The Leopard* (1963).

Lancaster lived with his wife, Norma, and his five children in an opulent Bel Air mansion, but it is hard to believe that he made them very happy. He combined workaholism with a remorseless pursuit of the body beautiful through austere diet and exercise.

When the Lancasters socialized, which they did rarely because Burt hates parties, he looked like a hood in black shirt and satin tie or a mis-matched electric-blue suit with canary-yellow tie and heavy brown shoes. The effect was topped off by his ferociously even teeth, the result of investing $10 000 in a "perfect bite" operation, the ultimate in preventative dentistry.

The resultant flashing grin lit up the lives of assorted ladies, among them the then blonde cutie, Shelley Winters, who recorded their affair in some detail in her autobiography. Nevertheless, the Lancaster marriage survived until 1969 when their youngest daughter was 15. Only then did Norma sue her husband for cruelty, nature unspecified, and free herself from his domination.

Controlled violence

Today, the veteran actor is enjoying an Indian summer, following triumphs in *Atlantic City* (1980) and *Local Hero* (1983). He lives in Los Angeles with his constant companion of 15 years, the ex-hairdresser Jackie Bone. She has

mellowed him mightily, as he admits.

"I have been a violent person. I am a violent person. But I control it. I'm not sure that I'm all that happy that I've conquered it, because it's not wise to alter your personality. But I had to change. I couldn't go around as I was. I was a terror."

Quite so, but the dictats keep coming, as he postpones retirement.

"People outside Hollywood don't understand how it is here. It's a battle to maintain a basic integrity. You have to fight all the time." And he is still making every single blow count.

Below: *An Oscar winning performance as the charlatan* **Elmer Gantry** *(1960).*

Bottom: *A gala outing with Jackie Bone, his long-time companion.*

Charles Laughton

Audiences were moved to tears by Charles Laughton's sympathetic portrayal of the hideously deformed Quasimodo in *The Hunchback of Notre Dame* (1939). There was, however, something painfully self-conscious in his identification with the underdog; Laughton was a superb character actor and could play almost any part but one—that of the romantic leading man. He considered himself fat and ugly and throughout his career was tormented by the knowledge of his homosexuality.

Feminine traits

British-born Laughton had built up a considerable reputation on the English stage before he found fame in Hollywood. Born in Scarborough on July 1, 1899, he was educated at the Jesuit Stonyhurst College. Renowned for its discipline and adherence to dogma, it was an unsympathetic background for a child who displayed so-called "feminine personality traits" and pupils were under surveillance for any sign of sexual activity.

Having completed his First World War service, in 1924 he was accepted by the Royal Academy of Dramatic Art, where he became a gold-medal student. He made his debut on the West End stage in 1926, and there was attracted to another celebrated stage performer Elsa Lanchester. They lived together before becoming man and wife in February 1929.

Disturbing incident

Lanchester had no idea about her husband's homosexuality until a disturbing incident occurred within a couple of years of their marriage. A young man was found loitering outside the Laughtons' apartment and taken in for questioning by the police. The man claimed he had been picked up and promised money by Laughton. The actor categorically denied that this story was correct.

Later, however, he confessed to his wife that he had been seeing other men for some time and that the allegation was true. The case came to court but Laughton was let off with a warning about misguided generosity. As a result of the court's leniency, bad publicity was avoided.

Their marriage survived this crisis,

Above: *A memorable Captain Bligh, in* **Mutiny on the Bounty** *(1935).*

but they both had affairs with other people and over the years followed their separate interests within the framework of their unconventional marriage.

In 1931, the Laughtons went to New York, where he gained good critical notices for his Broadway appearance in *Payment Deferred* and was signed to Paramount the following year. His Hollywood career was a remarkable success, although the social life did not always suit him. There were some disconcerting encounters with other stars—the outspoken Tallulah Bankhead for instance once called him "a big fat slob".

He traveled frequently between England and America over the next few years winning a best actor Oscar with *The Private Life of Henry VIII* (1933), a British film which established him as an international screen star of repute.

Like other expatriates, Laughton suffered at the hands of the British press for not returning home during the Second World War. In fact, he had been gassed in the First World War and, as a result of his injuries, he was unfit for active service.

In 1950 the Laughtons became American citizens, but his attitude to Hollywood remained ambivalent. He once said: "Hollywood is a goofy place. But I like it. It's the perfect mummer's home. If one weren't a little mad, one wouldn't be there."

Homosexual relationships

Laughton had several homosexual relationships but nothing lasting until, in 1941, he met actor David Roberts. Initially he persuaded Roberts to marry and lead a normal life, but after only

Right: *An impromptu tea party with Elsa Lanchester and Billy Merson.*
Middle right: *A pensive moment in the title role of* **I, Claudius** *(1937).*
Bottom right: *Directing his only film* **The Night of the Hunter** *(1957).*

four weeks of marriage Roberts' wife was killed in a car crash. Seemingly fated to return to Laughton, Roberts had at first a sexual, then later a platonic friendship with him.

Once again the Laughtons' marriage survived, although by the end of the 1940s relations between them were becoming strained.

Landmarks

A landmark in Laughton's career was his sole directorial effort: *The Night of the Hunter* (1955). Poorly received at the time, it is now regarded as a classic. One of the stars, Robert Mitchum, has since revealed that Laughton so disliked directing the children in the film that he asked Mitchum to take over during their scenes.

As an actor, his most notable films were: *The Big Clock* (1948), *Witness For the Prosecution* (1957) and *Advise and Consent* (1962).

Truly in Love

By the late 1950s Laughton's health was failing and his finances dwindling, although he and his wife had become close again. Then, in 1959, he fell truly in love. He met model Bruce Ashe in a London art gallery and established a teacher-pupil relationship with the young man. They lived together in Pimlico then traveled to Rome and America where Laughton's health took a turn for the worse.

In May 1960 he suffered a heart attack and then underwent two gall bladder operations. He was slow to recover and became depressed, even suicidal, when Ashe returned to England temporarily.

Once they were reunited he was a lot happier and took Ashe to Japan. For the first time he wanted to "come out" and make known his homosexuality. He wanted, he said, to "be with his own kind". This idyll was short-lived. He was ill again by the end of 1961 and early the next year slipped and broke a collar bone which took a long time to heal. Lanchester joined him at his New York hospital where doctors told her he had cancer of the bone. Heavily sedated during his last weeks, Laughton died on September 15 1962.

Vivien Leigh

Laurence Olivier called her "the possessor of this wondrous, unimagined beauty . . . She also had something else: an attraction of the most perturbing nature I had ever encountered."

Vivien Leigh was born Vivian Mary Hartley on November 5, 1913 in Darjeeling, India where her father was an exchange broker. She was convent-educated in England and Europe before joining London's Royal Academy of Dramatic Art. At 20, she married a rising lawyer, Leigh Holman, but the birth of their daughter Suzanne was barely a hiccup in her determination to be an actress.

She got her first line, appropriately, in *Things Are Looking Up* (1934) and an agent who, after pondering the stage name of April Morn, agreed to her altering the spelling of her first name and adding her husband's.

That year, the Holmans went to see the stage production *Theatre Royal*, and Leigh gazed on the dashing young actor Laurence Olivier for the first time. She was smitten. Olivier was in the audience when she played in *The Mask of Virtue* (1935), but they did not meet until they were introduced by Gladys Cooper's son.

Furtive Life

Leigh took to visiting Olivier at the New Theatre, where he was alternating Romeo and Mercutio with John Gielgud. So began what Olivier described as "two years of furtive life, lying life. Sneaky. At first I felt a really worm-like adulterer, slipping in between another man's sheets."

The secret was well kept for most of this time. When Leigh accepted a role in *Fire Over England* (1937), Alexander Korda's historical epic, she did not even know that she would be playing opposite her lover. It was while playing *Hamlet* together, that their affair finally became public.

Before their existing marriages were dissolved, Leigh's career suddenly soared. Against such formidable competition as Bette Davis, Katharine Hepburn, Paulette Goddard, Norma Shearer and Tallulah Bankhead, she landed the role of Scarlett O'Hara in *Gone With the Wind* (1939). As Olivier noted, "the odds against her getting the part would create a whole

new scale of betting at Ladbroke's today". She had followed him to Hollywood where Olivier now commanded influence. *Gone With the Wind* made Leigh a star also—and won her an Oscar. The pair became Hollywood's most famous lovers as a result of this success.

Miscarriage and depression

After a financially disastrous road-show of *Romeo and Juliet*, the couple filmed *That Hamilton Woman* (1941) in Hollywood. They had finally married in Santa Barbara in 1940.

When they returned to England, Olivier joined the Fleet Air Arm, while Leigh traveled to North Africa to entertain the troops.

Above: *The lustrous looks of one of the screen's most exquisite beauties.*
Right: *As Blanche Du Bois in* **A Streetcar Named Desire** *(1951) she won her second Academy Award.*

As the war ended, she suffered a miscarriage, a blow from which she took a long time to recover. When Olivier bought the stately Notley Abbey, his now depressive wife was overwhelmed by what she regarded as an inhospitable ancient monument. She took to her bed for a time with tuberculosis.

On resuming her career, however, she triumphed again, winning her second Oscar for her role as Blanche in *A Streetcar Named Desire* (1951).

Breakdown
On a British Council tour to Australia Sir Laurence and Lady Olivier, as they now were, met and took up the young actor Peter Finch. He followed them to London and Leigh told her husband: "I don't love you any more." When Finch and Leigh were paired for *Elephant Walk* in 1953, their affair began in earnest. But on location in Ceylon she went to pieces, her manic depressive illness taking hold. When Finch's wife flew in to break up the affair she found herself nursing her demented rival instead. Leigh was replaced by the young Elizabeth Taylor and Olivier had a nightmare flight bringing his wife home to England for treatment.

Public outbursts
Leigh learned to manipulate her condition, and grew crafty with her husband. She continued to pursue Finch, but when Olivier confessed an affair, she punished him mercilessly. There were outbursts in public; she had another miscarriage. But now Olivier had met Joan Plowright and Leigh ended the speculation while playing Broadway, by announcing that she would give her husband his freedom.

After the break-up of her marriage, she drifted into a tragically disreputable middle age. She set up home with actor Jack Merivale but had many flings, one with Warren Beatty, co-star on her penultimate film, *The Roman Spring of Mrs Stone* (1961). But tuberculosis and depression haunted her. At 53, she died in her sleep on July 7, 1967. Olivier came straight over and "stood and prayed for forgiveness for all the evils that had sprung up between us".

Jack Lemmon

Jack Uhler Lemmon III was born in a hospital elevator stuck between two floors. That first appearance on February 8, 1925 was a fitting one for the future star who was to make his name as Mr Average bungler, limping from incident to hazard.

Voted Number 1 box office star in 1967 by the Motion Picture Exhibitors, twice winner of the Oscar for Best Actor, the only actor ever to win it for both Best Actor and Best Supporting Actor for *Save The Tiger* (1973) and nominee of six Academy Awards, Lemmon is a great star.

First recognized as a master of the tragi-comedy when his Ensign Pulver in *Mister Roberts* (1955) won him an Oscar, he was a late starter in the film industry.

The son of affluent Boston stock, he graduated from Harvard with the intention of following his father into business. However, after three years wartime service aboard an aircraft carrier in the Navy, he decided that his true career lay in acting and, sponsored by a loan from his father, he worked in radio before progressing to become a television producer and actor. He arrived in New York just in time for television's "golden age".

Live panic

"In the early days of live television we had some horrendous experiences," he recalls. "Panic all the way, adrenalin pounding."

When he went to Hollywood on a Columbia contract in 1953, he had some 500 TV roles under his belt and a growing reputation as a comedy actor following his Broadway debut in *Room Service* (1953).

He made the big screen, opposite Judy Garland, in *It Should Happen To You* (1954). Three films later was his Oscar-winner, *Mister Roberts*. Since then he has made a steady succession of films, ranging from fraught-frantic comedy to intense drama.

"I never had a basic desire to be a comic actor," he comments. "It's just

Above right: *Leading a double life in Billy Wilder's* **Irma La Douce** *(1963).*
Right: *One of Hollywood's happiest couples: Lemmon and his actress wife, Felicia share a joke.*

that when I first went into movies I made comedies, and they seemed to work, thank God!"

Between Oscars
Between the two Oscars his run of films included classic hits such as *Some Like It Hot* (1959), *The Apartment* (1960), *Days of Wine and Roses* (1962), *Irma La Douce* (1963), *The Odd Couple* (1968) with frequent screen partner Walter Matthau, and *The Out Of Towners* (1970).

Friendly off-screen with director Billy Wilder and co-star Matthau, Lemmon has repeatedly worked successfully with them, most recently in *Buddy, Buddy* (1981). In 1971, making his directorial debut, Lemmon directed Matthau in *Kotch* – for which Matthau received a well deserved Oscar-nomination.

Fairly split
Since *Save The Tiger* (1973), in which Lemmon played an emotionally disturbed man in mid-life crisis, he has consistently selected more serious roles.

Returning to Broadway in 1978 in the hit play *Tribute* (which won him a Tony nomination and New York's Golden Apple Award) he was the

Sharing the action and the adulation (top) *with screen buddy Walter Matthau in* **The Odd Couple** *(1968) is a far cry from a day at home* (below).

fast-talking PR man trying desperately to achieve a relationship with his son – a theme poignantly close to his personal life. He and his son from his first marriage similarly drifted apart.

Hot on the heels of an Academy award nomination for his performance as a nuclear engineer in *The China Syndrome* (1979), *Tribute* (1980)

garnered him another. Again, for *Missing* (1982) he received a Best Actor nomination.

Lemmon has other gifts, too. He is a first-class pianist and singer. His album *A Twist of Lemmon* was released in 1958 and he contributed musically to two of his films: *Fire Down Below* (1958) and *Tribute*.

Dubbed the happiest star in Hollywood, Lemmon has been married to actress Felicia Farr since 1960. They live in Beverly Hills and also have a beach house in Trancas, California, next door to Wilder and Matthau.

"Ecology nut"
Now, following a career philosophy that "less is better", he regularly plays the professional celebrity golf circuit and spends time traveling and fishing.

A self-confessed "ecology nut", one of Lemmon's main concerns is physical pollution and he records narrations for television documentaries, and broadcasts on the subject.

He is currently back in the director's chair, working on a script based on an Off-Broadway play called *A Coupla White Chicks Sitting Around Talking*. Not obvious film material, he admits, but a good example of new challenges he's taking up.

Carole Lombard

Wise-cracking, trooper-outswearing Carole Lombard was one of the most lovable and most loved of stars, and if she were around today she'd probably be trading chat show insults with comedienne Joan Rivers.

Christened Jane Alice Peters, she was born October 6, 1908 in Fort Wayne, Indiana, the tomboy sister of two older brothers. When she was six, the family moved to Los Angeles where she was spotted on the street, "knocking hell out of the other kids" by director Allan Dwan who put the 12-year-old in *A Perfect Crime* (1921), a movie distinguished only for being her first. Thereafter she went back to junior high school.

When she eventually gained a Fox contract, she served her movie apprenticeship moving from Fox to Sennett to Pathé. Her only major setback during this time was a Bugatti crash that left her with a gashed cheek requiring plastic surgery.

Paramount and Powell
In 1930, Lombard signed a seven-year contract with Paramount. Though practically all her great movies were made elsewhere, it was this studio that provided her steady livelihood through 22 roles. Her fourth Paramount outing teamed her with William Powell, whom she married in summer 1931. But it didn't last long—she was 22, he 39 and they proved incompatible from the start. They divorced within two years but remained friends, even lovers.

Fun after hours
For Lombard, security at Paramount meant fun, fun after hours. The legendary parties began. At their height in the late 1930s a Lombard guest list became a more reliable barometer of who was up and who down than any production cast list. The hostess, with her taste for pranks and hoaxes, inclined to theme parties and many a star cavorted in ill-advised garb at the Lombard residence.

Lombard's lovers at this time included writer Robert Riskin, who had penned her melodramatic vehicle *Virtue* (1932), and the band-singer and former child prodigy, Russ Columbo, who, at 26, was accidentally killed by a shotgun.

Meanwhile, the workaday work at

The sophisticated, talented comedienne (far left) *who married two of the most eligible men in Hollywood – William Powell* (left) *and Clark Gable* (below left) *– before her early death. She is also seen preparing for work* (above) *on* **The Princess Comes Across** *(1936).*

Paramount continued through 1937—but there were successes with other studios, none more so than at Columbia where Howard Hawks cast her opposite John Barrymore in his first screwball comedy, *Twentieth Century* (1934).

That comedy was her métier most agreed, though not Paramount, until 1935 when Ernst Lubitsch was appointed production manager and promptly assigned Lombard to the excellent comedy-drama *Hands Across the Table* (1935). Henceforth the cycle of routine vehicles was punctuated by great movies—*My Man Godfrey* (1936), which reunited her with William Powell at Universal, *Nothing Sacred* (1937) with Frederic March for Selznick, and Lubitsch's own *To Be or Not To Be* (1942).

Enter Gable
More significant than any of these for Carole Lombard herself, however, was the little-remembered *No Man of Her Own* (1932). For the male lead, Paramount traded Bing Crosby for MGM's rising star Clark Gable. At the time, Lombard paid little heed to her co-star: "I was on my ear about a different number," she said later. But in 1936 when the pair renewed acquaintance, the flame was lit.

Marriage had to wait three years because Mrs Ria Gable would not divorce "The King". In the meantime, Lombard and Gable became Hollywood's most celebrated duo.

Tragedy strikes
"To the outside world," reported *Photoplay Magazine* "Clark and Carole might as well be married." The love affair changed Lombard continued *Photoplay*, "Clark doesn't like night spots or parties, social chit-chat or the frothy pretensions of society ... Carole, quite frankly, used to eat it up. She knew everybody, went everywhere. But look what happened —Carole has practically abandoned all her Hollywood social contacts."

Lombard's flippancy wasn't entirely expunged by Gable. Even the fact that they both desperately wanted children was treated lightly in public. "He's sure as hell working on it," she told David Niven but, though they were "forever checking sperm", Lombard could not conceive.

It was while returning on January 16, 1942 from a record US Bond-selling tour of the mid-West that the plane carrying Lombard, her mother and press agent crashed into a mountain near Las Vegas. Her death shocked the world and almost destroyed Gable.

Said President Roosevelt, "She brought great joy to all who knew her and to millions who knew her only as a great artist... She is and always will be a star, one we shall never forget nor cease to be grateful to." *To Be or Not To Be* (1942), arguably her finest work, was released a month later.

Sophia Loren

The tiger-eyed Sophia Loren received more coverage for her prison internment on a tax evasion charge than for her recent cinematic achievements, but even under those tawdry circumstances she remained the sophisticated international star.

A highly talented actress, Loren has a completely different persona from the Hollywood mold of leading ladies. Statuesque and with a face that actually failed early screentests because the nose was too long, the mouth too full, she made her name in her homeland, Italy, before Hollywood snapped her up in the mid-1950s. Cast as a fiery peasant girl opposite Cary Grant and Frank Sinatra in *The Pride and The Passion* (1957), her sultry sexuality caused a rush to cinemas to see her dance in revealingly tattered dresses.

Illegitimate
Loren was born in a charity ward for unmarried mothers in Rome in 1934, and christened Sofia Scicolone. She grew up, strictly Catholic, in the small town of Pozzuoli, near Naples, living in extreme poverty and enduring a German occupation.

In 1948, she was runner-up in a beauty contest and this encouraged her mother, herself the winner of an MGM Greta Garbo lookalike competition, to enroll the young Sophia for drama lessons. When *Quo Vadis* (1951) was being filmed in Rome, mother and daughter were both taken on as extras.

Loren continued to work as an extra until she was noticed by producer Carlo Ponti, who invited her to do a screen test.

Aided by Ponti, who was to fall in love with and marry his protégée, she changed her name to Sophia Lazzaro for two films and then settled on Loren in 1952. She made 20 more films in Italy before moving to America.

Pride and passion
There she found herself acting with the stars she had so admired as a child: Frank Sinatra and Alan Ladd in *Boy on a Dolphin*, John Wayne in *Legend of the Lost* (both in 1957), William

Right: *The sensuous beauty and overt sexuality that brought Hollywood to its knees during the mid-1950s.*

Holden in *The Key* and Anthony Quinn in *The Black Orchid* (both in 1958). She was also cast opposite Cary Grant, in *The Pride and The Passion* (1957) and *Houseboat* (1958), and they had a secret love affair.

Two Women (1960) was the film that established her as an actress. She played a young mother raped, along with her daughter, by invading soldiers, and won the Best Actress Oscar as well as a British Film Academy Award. Thus commenced an international career, working with top directors and actors.

With actor Marcello Mastroianni she made eight successful films, *A Special Day* (1977) scooping up awards internationally. They were the first couple since Fred Astaire and Ginger Rogers to appear in so many films together and the partnership was enormously popular with cinema-going audiences.

Debt to de Sica

Loren singles out Vittorio de Sica as the director who made the greatest impact on her career. For him she made *Two Women*, *The Condemned of Altona* (1962), *Yesterday, Today and Tomorrow* (1963), *Marriage Italian Style* (1964), *Sunflower* (1969) and *The Voyage* (1974).

"He taught me everything I know," she says. "I've never been to drama school, so de Sica was my drama school!"

Her more recent films include *Brass Target* (1978), *Blood Feud* (1979), and *Firepower* (1980).

In 1979 her memoirs, *Sophia: Living and Loving—Her Own Story* were published and she then played herself in the film that chronicled her dramatic rise to fame—*Sophia* (1979).

Condemned by the Vatican

Exposed by the Italian press as a "public sinner" because her marriage to Ponti (22 years her senior) was condemned by the Vatican—his Mexican divorce from his first wife was not recognized—the trials of Loren's life have increased over the years.

For many years she struggled to conceive, before finally giving birth to two sons. Now, for tax reasons, Ponti and Loren are exiled from Italy. The sixteenth-century villa outside Rome that he gave her when they married had to be abandoned; paintings and sculptures valued at $6½ million were seized to clear tax bills.

Now, her marriage to Ponti—who is reported to be in poor health—is said to be in trouble and the future of their homes in Paris, Zürich and Hollywood undecided.

While these uncertainties cloud her personal life, Loren is resuming her film-making life in *Something Blonde* (1985), co-starring Larry Hagman.

Also, her name has been used to launch a new brand of perfume and Loren has increased her enormous popularity touring the world to promote this latest venture.

Below: *Showing her true potential in* **Two Nights With Cleopatra** *(1954).*
Bottom: *Towering over her husband and mentor, Carlo Ponti, who discovered her when she was fifteen.*

Lee Marvin

Legendary hell-raiser Lee Marvin will go down in the annals of Hollywood not only as a snake-eyed, ruthless yet magnificent tough-guy at the center of bar-room fracas both on and off the screen, but also as the star who made legal history. He fought, and won, the internationally publicized palimony suit brought against him by his former mistress, Michelle Triola Marvin.

Meanest baddie
Always one to shoot from the hip, Marvin believes that in order to get ahead in the movie business you have to create an image. In his case he created the meanest baddie of them all.

"I did it damned well, perhaps too well. My image became larger than life," he growls.

The New York-born son of an advertising executive father and journalist mother, his background is very different from that suggested by his screen image. The brother of noted artist Robert Marvin, he was educated at various schools, among them St Leo's Benedictine Academy in Florida—from which he was expelled for throwing a classmate out of the window. The boy had called Marvin "a son-of-a-bitch".

Purple-heart hero
In 1943, he joined the Marines and became a real-life hero while fighting in the Pacific.

"I learned to be tough in the Marines. It was the only way to survive. And I've been giving the same act on and off the screen ever since," he says.

Hit by a Japanese shell splinter he was invalided home from the war and hospitalized for 13 months. He was duly awarded a disability pension— and the Purple Heart.

Marvin was recuperating in New York when a friend of actor John Barrymore met him at a party and suggested he read for a play. This he did and found himself in an Off-Broadway production called *Roadside*. He also enrolled at the American

Above right: *Puffing on a fat cigar as the train-riding hobo in the sadistic adventure,* **Emperor of the North** *(1973).*
Right: *A killer caught by Glenn Ford's cop in Fritz Lang's* **The Big Heat** *(1953).*

Theater Wing. A feature role came up in *Billy Budd* on Broadway and then he toured with various plays.

Director Henry Hathaway spotted him and signed him up for *You're in the Navy Now* (1951), but it took three dozen films, 117 episodes of TV's *M.Squad* and 15 years of playing the laconic, iron-hard thug, before *Cat Ballou* (1965) brought him public recognition. His drunken cowboy in the spoof Western won him an Oscar for Best Actor, and other awards.

The same year *Ship of Fools* (1965) was released, bringing fresh acclaim, and there were also leads in *The Professionals* (1966), *The Dirty Dozen* and John Boorman's *Point Blank* (both in 1967), the latter film being hailed as a cult classic.

Top of the Pops

His image as a character actor and hard-hitter was reinforced by his marathon drinking bouts with other of the industry's bar-room hell-raisers. Marvin was in danger of being typecast forever as the menacing anti-hero.

To break this pattern, he deliberately sought out more sympathetic roles, taking on the two-character film *Hell In The Pacific* (1968) with Toshiro Mifune and, quite out of character, the gold-prospecting, singing cowboy in the musical Western, *Paint Your Wagon* (1969), with Jean Seberg and Clint Eastwood. Much to his own astonishment his gravelly-voiced recording of the theme song took him to the top of the pop charts worldwide.

Palimony and after

Divorced from his first wife in 1964, for the next six years Marvin lived with Michelle Triola, who changed her name by deed poll to Marvin. When he refused to marry her however, she sued him for half of his total earnings during their years together. He won the multi-million dollar case, defended by Marvin Mitchelson, the lawyer who coined the term "palimony"

Marvin left Triola to marry his hometown sweetheart, Pamela Feeley, whom he first met in 1945. Since their marriage his films have tended to show him in a slightly less menacing light.

In the 1970s he made *Monte Walsh* (1970), *Pocket Money* and *Prime Cut* (both in 1972), *The Iceman Cometh* (1973) for the American Film Theater, *The Klansman* (1974) and *Shout At The Devil* (1976).

Increasingly now, Marvin picks and chooses roles, consequently making fewer movies. He has recently made his first film in France, *Dog Day* (1983), followed by *Gorky Park* (1983)—with a role that required him to look every inch the smooth, successful capitalist in expensively-tailored three-piece suits.

Now a grandfather many times over, the ageless Marvin spends part of the year fishing black marlin off the Great Barrier Reef. Back home on his ranch in Tucson, Arizona, he has an impressive collection of Australian art. He also half-owns a gold mine, whereabouts unknown. As always, the enigmatic Marvin likes to keep an ace up his sleeve.

Below: *With hometown sweetheart, Pamela Freely, now his second wife.*
Bottom: *As a drunkard in the musical,* **Paint Your Wagon** *(1969).*

Groucho Marx

Groucho was so blunt that he made bare-faced effrontery into an art form; when pelted with pennies by booing audiences, Groucho Marx turned round and asked for silver— "Our trip has been expensive," he said.

When a haughty woman mistook him for a gardener outside his Beverly Hills mansion and asked how much he was paid, Groucho calmly replied: "Oh, nothing in dollars. The lady of the house just lets me sleep with her." He also wrote in his autobiography: "When silent pictures started talking I interrupted."

Groucho's nickname (he was christened Julius) came from his cynical outlook on life. Unlike his scattier brothers, he resolutely refused to be taken advantage of and often upset sponsors of his radio and TV shows by flaunting competitors' products!

Asked to Detroit to give a talk at sponsor De Soto car works, Groucho told the audience: "I will be in there pushing the '54 De Soto as hard as I can. I only hope that I won't have to push it as often as I did my '52."

Hilarious disrespect

There can be little doubt that Groucho's hilarious disrespectfulness is connected with the grinding poverty of his early life. But whereas the childhood of Chaplin was tainted with misery, the five Marx brothers grew up in a zany atmosphere approaching that of their stage and film exploits. Their father was a good man but an exceptionally bad tailor—he preferred *not to measure* his customers—while their mother was a vaudevillian matriarch of comic proportions. It was she who encouraged her brood on to the stage.

Groucho joined his brothers in a comedy team, which ended up in a frantic Broadway revue, featuring Groucho as Napoleon. Though done on a shoe-string—"We cut enough corners to build a whole new street"— *I'll Say She Is* was a smash hit. The brothers were on their way and a string of crazed stage shows and riotous films were swiftly to follow.

Unholy ideas

In 1920, Groucho, forever the womanizer in his painted on moustache and lewd eyebrows, married Ruth Johnson—the first of his three wives. During the service, when the priest intoned: "We are gathered here to join this couple in holy matrimony," Groucho replied, "It may

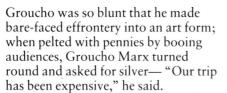

Left: *The fast-thinking comedian with his trademarks: steel rimmed glasses, outrageous moustache and thick cigar.*

be holy to you, but we have other ideas."

For a while the relationship was as successful as Groucho's films—*A Night at the Opera* (1935) and *A Day at the Races* (1937). Then, the marriage ran into trouble. "My wife's drinking was out of control and the whole town knew about it," Groucho said. By 1942 the situation was untenable and, after much agonizing, Groucho sued for divorce.

Groucho married an aspiring singer and dancer named Kay Gorcey in 1945 and had a daughter the following year but two years later was divorced again. The comedian coped in inimitable style: he grew a real moustache to replace his greasepaint trademark and threw himself into a new role as witty compère of a radio, and later a TV quiz show *You Bet Your Life*. To the critics surprise, the show was a hit with both the usual fans of quiz shows *and* would-be intellectuals. One socialite even took out an advertisement, asking friends not to telephone while the program was on!

Newly energized, the 64-year-old married Eden Hartford, a model less than half his age. He also took up his favourite pastime of letter writing in earnest—correspondents included the distinguished poet T.S. Eliot—and he wrote three uproariously funny and highly successful autobiographies: *Groucho and Me* (1959), *Memoirs of a Mangy Lover* (1964) and *The Groucho Letters* (1967).

Second wind
Marriage with Eden didn't last—few had thought it would. After *You Bet Your Life* Groucho lapsed into semi-retirement, living alone in Beverly Hills with his housekeeper, thinking the world had forgotten him. "I ran in to Maurice Chevalier," he wrote. "No one had been a bigger star. 'Do you get asked out much?' I asked him. 'Not so much,' he replied. 'The world has passed me by.' I knew what he meant."

For Groucho, however, there was going to be a second wind. Despairing at piles of unanswered mail he hired Erin Fleming, a not-too-successful actress, as a secretary. She moved in and revitalized the aging star, sorting through invitations, encouraging him to accept a request for a comeback appearance at Carnegie Hall and talk-show engagements. "Our relationship is purely physical," the 82-year-old comedian joked, but when

he was awarded a special Oscar in 1974 he dedicated it to Erin Fleming, among others, saying that "she makes my life worth living."

Final chapter
Not everyone felt this way about her. After Groucho became increasingly frail, his son Arthur claimed that she

Below: **A Night at the Opera** *(1935) with Margaret Dumont and Sig Rumann.* Bottom: *In 1964, with wife Eden and daughter Melinda.*

tormented, drugged and humiliated the old man, and was only interested in his money. A long and sordid series of court hearings followed, concerning who was to be Groucho's guardian. The wrangles continued even after the comedian's death in 1977.

Fortunately, Groucho knew nothing about this final chapter in his life. It would perhaps be better to commemorate the man with his own chosen epitaph: "Here lies Groucho Marx, and lies and lies and lies. PS. He never kissed an ugly girl."

James Mason

The biggest box-office draw in Britain in 1946, James Mason was more popular with British filmgoers than any of the top American stars, even the perennial Bing Crosby. The reason was simple—there has never been a sexier man in British films.

Born in May 1909, he was educated at exclusive Marlborough—where a fellow pupil was the spy Anthony Blunt—and Cambridge. He studied to be an architect, but the theater claimed him, and he made his professional debut in 1931 at the Theatre Royal, Aldershot, in *The Rascal*. Two years later he made his mark in *The Gallows Glorious*, which led to a spell at the Old Vic theater.

Hired and fired

His first venture into films was a disaster. Alexander Korda hired him to play a small part in *The Private Life of Don Juan* (1934), but after four days shooting, fired Mason. Fortunately, he was to have another crack at the cinema, in a B feature, *Late Extra* (1935).

He began to push his way to the top in the war years, when his dark, glowering good looks and resonant voice attracted a great deal of attention in films like *Hatter's Castle* (1941), *Secret Mission* (1942) and *The Bells Go Down* (1943).

Below: *In **A Star is Born** (1954) with Judy Garland.*

Arrogant sadist

Then his powerful brand of cultivated arrogance and charm were given full rein in Gainsborough's *The Man in Grey* (1943). Mason played the sadistic Marquis of Rohan, whipping his mistress Margaret Lockwood to death, to the evident approval of the readers of *Picturegoer* magazine—they voted him Actor of The Year. Women adored him as the vicious Lord Manderstoke in *Fanny by Gaslight* (1944), and as concert pianist Ann Todd's lame guardian in *The Seventh Veil* (1945), bringing his cane crashing down on her hands in a frenzy of impotent rage.

Then came a deserved critical success as the dying IRA gunman in Carol Reed's *Odd Man Out* (1947), a performance which marked him out for a Hollywood career.

Outraged rebuttal

But by the time Mason arrived in California, he was not such a hot property. Before sailing for New York with his wife Pamela and their precocious little daughter Portland, he attacked British films for their "lack of glamor", singling out J. Arthur Rank for particular criticism. When his liner docked, Rank's press agents had already been at work and the gossip columnists poured out a stream of stories about Mason's "uncooperative" behavior.

He further lowered his stock by

Left: *Showing little enthusiasm for a compulsory 20th Century Fox portrait during* **Island in The Sun** *(1957).*
Below: *Relaxing at home with his first wife, Pamela, and their daughter, Portland.*
Bottom: *Lord of the slave breeding plantation he views so autocratically in* **Mandingo** *(1975).*

writing an article which poked fun at the film capital. His jibes at the snobberies of the seating arrangements at Romanoff's, a favorite watering hole of the stars, resulted in an outraged rebuttal printed on the restaurant's menu.

Mason had fatally undermined his chances of becoming a major Hollywood star. He had to mark time until the early 1950s, when he played Rommel in *The Desert Fox* (1951) and gave a masterly performance in *Five Fingers* (1952) as "Cicero", the British embassy valet in Ankara who sold secrets to the Germans in the Second World War.

He then regained his rightful place as the suavest of villains, playing Rupert of Hentzau in the remake of *The Prisoner of Zenda* (1952), Captain Nemo in Disney's spectacular *20 000 Leagues Under The Sea* (1954) and almost stealing the show from Cary Grant in Hitchcock's *North By Northwest* (1959).

He showed his quality as an actor of distinction in *A Star is Born* (1954)—providing Judy Garland with the best support she ever had.

Outstripping mediocrity

Mason's talent has invariably outstripped the mediocre films which have punctuated his career. It was in the doldrums when he was cast as Humbert Humbert in Stanley Kubrick's *Lolita* (1962), a performance of immense skill in an uneven attempt to transfer Vladimir Nabokov's novel to the screen.

After *Lolita*, Mason applied himself with great success to a series of character roles. And in 1967, at the Montreal Exposition, he was named "Cinema Actor of the Century", a just tribute to his supreme professionalism.

In recent years this quality has seen him safely through a number of unlikely films: playing opposite Lee Van Cleef in a spaghetti Western, *Bad Man's River* (1971); cast as a French crime baron in *The Marseille Contract* (1974); as a Southern plantation owner in *Mandingo* (1975); a Nazi war criminal in *The Boys from Brazil* (1978) and Dr Watson to Christopher Plummer's Sherlock Holmes in *Murder by Decree* (1979).

Since his 1936 screen debut, Mason has appeared in well over 100 films. Sadly, he died on Friday July 27, 1984 of a heart attack.

123

Steve McQueen

Shortly before his tragic death in 1980, Steve McQueen speculated on where his acting ability and appeal lay. He concluded: "My range isn't very great and I don't have much scope. There's something about my shaggy-dog eyes that makes people think I'm good, but really I'm *not* all that good. I'm pretty much myself most of the time in my movies and I have accepted that."

His fine performances in *The Cincinnati Kid* (1965), *The Sand Pebbles* (1966), *The Thomas Crown Affair* (1968), *Papillon* (1973), and *Tom Horn* (1979) testify to the contrary. As for his appeal, his little-boy-lost looks and a pair of the bluest eyes in the business guaranteed McQueen a large female following, despite his own reluctance to consider himself as a sex symbol.

He tended to be most relaxed in the company of fellow car, motor-bike and airplane enthusiasts rather than show-business people; Hollywood played only a small part in his life.

Sent to reform school
Born on March, 24, 1930, McQueen had an unsettled childhood. After his parents separated when he was only six months old, he was raised by his great-uncle on a farm in Missouri. His mother came back into his life during his early teens and took him to Los Angeles, a new and alien environment which brought out the rebel in him. Keeping company with street gangs, the young McQueen was often in trouble with the police. One night, when he was only 14, he was caught stealing hub-caps. This led to 14 months in a reform school.

Shortly after his release, in 1947, McQueen ran away to sea. In Port Arthur, Texas, he jumped ship—working as an errand boy in a brothel, an oil rigger, a lumber jack and a salesman before joining the Marines as a tank driver.

When he returned to civilian life in 1950, he used the GI Bill of Rights to obtain a drama school scholarship. Later he recalled that the idea of becoming an actor had first appealed to him when working as a TV repair man in Greenwich Village.

McQueen was a natural actor and won a Broadway role in *A Hatful of Rain* in 1956, before making his film

A passion for all things mechanical (above right) *which was translated to the screen* (right) *for* **The Great Escape** *(1963).*

124

debut as a member of a street gang straight out of his own childhood in *Somebody Up There Likes Me* (1956).

Exciting lifestyle

Around this time, he met Neile Adams, a pretty young actress. As his future wife recalled: "It started out beautifully, very romantically, too. And exciting—he introduced me to a new lifestyle. I'd been brought up in convents and never been exposed to this kind of man."

The couple married with McQueen wearing a borrowed suit and with a $40 ring in his pocket.

After his appearance in the Western *The Magnificent Seven* (1960), McQueen became a household name, but curiously—considering the number of Westerns in which he appeared—his passion was hardly equinal. "Horses cannot be trusted. You never know what they'll do. I don't understand them. I don't like them," he once said.

Love of speed

His most popular films were those in which he indulged in his love of speed. In the famous motor-bike chase sequence of *The Great Escape* (1963), he performed his own stunts, appearing as both the escaping American prisoner-of-war and his German pursuer, because he was the only man on the set who knew how to make the chase look convincing.

The car chase to end them all was the highlight of *Bullitt* (1968), with McQueen insisting that he undertook the dangerous stunt of driving a car at breakneck speed along the streets of San Francisco, much against the wishes of Warner Brothers and his insurance company.

He co-starred with the darkly beautiful Ali MacGraw in *The Getaway* (1972) and married her the following year. But they separated in 1979 and eventually divorced.

Towards the end of his life, however, McQueen found peace and stability with model Barbara Jo Minty, whom he married only eight months before his death from cancer.

Struck down

Throughout his career, McQueen had worried that he might have chosen the wrong profession, explaining that although he liked his work, "acting doesn't have any dignity". In his penultimate film, *Tom Horn* (1979), he plays a man who faces death with dignity—a role made all the more poignant by the courage with which he faced his own end, barely a year later.

Although on screen he appeared to be the embodiment of physical fitness, this was only achieved by long hours of hard training. And at the age of 50, McQueen was struck down by mesothelioma, an incurable lung cancer. He underwent a controversial "nutritional" treatment in Mexico and fought the disease with dignity and courage.

No one realized just how serious his condition was and it came as a shock when his death was announced after an extremely grueling three-hour operation, on November 7, 1980.

Below: *Rough treatment for wife-to-be Ali MacGraw in* **The Getaway** *(1972).* Bottom: *With newly-wedded wife, Barbara Minty, six months before his premature death from cancer in 1980.*

Robert Mitchum

Robert Mitchum's life story reads like a film script. He has been a prisoner on a chain gang, arrested on a narcotics charge, and wandered destitute around Depression America. In spite of all that, he has become one of Hollywood's best known leading men and has remained married to his childhood sweetheart.

Mitchum was born in Connecticut on August 6, 1917. His father was killed when he was 18 months old, and after a tough childhood he ran away to sea at 14. Then he traveled around America by jumping trains and sleeping rough. Jobs were scarce and he endured claustrophobia to work as a miner in the Pennsylvania coalfields.

Sent to prison

At 15 he was arrested in Georgia for vagrancy and was nearly framed on a burglary charge. Sent to prison, he was made to work on a chain gang, shackled at the ankles, and nearly lost a leg when injuries caused by the shackles became infected.

Recovering at home, he met 14-year-old Dorothy Spence, fell in love and vowed to marry her, which he did in March 1940. In the meantime, he worked in a variety of jobs, including heavyweight boxing.

Living in California, he drifted into the film industry and after taking small parts in Western—he made 9 in 1943—was spotted by director William Wellman, who offered him the lead in *G.I. Joe* (1945). For this role Mitchum received an Oscar nomination. Before the film's release he joined the army, and when he came out he was a star.

Growing notoriety

Mitchum made a string of excellent films in the late 1940s but as his reputation grew, so did his notoriety. The press labeled him rebellious and unco-operative but he was simply unimpressed by the glamor and sparkle of Hollywood and did not take his own screen image very seriously: "People started talking about Mitchum-type roles, but I still don't know what they

Top: *The rugged, nonchalant leading man with the sleepy eyes women loved.* Right: *Locked in romantic action with Greer Garson, in* **Desire Me** *(1947).*

meant. They'd paint the eyes on my eyelids and I'd walk through it. The least work for the most reward."

In September 1948 he was involved in a police raid at the home of an actress friend. Marijuana and benzedrine tablets were found and he was charged with conspiracy to possess and actual possession of marijuana. The raid was part of a drive to rid Hollywood of drugs and to have caught a "famous name" was considered a coup.

Mitchum's fans stuck by him, and his wife, who had wanted to leave Hollywood for New York, immediately came back to him. He was found guilty only on the conspiracy charge and received a one-year suspended jail sentence and two years of probation, of which the first 60 days had to be spent in custody. Afterward he commented, "It's been the finest vacation I've had in seven years."

Complaint dismissed
Amazingly the affair did not damage his career; he survived the crisis and got back to work quietly. Rumors about the circumstances of the raid persisted and in 1951 the complaint against Mitchum was dismissed, but this verdict was never publicized.

Sometimes he lived up to his "difficult" reputation. Wellman fired him from the set of *Blood Alley* (1955) when a prank misfired. With every incident reported by the media, however, the publicity placed a strain on Mitchum's family.

Brilliant performances
Mitchum has made in the region of 100 films and put in brilliant performances in a variety of genres—from melodrama in *Home From the Hill* (1960) to modern-day gangster in *The Friends of Eddie Coyle* (1973). He has twice played the part of Chandler's famous private eye Philip Marlowe in re-makes of *Farewell My Lovely* (1975) and *The Big Sleep* (1978).

He has talked of retirement for some time and still maintains a cynical detachment from the glamorous side of his profession. "I was usually in Mexico sliding my backside down some mountain or getting burnt to a crisp on some location in a place like Death Valley. And as for the beautiful girls I was supposed to work with—John Wayne, Dean Martin, Kirk Douglas. These are beautiful dames? Anyway, they always got the girl. I got the horse!"

Early in the 1980s Mitchum turned his attention to television, starring in the lucrative blockbuster *The Winds of War*, scorning artistic pretensions. As far as he is concerned—"I got into movies because I needed the money—and the situation hasn't changed."

127

Marilyn Monroe

No star's life has been so minutely analyzed as that of Norma Jean Mortensen, who grew up to be Marilyn Monroe. Not that all this analyzing has brought us nearer to the truth. The facts are disputed, opinions vary, but on one thing all agree: her own account is not to be relied upon.

Fantasy—or fact?
Her birth date at least is known: June 1, 1926 in Los Angeles. Older sources have her registered as Norma Jean Baker. Her mother, born Gladys Monroe, and becoming successively Gladys Baker and Gladys Mortensen by marriage, had little hand in her daughter's upbringing. The child was fostered when Gladys succumbed to paranoid schizophrenia.

Monroe later claimed that her grandmother had tried to asphyxiate her, that her mother stabbed Grace McKee to whom Monroe was made ward, that McKee's husband molested her and that she was raped at 9 by a lodger at another foster home. However, James Dougherty, a blue-collar worker who married her fresh from high school, maintained that he married a virgin.

Monroe also attested that her childhood retreat was the movies—she dreamed of Clark Gable being her father. Her own route to stardom began in 1944, when she drifted into photographic modeling. This led to a

Above: *Posed to attract attention: Norma Jean Baker at the start of her short, glorious reign as a sex goddess.*

contract with 20th Century-Fox and a name change, the Marilyn taken from musical comedy star Marilyn Miller.

The Dougherty marriage ended and there followed a relationship with Joseph M. Schenck, executive producer at Fox and nearing 70. Some commentators portray Schenck as Monroe's sugar-daddy, others point out that her lack of progress at Fox belies this.

More certain is that Johnny Hyde, vice president of the William Morris Agency, left his wife and four sons for her, and managed her career. The actress duly got her first decent parts in *The Asphalt Jungle* and *All About Eve* (both in 1950), and a seven-year contract.

At Hyde's behest, she had her jaw remodeled and her nose-tip bobbed. But Hyde had a bad heart condition and he begged her to marry him so that she would be a wealthy widow. Monroe confounded the gossips by declaring that she could only marry for love, not simply for security.

Too hot to publish

After Hyde's death in 1950, Monroe's career trod water—steady but no splash. She survived and eventually thrived on initially bad publicity over a nude calendar portrait for which she earned $50 and netted the publishers $750 000.

Joe DiMaggio was 37 and retired from baseball when he and Monroe became an item just as her career was taking off. She was top-billed in *Niagara* and clinched her stardom in

Below: *A pause for thought with Yves Montand in* **Let's Make Love** *(1960).*

Above: *With playwright Arthur Miller during her third unhappy marriage.*

Gentlemen Prefer Blondes (both in 1953). Marriage followed in 1954.

Her wedding gift to DiMaggio—a portfolio of the calendar shots considered too hot to publish—showed how badly she misread his character. DiMaggio was a home body who disapproved of showbiz shenanigans. As his profound stability asserted itself, her incipient instability began to claim her. She began drinking and analysis.

The last straw for DiMaggio was when he appeared on a New York street to watch location filming for *The Seven Year Itch* (1955), only to see a wind machine blowing up his wife's skirt and crowds of onlookers cheering from the sidewalk. The nine-month marriage ended.

No dumb blonde

Tiring of dumb blonde type-casting, Monroe went to New York. There she joined Lee Strasberg's Actors' Studio, formed her own production company and renewed acquaintance with writer Arthur Miller, with whom she'd had a fling in 1951. Miller was currently being pursued by the House of Un-American Activities Committee, this being the height of the witch-hunts for Communist sympathizers; marrying Monroe would certainly take the heat off. For her, Miller was a passport to intellectual respectability. They married in June 1956 and promptly left for London—where she joined forces with Laurence Olivier in *The Prince and the Showgirl* (1957), a piece of fluff far removed from the heavyweight roles she'd aspired to.

Troubles galore

Monroe's problems grew more acute. The first of two miscarriages bitterly distressed her. She was now a habitual user of barbiturates, easily inclined to overdose. And for all his intellectual accomplishment Miller was no more tolerant than her previous husbands.

Her insecurities redoubled, so did her reputation as trouble on the set. She worked with an entourage that also made itself a nuisance. Even so, one of the most fraught shoots that Hollywood ever hosted produced one of its most successful comedies, *Some Like It Hot* (1959).

Monroe had an affair with her next co-star, Yves Montand in *Let's Make Love* (1960), but he returned to his wife. The end of Monroe's marriage was delayed by John Huston's shooting of Miller's script *The Misfits* (1961) which teamed her with Clark Gable, then near to death. The divorce went through on the day of President Kennedy's swearing in.

The Kennedy-Monroe affair could only continue while her silence could be relied upon. Kennedy's brother Robert, then Attorney General, became her next lover, but he too found her emotional and mental instability a liability.

Sacked from her latest movie, fitfully a psychiatric patient, abandoned by her lovers, Monroe took her last overdose on August 5, 1962. Whether it was accidental or deliberate—or whether, more fancifully, the CIA killed her—will never be known. Unquestionably, though, Monroe could no longer cope with being, as Norman Mailer put it: "Every man's love affair with America."

Paul Newman

When Paul Newman's first film, *The Silver Chalice* (1955), played for a week on television in America recently he took out an advertisement saying "Paul Newman apologizes every night this week", because it was so awful. It was the latest of many quirky Newmanisms, which have included having Robert Redford's face printed on every sheet of 150 cartons of toilet paper and giving director Robert Altman a baby goat labeled: "Your Own Vineyard", following years of complaining that Altman's wine tasted like goat urine.

Selling popcorn
Now he's marketing *Newman's Own* Salad Dressing, Organically Grown Popcorn and Industrial Strength Venetian Spaghetti Sauce.

Born in January 1925, in an upper middle-class suburb of Cleveland, Ohio, Newman is the son of a Jewish sports shop owner and a Hungarian-descended Catholic mother. Raised as a Christian Scientist, he now calls himself a Jew.

As a teenager, he worked briefly in summer theater before studying at Kenyon College, Ohio. Soon after Pearl Harbor he tried to enlist in the Navy but failed the medical: his famous blue eyes proved to be color blind. Undeterred, he served as a radioman.

After the war Newman returned to college, graduated and, when his father died, took over the shop. Unhappy as a

Resting between shots (top right) *and turning it on as the rebel prisoner on a chain gang* (right) *in Stuart Rosenberg's* **Cool Hand Luke** *(1967).*

salesman, he eventually sold up and enrolled at the Yale School of Drama—where he met and married his first wife, actress Jacqueline Witte.

Knobbly knees
By the time he broke into acting in New York he had three children. Understudying the lead in the Broadway run of *Picnic*, he impressed enough to land a feature role in the play and joined Lee Strasberg's Actors' Studio. Then Warner Brothers placed him under contract for the *Silver Chalice*. After seeing himself as a Greek slave with knobbly knees, however, he wanted only to return to New York.

Fortunately he bounced back in better roles and received his first Oscar nomination for *Cat On A Hot Tin Roof* (1958). His career has zig-zagged onward through dozens of films, from excellent to less-than-memorable. He has also directed—notably his second wife, Joanne Woodward, in *Rachel Rachel* (1968) and *The Effect of Gamma Rays on Man-in-the-Moon Marigolds* (1972).

His second Oscar nomination came with *The Hustler* (1961), the third for *Hudd* (1963) and the fourth for *Cool Hand Luke* (1967). Fifteen years later *The Verdict* (1982) brought him a fifth. He has also given unforgettable performances in two big box-office hits, *Butch Cassidy and The Sundance Kid* (1969) and *The Sting* (1973).

Sex symbol
From the start Newman has been a sex symbol, always representing traditional masculinity of a cerebral rather than muscle-bound kind.

His image has been enhanced by his happy marriage to Woodward, whom he met in *Picnic* (1953). They have three daughters, and three homes.

Of their marriage Woodward has said: "For two people who have almost no interest in common, we have an unusually good marriage. Paul likes fast cars, swimming, fishing and playing pool. I love ballet, the theater, opera and museums."

Newman put it his way: "We have a deal: I trade a couple of ballets for a couple of races."

On their twenty-fifth wedding anniversary the couple renewed their

Right: A moment of peace with Joanne Woodward who describes their marriage as "unusually good for two people with almost nothing in common".

wedding vows at a party held in their Connecticut home.

Newman has been active in liberal politics since the 1960s. As a US delegate to the United Nations on disarmament he was on Nixon's list of particular enemies. He supports nuclear freeze, more rights for gays and compulsory wearing of seatbelts. He also donates to education funds, consumer groups and the Scott Newman Foundation—started to promote accurate film portrayal of drug problems following his son Scott's death by accidental overdose of a combination of drugs and alcohol.

Experimental films
He has also made experimental films like *WUSA* (1970), a melodrama about a right-wing radio announcer, and *The Life and Times of Judge Roy Bean* (1972), a fantasia on the Old West outlaw judge.

Each summer he devotes to

motor-racing on the amateur circuits. Twice he has notched up the national champion title in his class.

He combined work and play in *Winning* (1969), as a racing driver, and in his documentary for ABC-TV *Once Upon a Wheel* (1971), about the stock car circuit.

Newman's last three films, *Absence of Malice* (1981), a virtual indictment of the press, *The Verdict* (1982), in which he plays a washed-up lawyer, and *Harry and Son* (1984) which he produced, directed, co-scripted and starred in with his wife, playing a neurotic unemployed widower, have shown his determination to get away from the popular mold—and be involved in projects that actively interest him.

Future plans include a film about the death of his son, and a film version of *The Front Runner*, a best-selling gay love story about a track coach who falls in love with his star runner.

Jack Nicholson

Jack Nicholson wears sunglasses like a shield, even indoors on the darkest day. They serve to emphasize his flashing barracuda smile and the New Jersey drawl that makes him irresistible. His hair recedes, his belly hangs over his belt and his words come very slowly, but nobody turns away because Nicholson has the same charisma off screen as on.

He was born in New Jersey in April 1937, the son of an Irish-American part-time window dresser and full-time alcoholic, who moved out of the house when his only son was still a boy. Fortunately, his wife's beauty shop provided "a comfortable middle class existence" for her and her three children.

Learning his trade

Although a natural learner who earned a place in the top 2 per cent nationally for the college entrance exams, Nicholson rejected University in favor of the Hollywood dream.

His first job as a $30 clerk in the MGM mailing room led precisely nowhere however, so he signed on for acting lessons. These did not help as much as he had hoped and he found himself locked into a series of low budget movies. Some—like the drug-cult rave up, *The Trip* (1967)—he wrote and directed himself. He appeared in 15 such productions, with barely a favorable notice to show for it, before Peter Fonda cast him in *Easy Rider* (1969).

"Before, I was an actor-director-writer-producer looking for work. Suddenly I was much sought after. Your name becomes a brand image like a product ... with 37 different varieties of roles you can play!" he said at the time.

He established his screen persona in films like *Five Easy Pieces* (1970), *Carnal Knowledge* (1971), *The Last Detail* (1973), *Chinatown* (1974) and *One Flew Over the Cuckoo's Nest* (1975), for which he won an Oscar. He went on to confirm his position in *The Shining* (1979), *The Postman Always Rings Twice* (1981) and *Reds* (1981), with *Goin' South* (1978)—a film he

Left: *In characteristic manic mode as the unhinged writer in Stanley Kubrick's,* **The Shining** *(1979).*

directed himself—among his rare failures.

Despite the manic nature of the characters he plays, Nicholson's presence on a set is a guarantee that excellent work gets done. He likes to party all night, so the cameras don't turn until 11a.m., but his relaxed good humor ensures that everyone enjoys working with him.

Reformed degenerate
His extraordinary charm is that of the degenerate who has only partly reformed, the kind you hope will never quite complete the process. The habits that have turned him on include drugs, alcohol, gambling and girls. Some of them he's kicked.

"I gave up drugs when Dennis Hopper and I found ourselves up a tree after spending the night before on the top of D.H. Lawrence's tomb. I quit gambling when I had lost so much and I was so dazed from drink that I couldn't find my own car in the parking lot."

Some of them he hasn't kicked. "I love women. It's not true that I'm a womanizer, but I'll admit to being something of a male chauvinist pig. When women throw themselves at you all the time, the only way to treat them is badly … there are times when I prefer to make the play."

Live-in romance
Nicholson was married in his pre-*Easy Rider* days to actress Sandra Knight, who bore him a daughter, Jennifer, but their relationship didn't survive his elevation to star status. After its failure, the lucky ladies who get through on the Nicholson line read like a Hollywood register, but pride of place belongs to Anjelica Huston, daughter to director, John Huston, with whom he's shared a stormy decade of live-in, live-out romance.

In one of the out phases, Nicholson didn't hesitate to detach Diane Keaton from his best mate, Warren Beatty. However, such a minor misdemeanor didn't break up their friendship.

Enjoying the spoils
Recently he's been reducing his work load, the better to enjoy the spoils. As he collects a seven figure pay check for the kind of Oscar-winning cameo he performed so effortlessly in *Terms of Endearment* (1983), these are considerable.

Nicholson takes a pretty balanced view of his good fortune: "Money, as someone once said, isn't everything. The very first year I started making movies, I earned $1400 which is nothing at all. But I survived. I was happy. I knew I'd make money some day. What I didn't expect to happen

The lucky ladies in his life: in bed with Faye Dunaway (below) in **Chinatown** *(1974), and escorting his long term girlfriend, Anjelica Huston (bottom).*

was to find myself a superstar. It's unreal!"

For reality, he turns to Aspen, Colorado where he has a house overlooking mountains and lakes which he uses as a base for skiing. "When I'm racing down these slopes, with the wind behind me and my body exploding with the speed of it all, I know I'm a human being again, not a superstar. It's very good for the sanity!"

David Niven

With the death of David Niven in 1983, Hollywood lost one of its best-loved figures—he had appeared in over 80 films in a career that spanned six decades and remained charming and debonair to the end.

A man who really enjoyed his work, he could never fully accept the stroke of good fortune that brought him into acting, once saying, "I expect at any moment to have some serious looking gent walk up to me and say 'All right, Niven, it's all over. You've been found out'."

Niven was born in Scotland in March 1909 and educated at a succession of boarding schools where his self-appointed role of school clown did little to endear him to his teachers. His father had been killed in action in the Dardanelles during the First World War, when Niven was five.

Later, deciding on a military career himself, Niven attended the Royal Military Academy at Sandhurst, after which he was commissioned a second lieutenant in the Highland Light Infantry.

He made his first trip to America when, on leave for a month, he accepted an invitation from Barbara Hutton, having met her while based in Malta.

On his return from the States, disillusioned with army life, he resigned his commission and sailed to Canada, hoping to make his fortune.

Shenanigans

Before his eventual break into movies, Niven was a post-prohibition liquor salesman, indoor pony racing promoter and a technical adviser to Cuban insurgents. With typical bravado, he registered as an extra in the belief that the shenanigans which had endeared him to his fellow-schoolboys would make him a suitable candidate as an actor.

He was to find out the hard way that this was not the case, instead working long hours for meager returns. And despite his classification of "Anglo Saxon Type Number 2008", his first part was decidedly Hispano-American—as a Mexican obscured by a poncho in a Hopalong Cassidy film.

Niven came to the attention of Samuel Goldwyn, who placed him under contract and cast him opposite

Above: *The perfect English gentleman, enjoying all the good things in life in* **The Toast of New Orleans** *(1950)*.

Laurence Olivier in *Wuthering Heights* (1939). During this period, he formed a lasting friendship with screen idol Errol Flynn, with whom he had co-starred in *The Charge of the Light Brigade* (1936) and *Dawn Patrol* (1938). The parties they held at their shared Beverly Hills house have long since become part of Hollywood folklore.

Distinguished service

In 1939, he became the first British actor in Hollywood to volunteer for active service and returned home to rejoin the army, where he distinguished himself as a commando, attaining the rank of colonel.

For a brief period Peter Ustinov was assigned as his batman so they could work together on the wartime British moral booster *The Way Ahead* (1944), released in the USA as *Immortal Battalion*. Niven seldom spoke of his wartime experiences, and, despite being one of the few British servicemen to be awarded the American Legion of

Romance off the screen (right) *with his second wife, the Swedish-born Hjordis Tersmeden, in 1948, and on* (below right) *with Jean Seberg, in Preminger's* **Bonjour Tristesse** *(1958).*

Merit, he spoke of his exploits in a self-depreciatory manner, commenting that he had done "nothing brave, but no one caught me running away".

Shortly after his discharge and return to Hollywood, his wife was tragically killed in an accident. This was the start of an unhappy period in Niven's career: he fell out with Samuel Goldwyn and their contract was dissolved by mutual consent.

Cavalier

Niven's attitude to film making could be cavalier: "I'm naughty. Whenever I'm offered a part, I ask three things: Where is it being made? Who else is in it? How much are they paying? Only then do I read the script."

With his starring role in *Around the World in 80 Days* (1956) and Oscar-winning performance in *Separate Tables* (1958), in which he played brilliantly against type, Niven's career began to pick up. But in 1960, following the death of his close friend Errol Flynn, he felt as though some of the magic of Hollywood had died too. He decided to move with his family—Niven remarried in 1948—to Europe where he set up homes in France and Switzerland. His film output remained unaffected by the change of scenery and he was as prolific as ever.

Natural raconteur

Expanding on his talent as raconteur, Niven penned the first part of his memoirs, *The Moon's a Balloon*, in 1971, followed by *Bring on the Empty Horses* in 1975. The two books have sold millions of copies throughout the world, and they enjoy the status of being the most successful autobiographies ever written by an entertainer.

David Niven died at the age of 73 after a typically courageous and played-down battle against unbeatable amytrophic lateral sclerosis, a neuromuscular ailment. Shortly before his death, he shot a few scenes for the film *The Curse of the Pink Panther* (1983), despite his devastating illness, continuing to work with the stoic professionalism for which—coupled with a sincere geniality—David Niven is best remembered.

Laurence Olivier

Now in his late seventies, Laurence Olivier has a title—Lord Olivier of Brighton—and the Olivier auditorium at the National Theatre, London to prove his pre-eminence in the profession he once described as "a masochistic form of exhibitionism, not quite the occupation of an adult."

However, the records suggest that he never considered any other—at least from the age of ten, when his appearance in a school production of *Julius Caesar* prompted Ellen Terry to write in her diary: "The small boy who played Brutus is already a great actor."

Child bully

In all other respects, Olivier's childhood was unremarkable. He was a thin, unattractive boy, who endured the persistent dislike of his stern Victorian father, a High Anglican cleric. The family moved constantly from parish to parish, so young Larry had few opportunities to make friends. At school he tended to bully his peers, whenever he couldn't avoid them altogether by playing truant. "I just hated school," he has said. "Without wanting to pull out any violins, I think I can say I was vastly unpopular."

Coming alive

In due course, the gauche boy turned into a glowering, undernourished young man, who only really came alive on stage while he was learning his trade at the Central School and the Birmingham Rep. However, he was intelligent and soon acquired tact and polish to match his talent.

The catalog of Olivier's triumphs is legendary. He developed into a very physical actor, given to huge leaps and bounds, with a robust delivery to match—characteristics that enabled him to make definitive interpretations of *Henry V* (1944), *Hamlet* (1948) and *Richard III* (1955) in both theater and cinema.

Although his early days in Hollywood were marred by his much publicized rejection as Garbo's leading man in *Queen Christina*, he has carved himself a career in American films that

The greatest actor of his generation (above right) *in his own production of* **Hamlet** (1948), *and as Professor Van Hesling* (right) *in* **Dracula** (1979).

ranges from magnificent, as in *Wuthering Heights* (1939) and *Rebecca* (1940) to dire.

Incurable romantic

In his youth, Olivier was incurably romantic which led to his marrying for the first time when he was only 23. His bride was Jill Esmond, an actress who was rather more famous than he was at the time and believed that marriage was an equal partnership, rather than a form of slavery. But neither her enlightened views, nor the fact that she bore him a much-wanted son, Simon Tarquin, in 1936 saved her once Vivien Leigh came into her husband's life.

Two out of three wives: with Vivien Leigh (below), while filming **The Divorce of Lady X** *(1938); socializing with Joan Plowright (bottom).*

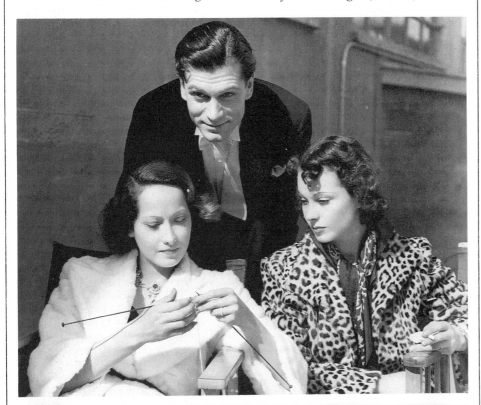

Lavish entertainer

Olivier's second wedding was a quiet affair in Santa Barbara, California, witnessed only by Katharine Hepburn and Garson Kanin, after which the couple began a glittering 21-year progress from triumph to triumph, until Leigh's mental illness led to a breakdown of their marriage, too. Back in England for the duration of the war, they set up house in twelfth-century Notley Abbey, Buckinghamshire. There they entertained the élite of the theater world on a lavish scale.

In 1957, when his beautiful wife's recurring depressions and increasingly oppressive demands were already taking their toll on the marriage, Olivier met the actress Joan Plowright, at the Royal Court, where they were to appear together in John Osborne's *The Entertainer.* "Delighted to have you with us," he said graciously, before disappearing upstairs to rehearse alone but, on closer acquaintance, he recognized her sterling qualities, and she eventually became his third wife.

Proud father

They were married in 1960 and established themselves in an elegant, four-storey Regency house in Brighton. There, Olivier at last found a real home. Four children were born in quick succession: a boy, Richard, then three girls, Tamsin, Agnes Margaret and Julie Kate.

"I know nothing more beautiful than to set off from home in the morning in a taxi, look back and see your young held to a window, to wave to you. It's sentimental and it's corny but it's better than poetry, better than genius, better than money," said the proud father.

His new-found domestic bliss coincided with two major administrative triumphs, the establishment of the Chichester Festival Theatre in 1961 and the National Theatre at the Old Vic two years later. It was his 10-year reign that laid the foundations for the company's establishment in its permanent South Bank home, though ill health forced the newly elevated Baron to retire before the transition was actually made.

Today the old lion still supports his young family with a succession of film roles which add nothing to his stature as an actor, perhaps to prove the point that he has nothing more to prove.

Al Pacino

Just as his film fans feel they're getting to grips with Al Pacino, the five-time Oscar nominee and twice winner of a Tony Award slips off to do a stage production Off-Broadway or in a tiny theater out of town.

In spite of becoming one of the superstars on the strength of only a few performances, he retains a certain streetwise attitude.

Growing up
Born in 1939 in the South Bronx area of New York, he was raised by his tradition-bound Sicilian mother and grandparents after his father left home when he was two. Not allowed out of the house until he was seven, other than to go to church or the cinema with his mother, his only means of release and expression was to act out the movies he saw.

At 15, Pacino was accepted by

Above: *A star for the 1970s in* **Serpico** *(1973), a true tale of an honest cop.*

Manhattan's High School of Performing Arts, but left after just a couple of years, to support himself by doing temporary work while he waited for his first break. While still a teenager he joined the Herbert Berghoff Studio, where he met Charles Laughton who proceeded to "educate" him.

Four years later Lee Strasberg accepted him into his Actors' Studio and a friendship developed between them that was to last until Strasberg's death.

Pacino began finding roles in Off-Broadway plays. *The Indian Wants The Bronx*, won him an Obie Award and the next year *Does A Tiger Wear A Necktie?* on Broadway won him a Tony. On the strength of that he was given a small role in the film *Me,*

Natalie (1969) and then the lead in *Panic In Needle Park* (1971) playing a desperately unattractive heroin addict.

Anti-hero
Pacino seems almost to have typecast himself as the anti-hero. In *Scarecrow* (1973) he was one of the world's losers. In *Serpico* (1973) he was a New York cop exposing police corruption, in *Dog Day Afternoon* (1975) a homosexual bank robber.

The first signs of romance came as a Grand Prix driver in *Bobby Deerfield* (1977) but then he went back to the unloved parts.

He played the lawyer at odds with the legal system in *And Justice For All* (1979); the cop, possibly gay, investigating homosexual murders in *Cruising* (1980); the shed husband and father of five in *Author! Author!* (1982) and the gangster-turned-

138

cocaine king in *Scarface* (1983). Even in *The Godfather* (1972) and *Godfather Part II* (1974), in the role of Michael Corleone, he was the understated outsider who turns killer and becomes the Godfather's successor.

His performance in *The Godfather* earned Pacino a National Society of Film Critics Award for Best Actor and an Oscar nomination for Best Supporting Actor. Three films in a row (*Serpico, Godfather Part II* and *Dog Day Afternoon*) then won him Best Actor nominations as did *And Justice For All* but, as yet, he has never been awarded the prized golden statue.

Dedicated
The most dedicated of the New York stage actors working in Hollywood, he returns consistently to theater.

"I am more alive in the theater than anywhere else," he comments, "but what I take into the theater I get from the streets."

He believes that an actor should not turn down a good part, however little the financial reward offered. Still lit by the glory of *The Godfather* he joined an experimental theater company in Boston on a $200 a week fee at a theater with an audience capacity of only 85. Ten years later he repeated his performance in the same play, *Pavlo Hummel*, but this time on Broadway. For his superb acting he was awarded his second Tony.

Shy recluse
"No serious actor can develop without staying in touch with the stage and experiencing the feedback," he comments. That feedback is vital for Pacino who leads a largely reclusive life, believing that being an actor and a celebrity are not necessarily the same thing.

He seldom speaks of the two women who have shared his life, actress Jill Clayburgh, with whom he lived for four-and-a-half years and Marthe Keller, his *Bobby Deerfield* co-star.

Apart from his passion for baseball, Pacino is a talented magician and illusionist. Lee Strasberg's widow, Anna, recalls how the actor would turn up at their apartment wearing a huge overcoat laden with paraphernalia and then proceed to treat them to an evening show of his latest tricks. "We were amazed not so much by his tricks but by his total absorption," she comments.

As with his acting, it's a case of completely immersing himself in the role body and soul, applying his great drive and intensity to bring out that extraordinary Pacino magnetism.

Gregory Peck

It was once said of Gregory Peck that he was "the nicest man in Hollywood, and the dullest". After seeing his performance in *On The Beach* (1959), Stanley Kauffman went very much further, observing that he was "wooden to the core".

A monument to handsome decency—he photographs like Abraham Lincoln—Peck has consistently fought shy of his extraordinary good looks, camouflaging sex appeal with lanky, boyish reserve. He was born in La Jolla, California, in April 1916, and his father had plans for young Eldred, as he was christened, to become a doctor. But he dropped out of pre-med school to seek fame and fortune in New York.

Male model

He found work as a barker at the 1939 New York World Fair, then won a two-year contract with the Neighborhood Playhouse, and modeled for the Montgomery Ward mail order catalogue and Palmolive soap advertisements.

After a spell at the famous Barter Theater in Virginia—where farmers could buy tickets in exchange for farm produce—he made his Broadway debut in Emlyn Williams' *The Morning Star*. He was screen tested—and turned down—by David O. Selznick, but then scored a big hit in a dual role in *The Willow and I*. This led to his film debut as a Russian partisan in RKO's *Days of Glory* (1944).

The film was a flop but Peck was instantly marked out as a hot property and 20th Century-Fox cast him as the high-minded missionary-priest hero of A.J. Cronin's *The Keys of the Kingdom* (1944).

Now launched as a major star, Peck resisted all efforts to tie him down to a long-term contract. As a result he was able to choose his own films, unhampered by studio pressure, although the results were not always to be happy.

The Keys of the Kingdom established Peck as the champion of uncomplicated emotions and noble causes: playing Claude Jarman Jnr's homesteading father in the *The Yearling* (1946); fighting anti-Semitism in *Gentleman's Agreement* (1947); striding the quarterdeck of a schooner

in the title role of *Captain Horatio Hornblower* (1951).

Hitchcock's *Spellbound* (1945) cast him as an amnesiac, suggesting flaws beneath the handsome surface. In *Duel in the Sun* (1947) a bloated sex Western dubbed "Lust in the Dust", he also tried his hand none too convincingly at villainy—kicking Jennifer Jones in the face, shooting his brother Charles Bickford, and blowing up a train before riding off singing, "I've been working on the railroad".

Best performances

After the disaster of *The Great Sinner* (1949), he gave two of his finest performances, both for the veteran director Henry King. In *Twelve O'Clock High* (1949) he was the

Above: *The decent face of Hollywood: handsome and sincere, as he strides the quarterdeck in the title role of* **Captain Horatio Hornblower** *(1951).*

martinet commander of a wartime bomber station, restoring his men's shattered morale at the personal cost of a nervous breakdown. In *The Gunfighter* (1950) he adopted a pudding basin haircut and wispy moustache to play an aging hired gun weary of defending his reputation as the fastest man in the West.

Darryl F. Zanuck was furious when he learned about this anti-romantic image and even more angry when he was told that it would cost $300 000 to remove the offending moustache and start filming again from scratch.

Peck went on to score a big hit in *The Snows of Kilimanjaro* (1952) and romance Audrey Hepburn in *Roman Holiday* (1953).

Three years later he strapped on a whalebone leg to play the doomed Ahab in *Moby Dick* (1956), and had an encounter with a "rogue" whale that nearly proved fatal.

Danger afloat

Location shooting in 12-foot seas off the coast of Western Ireland, he floated off into the fog clinging to the huge rubber model of Moby Dick. Fortunately rescue was at hand and newspapers were denied the headline "Actor Lost on Rubber Whale".

After *The Big Country* (1958), which he co-produced, there was a commercial and critical disaster: *Beloved Infidel* (1959), in which he was hopelessly miscast as F. Scott Fitzgerald. He came back with a strong performance in a classic actioner, *The Guns of Navarone* (1961).

In *To Kill a Mockingbird* (1963) he slipped back into a portrayal of integrity as easily as if he was pulling on a comfortable suit of old clothes, playing a liberal Southern lawyer defending a Negro accused of rape. It won him the Oscar which had proved so elusive despite the four nominations he had received in the 1940s.

Liberal causes have always been close to Peck's own heart. He produced *The Trial of the Catonsville Nine* (1972) as a protest against the Vietnam war, and earned himself a place high on President Nixon's White House "enemies" list.

Battle with demons

Peck has made few good films since *To Kill a Mockingbird*. A tense Western, *The Stalking Moon* (1969), was the best of a bad bunch. However, his dignified bearing was put to good use as the US ambassador with a demonic son in *The Omen* (1976). Eight years before, Lyndon Johnson had toyed with the idea of appointing Peck US ambassador in Dublin.

His restored box-office appeal led to the title role in *MacArthur* (1977), an honest attempt to portray America's most brilliant and complex fighting man, and then he made another ill-fated shot at deep-dyed villainy—as the Nazi doctor Mengele—in *The Boys from Brazil* (1978). It seems he's fated to be good only when he is not hell-bent on playing baddies!

Above: *At the première of* **Some Came Running** *(1958) with his wife.*

Below: *As the liberal southern lawyer in* **To Kill A Mockingbird** *(1962).*

Mary Pickford

There are often discrepancies between the roles film stars play on screen and their behavior in real life, but rarely has the contrast been as extreme as it was with Mary Pickford—known to millions as "America's sweetheart". Her angelic looks and golden curls hid one of the shrewdest business minds in silent Hollywood and she became one of the world's richest and the film industry's most influential women. At her death in 1979, her fortune was estimated at $50 million.

Pickford always attributed her brilliant business sense to her harsh childhood. "A little financial anxiety in childhood gives you drive and ambition," she told one interviewer.

Working at five

Gladys Marie Smith, as Pickford was christened, after her birth in April 1893, started contributing to her impoverished and fatherless family's income at five as the child star "Baby Gladys Smith". At 14 she slipped past the doorman at a theater where Broadway promoter David Belasco was rehearsing a play—and having trouble with his child star. Pickford charmed Belasco, changed her name and replaced the child star. In later years she said that she had very much liked child parts, "Because I didn't have much of a childhood."

Grit and guile

Pickford used the same combination of grit and guile two years later when she asked D.W. Griffith for a movie role. Griffith said that she was "Too little and too fat," but Pickford went ahead with the day's trial shoot, undeterred. When Griffith offered her $5 a day to continue, she demanded, and got, $10.

At this time no names appeared with the title of films and there were no Hollywood "stars". But the public began to clamor to see films which featured "Little Mary" and Pickford realized that she could use her public popularity to push up her wages by playing the studios against each other.

Her earnings increased from $175 a week in 1910 to $10 000 a week plus a share of the profits in 1916. By this

Right: *America's Sweetheart — wearing the innocent smile that concealed one of the astutest brains in the business.*

time Pickford had eloped with Owen Moore, a handsome but drunken actor. She quickly realized that for once she had miscalculated: "As the ring went on my finger I thought 'Why, I don't love him. What am I doing here?' " Professional jealousy increased Moore's drinking, and five years later Pickford gave him the ultimatum that either she, or the liquor, would have to go. Moore chose liquor and she went.

In 1919 Pickford joined with the dashing Douglas Fairbanks, Charlie Chaplin and Griffith to form the United Artists Corporation. Now 26, she secretly yearned to play adult parts, but yielded to the public's desire to see her as a spunky but winsome little girl in films like *Pollyanna* and *Suds* (both in 1920) and *Tess of the Storm Country* (1922).

Hostess to royals

If anything though, the seal on Pickford's elevated status was set not by these roles, but by her marriage to Fairbanks, the most adored male actor of the period. "The King and Queen of Hollywood" built Pickfair—a vast white-gabled mansion surrounded by swimming pools, and with "beaches" of specially imported sand. Guests— including film world luminaries and crowned heads of Europe—mingled on the lawns and ate off solid gold plate, or the dinner service given to Josephine by Napoleon.

The idyll was disturbed by the advent of "the talkies". Pickford attempted to adapt to the new technology and change her image, but it was too late. Although she won an Oscar for her first "talkie" *Coquette* (1929), her next three films: *Taming of the Shrew* (1929) co-starring Fairbanks, *Kiki*

Above: *Directing Douglas Fairbanks in* **Robin Hood** *(1922).*

(1931) and *Secrets* (1933) were all extremely expensive failures.

At the same time, an era was ending at Pickfair. Fairbanks had revealed an almost fanatical jealousy, ejecting male friends from Pickfair with considerable rudeness and demanding that Pickford should never, ever dance with another man—kings and princes included. "I have never known a man to read as much as Douglas did into a simple look of masculine approval," Pickford wrote in her autobiography.

Finally, when a swift infatuation led to Fairbanks's appearance as

Below left: *Pickfair, the hilltop mansion she built with Fairbanks.* Below right: *A rare glimpse of the older woman; a recluse.*

co-respondent in a divorce case, she disregarded his repentant pleas and divorced him.

Eccentric recluse

Pickford then married the devoted Charles "Buddy" Rogers, a bandleader, and retired from films at the age of 33.

Rumors of comebacks flourished, but never became reality and Pickford became an eccentric recluse living amongst the glorious remnants of Pickfair. After a 1965 visit to Paris she announced that she was tired and took to her bed, where she remained until she died, drinking whisky and watching TV. Visitors were only talked to by telephone and photography was banned. "People remember me as a little girl with golden curls," she said before becoming a recluse. "I don't want them to see me as an old lady."

Anthony Quinn

There was a long apprenticeship in B movies before stardom came to Anthony Quinn in the early 1950s. Now, approaching 70, his energy remains undiminished, and can be summed up in the title of one of his films—*Lust for Life* (1956)—the driving force which has fueled his overblown screen personality.

He was born in Chihuahua in 1915, to a Mexican mother and Irish father, and was still just a baby when his parents rode a cattle car to California, where they found work picking walnuts. Later Quinn said: "My youth was all whirlwinds of sand and threatening rain." Poverty left a permanent and profound mark on the actor: he once told Marlon Brando, "When you buy shoes, you buy one pair. When I buy shoes, I buy 18."

Speech defect

At 14 he escaped to work with the colorful evangelist Aimee Semple McPherson. Three years and dozens of jobs later he was sparring with heavyweight boxing champion Primo Carnera.

When he was 18 he had a speech defect remedied by an operation paid for on an installment plan and embarked on an acting career. In 1936 Mae West hired him to play an eccentric 65-year-old man in *Clean Beds*, the character being closely modeled on John Barrymore, who subsequently became a close friend.

The play led to a small role in a Universal B feature, *Parole!* (1936)— Quinn was on screen for only a few seconds before getting a knife in his back. After a couple more bit parts and a spell digging ditches, he bluffed his way into Cecil B. DeMille's Western epic, *The Plainsman* (1936) by passing himself off as a Cherokee Indian.

Drowning tragedy

While filming *The Plainsman*, Quinn met his first wife, Katherine, one of DeMille's four adopted children. Tragedy struck in 1941 when their three-year-old son Christopher drowned in a lily pond at W.C. Fields' home, so distressing Fields that he immediately sold the house.

At Paramount, Quinn was quickly typed as an all-purpose exotic—a Red Indian, blustering pirate or menacing mobster. A stalwart of the studio's thriving B unit, he was frequently cast as a hood, inevitably stopping a bullet just before the gang boss got his. He had a heroic role in *Guadalcanal Diary* (1943), and in the following year— in his thirty-ninth film—finally received his first screen kiss, in *Ladies of Washington* (1944). He had to wait another three years for his first starring role, in *Black Gold* (1947) and then, frustrated by typecasting, he returned to the theater, as Stanley Kowalski in the Broadway production of *A Streetcar Named Desire*.

The Brave Bulls (1951) marked his screen comeback and in the following year he won the Best Supporting Actor Oscar for his performance as Marlon Brando's lecherous bullying brother in *Viva Zapata!* (1952). It was a full-blooded version of the kind of role Quinn had been playing for years in smaller films and established his personal copyright on shaggy, roistering romantics.

Emotional melodramas

He had been in films for 17 years and had made 62 movies when he went to Italy to play Zampano, the brutal street performer and strongman in Federico Fellini's *La Strada* (1954). Whether his performance is great acting or an inspired piece of hamming depends on your point of view, but his success in the role drained all the humor from Quinn, and he set his sights on performances dripping with significance.

For his Paul Gauguin in *Lust for Life* (1956), he won a second Best Supporting Actor Oscar. Then, after a botched attempt at Quasimodo in a remake of *The Hunchback of Notre Dame* (1956), he threw himself into a string of emotional melodramas, going over the top in his quest for earthy pathos.

He was also given the thankless task of directing another remake, *The*

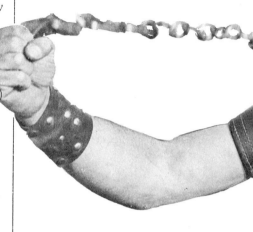

Above right: *His role as a brutal street performer and strongman in Fellini's* **La Strada** *(1954) proved to be a turning point in his career.*

Right: *A grim moment over the caviar during his marriage to the boss's daughter, Katherine de Mille, at the gala première of* **Beau James** *(1957).*

Buccaneer (1958), by his father-in-law Cecil B. DeMille. Unfortunately the results were not very successful.

Coming full circle

When he exercised some restraint, however, Quinn showed his quality as an actor, notably as the Eskimo Inuk in *The Savage Innocents* (1960), a performance of quiet, moving simplicity.

But by now he was becoming virtually rooted to the spot in the role of earth father, suffering spectacularly in the title role of *Barabbas* (1961) and bringing the process to a triumphant conclusion in *Zorba the Greek* (1964). Michael Cacoyannis' film caught the public imagination and from then on both the critics and the public tended to see all of Quinn's screen roles as variations on the old Greek reprobate he had played so convincingly.

In the 1970s Quinn was cast as an Arab in *The Message* (1976); a thinly disguised version of Aristotle Onassis in *The Greek Tycoon* (1978) and in *The Children of Sanchez* (1978), he played a Mexican. He had returned to square one, employed as a general-purpose actor in exotic roles, albeit starring ones.

With Virna Lisi and his second wife Jolanda (below left), *while making* **The Secret of Santa Vittoria** *(1968), and at work in his studio (below).*

Robert Redford

Unlike the other kids on his block, Robert Redford did not want to be a movie-star. As a child, his first love was sport, with art as a close second. As far as the cinema was concerned, on the rare occasions he went, it was as a heckler. He stumbled into acting as a means of enhancing his studies as a theatrical designer at the American Academy of Dramatic Arts.

Today Redford is one of the most popular actors in the world, a position he achieved not only through talent, but sheer competitiveness. Once he decided that he wanted to be an actor, he set about becoming one of the best.

No illusions

Redford was born in Los Angeles in August 1937 and realized at an early age that the Hollywood portrayed on the big screen had little in common with the Hollywood in which he lived.

"Hollywood was never any big deal to me. It was never the end of the rainbow. The first thing I noticed was that no one looked the same as they did on the screen. I saw them for real on the street without make-up," he later recalled.

He also became disillusioned with formal education and dropped out of college, drifting through several manual jobs until he saved enough money to travel to Europe, where he lived a hand-to-mouth existence, hitch-hiking from country to country, living off the money he earned through selling his sketches.

Broke and uncertain

He returned to the States broke and uncertain about his future. But after moving into an apartment block in Los Angeles, he became friendly with one of his neighbours, Lola Van Wegenen, a pretty 17-year-old Mormon. Redford, who had been desperately lonely in Europe, had found a friend and confidante. They fell in love and eventually married.

In an industry where rocky liaisons abound, the Redfords appear to have one of Hollywood's most stable marriages, something which Redford attributes to the years they spent together before he became famous. "The couple that struggles together usually stays together. The bond between Lola and me is far too strong

Above: *All smiles; with Jane Fonda in a Rocky Mountain scene from the* contemporary western, **The Electric Horseman** (1979).

Above: *Behind the cameras, on* **Ordinary People** *(1980) which won him an Oscar first time out.*

Below: *The ecology-minded actor rides his own range in the Utah uplands with his wife, Lola, and their daughter.*

for any one human being to fracture."

Through his studies as a theatrical designer, Redford soon became aware of his talent as an actor, which, coupled with his copper-blond hair and deep blue eyes, made him an obvious candidate for movie stardom. In 1959, he was offered a walk-on role in a Broadway production, followed by some television work. He appeared in episodes of *The Twilight Zone* and *Perry Mason*, his break into movies coming with a supporting role in *War Hunt* (1962).

Superstardom

Not until the late 1960s was Redford firmly established in the superstar stakes with his role in *Butch Cassidy and the Sundance Kid* (1969).

Competition, whether it be on the ski-slopes or in front of the camera, is a key component in his make-up. He desperately wanted the role of Sundance and fought off stiff competition from Warren Beatty, Steve McQueen and Marlon Brando, not to mention the producer's wish to cast a better known actor.

With this success behind him, however, Redford himself became one of the most popular box-office stars of the 1970s, a position he was to consolidate with *The Candidate* (1972), *The Way We Were* and *The Sting* (both in 1973) *and The Electric Horseman* (1979).

His friend Paul Newman affectionately points out: "Bob Redford is the superstar and I'm not. He is a star in the shower, in the morning. No water spray would dare give him a hassle. The water would never be too hot or too cold and the eggs at breakfast would always come out perfect. That is what being a superstar is."

Not only has his acting ability been praised—Redford's spontaneity has been likened to that of Spencer Tracy—but his debut as a director, *Ordinary People* (1980), was justly rewarded with an Oscar.

Splendid isolation

He has invested the millions made from his films by buying hundreds of acres of land high up in the Utah mountains. Here the ecologically minded actor has built a beautiful cedar house, equipped with the latest solar energy devices and has his own personal ski-slopes. Away from the noise of Hollywood, he lives in splendid isolation.

Burt Reynolds

Burt (Burton) Reynolds has the distinction of having been the world's most popular box office star for five years running yet, apart from winning the Florida Drama Award as Best Actor in 1956 and the Charles Chaplin Award for Film Excellence in 1980, his acting merits have frequently been overlooked in favor of his colorful off-screen antics.

He cheerfully admits that, with the exception of John Boorman's *Deliverance* (1972), he has never had a *tour de force* role as an actor, usually being cast as a virile comedian.

"Most of the roles I've done have been the kind where I've reacted rather than acted," he said recently, talking about a career which spans 25 years.

Walking wounded
Although born in Virginia, in February 1936, Reynolds was raised in Palm Beach, Florida, where his mother ran the local drug store and his father ran the local jail.

A high-school football star in his teens he was signed up to play for the Baltimore Colts but, thwarted in this seemingly promising career by a car accident and damaged knee, he turned his attention to college theatrical productions and made his debut in *Outward Bound*, winning a scholarship to the Hyde Park Playhouse, New York.

His professional debut was at the New York City Center, in *Mister Roberts*, with Charlton Heston. Then he headed for Hollywood, where he was contracted for seven years to Universal, playing "Indians, eager young men in the background or half breed mongrels" for television.

Stuntman
Following a stint spent hurling himself through windows for $110 a time he began to make his way as an actor with three years in the popular TV series *Gunsmoke*, which led to title roles in prime-timers, *Hawk* and *Dan August*.

From 1960 until 1972, he appeared as the poker-faced, high-actionman— always doing his own stuntworks—in some fairly forgettable films. Then, following his forceful performance in *Deliverance*, his career took a sharp spiral upwards.

Other successful Reynolds films of

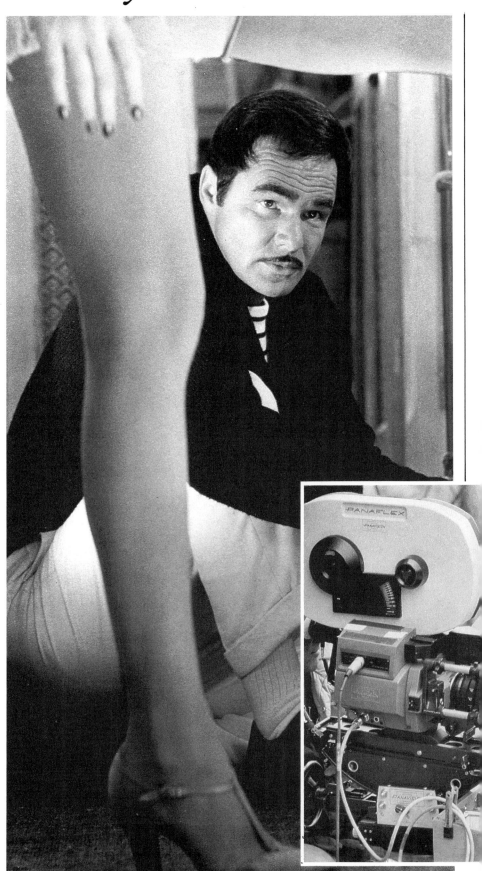

The man who loves women (he became a pioneering male centrefold in 1972 in Cosmopolitan *magazine) is as happy at work or at play. Appreciation is the name of his game as he gives Liza Minnelli's legs the glad eye (left) in* **Lucky Lady** *(1975), while his leisure pursuits include Sally Field (below) and Dinah Shore (right). But there are times when his career comes first, as he demonstrates when directing himself (bottom) in* **Sharkey's Machine** *(1981).*

the·1970s include the comedy *The Mean Machine* (1974), in which he played a football star who trains up a team of prisoners.

His first film as a director was *Gator* (1976), which showed his hitherto unrealized all-round potential.

Three quick successes followed: in *Smokey and The Bandit* and *Semi-Tough* (both in 1977), again as a footballer, and *Hooper* (1978). Then he directed again, this time a black comedy on the risky subject of death, *The End* (1978).

High praise
In an attempt to tackle meatier parts he starred in *Starting Over* (1979) for Alan J. Pakula, the film he's reported to be most proud of and for which co-stars Jill Clayburgh and Candice Bergen both received Oscar nominations.

Clearly at home in the humorous mold, he has also starred in a run of successful, usually wild-action comedies over the past few years.

After making *Rough Cut* (1980), in England with Lesley Anne Down, in the same year he reprised his role for Part II of *Smokey* and *The Cannonball Run*.

He directed, executive produced and starred in *Sharkey's Machine* (1981), followed by *The Best Little Whorehouse in Texas* and *Best Friends* (both in 1982), both huge hits. *The Man Who Loved Women*, with Reynolds depicting the ultimate womanizer, was released in 1983.

Renewing his links with the stage, in 1979 Reynolds opened the Burt Reynolds Dinner Theater, in Jupiter, Florida. He also formed the Foundation for Theater Training for College Students and the Burt Reynolds Chair in Professional and Regional Theater. He has both directed and starred with some of America's top actors at the Dinner Theater, as well as appearing in stage productions for other companies.

Superstar
Generally considered one of the world's most successful stars ever—he now commands a minimum fee of $5 million—the toupeed Reynolds still attracts crowds of fans.

He talks quite openly about his romantic liaisons, which include a three-year marriage to British comedienne and *Laugh In* star Judy Carne. There have also been long-standing relationships with singer Dinah Shore (18 years his senior), and actresses Catherine Deneuve, Loni Anderson and Sally Field.

Referring to himself as "Burt the Flirt", Reynolds has kept the popular press happy with his escapades such as driving his car into the swimming pool and posing for the very first nude beefcake spread in American *Cosmopolitan*, way back in 1972.

Now, on the threshold of his fifties, he says, "I've reached the stage where I'd be glad to work once a year, or less, if it meant preparing for a big role in an important film with a great director." Reynolds concludes, "It won't be long before I'm put out to pasture."

Edward G. Robinson

In 1956, one of the largest private art collections in the world was sold for $3¼ million. The money was needed to cover a divorce settlement by a man who, as he put it, "didn't want to be remembered as a crook". The man was Manny Goldenberg, the ghetto kid from Romania who grew up to be Edward G. Robinson.

Born December 12, 1893, Robinson changed his name while attending the American Academy of Dramatic Art on a scholarship in 1912.

Quickly successful at his chosen profession, he served 15 years on the stage, playing an astonishing range of character parts in all kinds of theater—mainstream and experimental, boulevard and classical, gentile and Jewish. A role he especially enjoyed was that of a store owner in a play he co-authored with Jo Swerling, *The Kibitzer*.

Murder and mayhem

But Robinson's most significant characterization was the gangster lead in *The Racket*, which he closely modeled on Al Capone. When a tour took the production to Los Angeles he was noticed by Hollywood scouts, and though he had no love for his gangster role, it was in such parts that he broke into films. Like many a stage actor, he returned to Broadway whenever he could, but one gangster role in the movies was to change all that: Caesar Enrico Bandello.

Little Caesar (1931) was the first of the hugely successful crime cycle of the early 1930s, and made Robinson a big star. He was placed under long-term contract and didn't appear on stage again for 20 years.

Fabulous art collection

In 1927 he married Gladys Lloyd, an unsuccessful actress, Quaker divorcee and, it later transpired, a manic depressive. But initially they were happy in the big house in Beverly Hills which Robinson began to fill with choice paintings, works then still available for five-figure sums.

He worked hard on the Warner production line: 26 films in the 1930s, 24 more through the 1940s. And, though he disliked being typecast as a crook, it financed his increasingly fabulous art collection of Renoirs, Cézannes, Matisses, Gauguins, Monets. and Pissarros.

"My paintings cannot be valued in dollars," he once said. "Late at night, when the house is quiet, when the last guest has gone, I go into my living room and sit down among these quiet friends."

There were occasional roles that gave Robinson satisfaction—the name parts in *Dr Ehrlich's Magic Bullet* and *A Dispatch from Reuters* (both in 1940) for director William Dieterle, and his movies with the great Fritz Lang, *The Woman in the Window* (1944) and *Scarlet Street* (1945), but

Bottom left: The greatest screen gangster of them all in **Operation St. Peter's** *(1967).*
Below: Holding the golden calf aloft in **The Ten Commandments** *(1956).*
Above right: Making his name as the gangland boss in **Little Caesar** *(1931).*
Right: Happy days with his first wife, Gladys, in their elegant Beverly Hills Home – but it was not to last.

by then he had left Warners. Meanwhile, things were not well at home. His only child, born in 1933, was even more difficult and unstable than Gladys, and engendered bad publicity. For the rest of Robinson's life—his son outlived him by only a year and was dead at 40—the dignified, cultivated movie star bailed him out, paid his fines and bills, cleared up after his frequent and uncontrollable drunken sprees and prayed that the latest suicide attempt might not be fatal.

Blacklisted by studios
A different kind of crisis engulfed Robinson in the early 1950s. A member of the Anti-Nazi League from way back, he fell victim of the witch-hunting House Un-American Activities Committee. Unjustly labeled "a Communist sympathizer", he was promptly blacklisted by the studios.

To clear his name, he volunteered himself to the committee. The "evidence" largely consisted of his support for international charities. He said: "I have been an extraordinarily good citizen . . . I may have taken money under false pretences in my own business and I may not have been as good a husband or father or friend as I should have been, but I know my Americanism is unblemished." After three hearings, spread over two-and-a-half years, he was exonerated.

Robinson's run of B movies and trivial supporting roles ended when that paragon of reactionary virtue Cecil B. DeMille cast him in *The Ten Commandments* in 1956. And that year Gladys, in and out of psychiatric clinics, persuaded him to end the marriage. Again the press had a field day: as settlement, Gladys won half of Robinson's estate and the collector was forced to break up his gallery.

Happier times
After that however, Robinson saw happier times, married to Jane Adler, 26 years his junior. He made a few pictures and bought a few pictures and, on his deathbed, he was shown the special Oscar in recognition of his achievement in films, to be formally presented to his widow the following month, April 1973.

He always hoped he would not be remembered only for his gangster roles. Indeed, he endures as a great character actor who became a top-flight Hollywood star without being a hero.

Ginger Rogers

"I certainly never dreamed about being an actress, of all things! I never thought about movie stars and their fabulous lives at all," confided Ginger Rogers, when interviewed for a magazine feature way back in 1936. The facts suggest otherwise...

Born on July 16, 1911 in Independence, Missouri, she was christened Virginia Katherine McMath and the contraction to Ginger followed. Her parents parted when she was still a baby, a gruesome tug-of-love ensuing until her father bowed to the inevitable court ruling. She got the surname Rogers when she was adopted by her mother Lela's second husband, John. After this marriage also ended, the future star was inevitably dominated by Lela, a showbiz-orientated journalist who had written Theda Bara vehicles at Fox.

Often cited as the archetypal backstage Mom, Lela said "no", however, when her 6-year-old was offered a contract. She was also loudly opposed to Ginger entering a Charleston contest, until she saw how well her then 14-year-old daughter could dance. Ginger won and began her vaudeville career. Thus she met again Jack Culpepper, a vaudeville dancer she'd known as a child. To Lela's horror, the pair married, but the partnership lasted a mere 10 months.

Launch in a billion

"All my breaks came in New York," Ginger said later. "I am really a Broadway Babe." Her second Broadway musical *Girl Crazy* (1930) had her introducing Gershwin songs, playing with Ethel Merman and singing to a pit orchestra that included Benny Goodman, Jimmy Dorsey, Gene Krupa and Glenn Miller. You can't have a better launch than that!

Already she was filming. In *Young Man of Manhattan* (1930) she started

Right: Ingénue hopeful in Hollywood: the dancer poses in 1932.

the catchphrase "cigarette me, big boy". Through a romance with Warner director Mervyn LeRoy, she was later featured in the Busby Berkeley-choreographed musicals *42nd Street* and LeRoy's *Gold Diggers of 1933* (both in 1933). That year—during which she made a staggering nine movies—turned out to be a vintage one. She met her second husband, actor Lew Ayres, and she was teamed professionally with a thoroughbred dancer she'd first met in New York, a newcomer to the movie world. His name? Fred Astaire.

Tensions with Astaire

Astaire was nervous about carrying the dancing burden of *Flying Down to Rio* (1933) but Rogers reassured him: "We'll have fun." And they did.

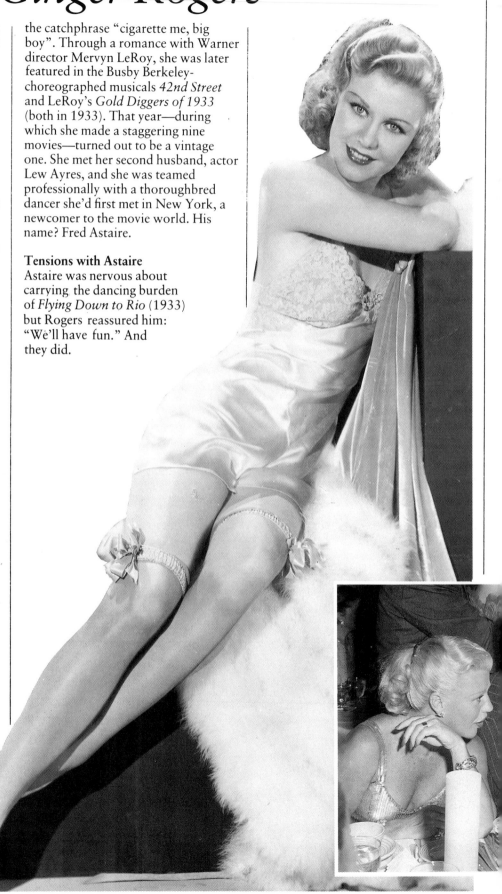

Thus began the cycle of 10 films with Astaire that made them the most famous dance duo in the world.

In the 1960s Rogers told a journalist, "I think that experience with Fred was a divine blessing. It blessed me, I know, and I don't think blessings are one-sided." The gossips had it differently however, and reports of rifts punctuated the partnership.

One of the tensions arose because Astaire was a perfectionist about dance and modest about his achievements beyond it, while Rogers regarded dancing as just one of the things she did and had ambitions as an actress. Inevitably, they split the moment their peak was over. The Ayres marriage ended too, much to Lela Rogers' relief. Her attitude to her daughter's involvement with Howard Hughes goes unrecorded but she adored the movie successes.

The role of *Kitty Foyle* (1940) brought Rogers an Oscar. This and *Primrose Path* (1940) were the films the actress most enjoyed.

Mother knows best

Lela's booklet about the star recorded that "when business permits Ginger to be at home, she need look no further for relaxation . . . or amusement. In her spacious play-room is a motion picture theater and the 30-foot comedy mural by Zube that tells the story of Hollywood . . . Her library contains a set of tooled-leather-bound volumes of all her motion picture scripts, her trophies and awards. On one wall, on its own shelf, sits the alabaster bust of her mother: the work of her own

hands. Throughout the house, among other famous painters, one comes upon canvases by Ginger Rogers."

In 1943 Rogers married struggling actor Jack Briggs; this mistake puttered on until 1949. There were two further husbands: actor Jacques Bergerac, 16 years her junior, and producer William Marshall. There were also many more movies and, after 34 years, a triumphant return to the stage—taking over *Hello Dolly!* in New York and playing *Mame* in London. She's still working, hale and hearty, in her seventies.

Lela continued to exert her influence for the whole of Ginger's movie career, and only once did Rogers sound less than beholden to her: "My first picture was *Kitty Foyle*. It was my mother who made all those pictures with Fred Astaire." Come to think of it, that's not very gracious about Fred either . . .

Below left: *With club owner Charlie Farrell and husband Jacques Bergerac.*
Below: *The popular partnership with Fred Astaire in* **Roberta** *(1935).*
Above right: *Forty years on briefly reunited in* **That's Entertainment** *(1974).*

Mickey Rooney

All child stars have to grow up, but Mickey Rooney—the most famous of them all—took the longest. Short, 5ft 3in, chunky and well into his twenties, he was still playing Andy Hardy, the all-American small-town teenager. When he made *Love Laughs at Andy Hardy* (1946), he was 26 years old and had been a performer for 24 of them.

This non-stop trouping produced a lopsided view of life. A close friend remarked that Rooney knew more about showbusiness and less about women than any man he had ever met. Rooney has survived eight divorces, bankruptcy and scandal, and now well into his sixties has lost none of his bumptious energy.

He was born in September 1920, the son of vaudeville entertainers. At the tender age of two he joined their act, and three years later was touring with song and dance man Sid Gold. In Chicago he played a midget in a melodrama, *Mr Iron Claw*, and this led to similar roles in two films *Not to be Trusted* (1926) and *Orchids and Ermine* (1927).

Shortly afterwards, he changed his name from Joe Yule Jnr to Mickey McGuire, the comic strip character he played in over 40 RKO shorts between 1927 and 1933. When the series ended, he changed his name again and for the last time—to Mickey Rooney.

Veteran at fifteen

The cocky youngster caught the eye of MGM's boss Louis B. Mayer, who hired him—on a week to week basis—to play Clark Gable as a boy in *Manhattan Melodrama* (1934). In 1935, MGM put Rooney under contract. He was 15 and, after eight years of hard slog in the movies, a veteran of 20 features and dozens of serials and shorts.

The studio cleverly cast him as a streetwise urchin opposite priggish child star Freddie Bartholomew in *Little Lord Fauntleroy* and *The Devil is a Sissy* (both in 1936), *Captains Courageous* (1937) and *Lord Jeff* (1938). He was an enchanting Puck in *A Midsummer Night's Dream* (1935)

Above right: *Top box office in* **Men of Boys Town** (1941).
Right: *With Elizabeth Taylor in the racing story,* **National Velvet** (1944).

154

and moving as the young tough reformed by Spencer Tracy in *Boy's Town* (1938).

By now Rooney had graduated from being the best scene stealer in the business to stardom in his own right. The catalyst was a modest B feature, *A Family Affair* (1937), in which he played Andy Hardy for the first time. There were many subsequent Andy Hardy films, cunningly crafted and immensely popular celebrations of Louis B. Mayer's sentimental notions of family and small-town life.

Exploited twosome
A regular co-star in the series was Judy Garland. They made eight films together—Rooney mischievous and brash, Garland wistful and appealing. Hindsight has lent the partnership a tragic quality. Their charm and talent were exploited by a studio system of sweated labour which ultimately destroyed Garland and left Rooney scarred for life.

By the time they were paired in the musical *Babes in Arms* (1939), Rooney was number 1 in the *Motion Picture Herald's* ratings. In 1938, along with Deanna Durbin, he received a miniature Oscar.

Expensive habit
In the early 1940s, Rooney wrote a song, prophetically entitled *I Can't Afford to Fall in Love*. He met his first wife, 19-year-old starlet Ava Gardner,

on the set of *Babes on Broadway* (1942). They were married on January 10, 1941 and eight months later had separated. After the divorce Gardner said that Rooney had been wonderful but behaved "like a child".

It was the first of nine marriages, an expensive habit which 10 years and four divorces later had cost Rooney a cool $1m in alimony.

His last MGM film before call-up was the hugely successful *National Velvet* (1944), but when he returned to Hollywood to make *Love Laughs at Andy Hardy* (1946), he was too old for the part and the cosy pre-war fantasy of the series was out of step with the spirit of the changing times.

The skids
The skids were under him, and in the next four years he made only four films. After *The Big Wheel* (1949), he went freelance. Now there was no longer an indulgent studio to ply him with gifts, pay him a vast salary and cater to his every whim. He was 29 but looked like an elderly 18-year-old, his manic energy transformed into embittered truculence.

With characteristic dynamism he set about rebuilding his career, taking his act in to night-clubs and on to television. He made a great many terrible films, including a feeble outing with Francis the Talking Mule in *Francis in the Haunted House* (1956), and a few good ones. He got good

Above left: *Veterans on Broadway – with Ann Miller in the hit musical* **Sugar Babies**, *in 1979.*
Above: *He may be small, but he's got stamina, as he shows with his eighth wife at a restaurant opening in 1980.*

notices for *The Bold and the Brave* (1956) and then scored a success in the title role of *Baby Face Nelson* (1957).

Bankrupt
But financial and marital problems continued to plague him. In June 1962 he filed a petition for bankruptcy, listing assets of $500 and debts of almost $1 million—in the war years he had earned nearly $12 million.

In February 1966 he discovered the body of his fifth wife Barbara Ann in their bedroom alongside the corpse of her Yugoslavian lover Milos Milosevic, who had shot her and then turned the gun on himself.

Rooney worked on. In 1970 it was reported that when MGM ran into difficulties he offered to take over the ailing studio with a plan to make 20 films for $20 million dollars. At the end of the decade—1979—he was on Broadway, co-starring with veteran dancer Ann Miller in a smash hit musical *Sugar Babies*. Given a strong director and some imaginative casting, "the oldest has-been in the business" undoubtedly still has a few tricks left up his sleeve.

George C. Scott

When asked to describe himself, George C. Scott, one of the most intelligent, but also one of the angriest, most difficult of Hollywood actors replied that he was a "kind of aging, wild-eyed maverick who has more or less sour-graped his way through a checkered career, sometimes good, sometimes bad, always rather contemptuous of it all."

Verbal terrorist

It is a blisteringly accurate and truthful assessment. Scott has never hesitated to show his disdain for Hollywood glitter and has been described as a "verbal terrorist". Notorious for drinking and brawling, his nose has been broken in fights during periodic bouts of heavy drinking. He has also twice smashed his hand by striking walls with it during rages: "I either thumped the set or I thumped the actress," he explained after one such injury.

Veteran director John Huston has said that he rates Scott as "one of the best actors alive. But my opinion of him as an actor is much higher than my opinion of him as a man."

Scott makes no secret of the fact that he has hovered on the edge of complete breakdown. He describes his childhood as "completely unloved" and after his mother died when he was eight he spent much of his time "being terrified of my father", a self-made mining engineer.

After high school, and active service in the Marines, he was posted to burial duty in Arlington Cemetery, Washington and here the drinking began. "You can't look at that many widows in veils and hear that many taps without taking to drink."

Self-hatred

Acting was a way out. "I became an actor because I couldn't stand myself. Acting is the only job that gives you a chance to be somebody else most of the days of the year. And you get paid for it."

After a long grind of unsuccessful auditions and tours with failing repertory companies Scott won critical acclaim for his first Shakespearian performances and went to Broadway, then Hollywood.

"Acting saved me," he said in later years. "If I hadn't been able to get work as an actor I would have hit one too many guys and wound up with a knife in my back." His reputation as a consummately skilled actor increased, but so did the stories of how impossible he was to work with. Given a second Academy Award nomination, for *The Hustler* (1961), he curtly demanded that his name be withdrawn.

Lowest point

Neither was his image helped by his tempestuous love-life. Scott, who by this time had married, divorced and then re-married actress Colleen Dewhurst, became obsessed with Ava Gardner, his co-star in John Huston's *The Bible* (1966). Gardner did not return his ardor and Scott followed her around Europe before retiring to a nursing home to dry out when she finally rejected him.

"The lowest point I hit was around 1964," Scott remembers. "I had terrible emotional problems. I was drinking heavily . . . and I was being divorced for maybe the second or third time."

As before, he survived by channeling his rage and self-loathing into acting. His portrayal of the crazed General Buck Turgidson in *Dr Strangelove Or How I Learned To Love The Bomb* (1963) still chills and delights present-day audiences. And his characterization of the manic, obsessive "General Blood and Guts" in *Patton* (1970) was the most superb performance of the year.

Snubbing the Oscars

Despite his customary snub of asking for his name to be removed from the nominations, Hollywood awarded him an Oscar. Scott remained unimpressed and boycotted the ceremony saying, "I don't give a damn about it, I'm making too much money anyway."

In a later statement he was more expansive: "Life isn't a race. It is a war

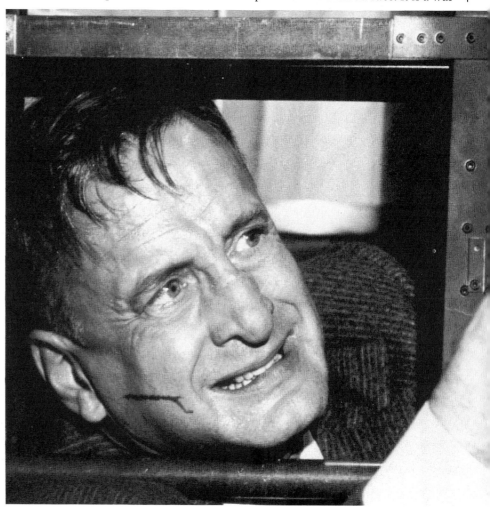

of survival and there are many who get crippled and injured on the way. And because it is not a race I don't consider myself in competition with my fellow actors for awards or recognition."

War of survival

Scott clearly includes himself amongst those maimed in the war of survival. "The pressures in this business can rend you," he says, "They tear you apart, which is why so many actors

Below: *Proving he's a man of action, as well as an intelligent, instinctive actor, as befits an erstwhile Marine.*

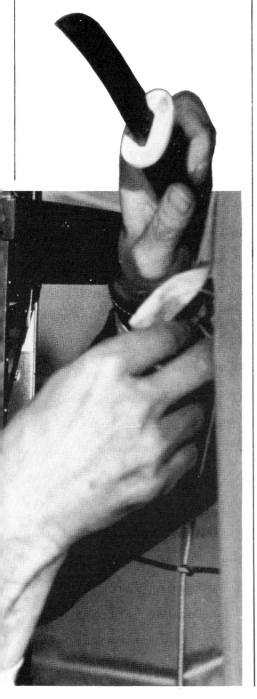

take the pills or put the gun in their mouths. Or drink. I spent three cold, long years in New York, looking for work as an actor."

The passing years have mellowed Scott only slightly. His acting and his temper remain as hard-edged as ever but he no longer drinks so much and has stayed married to his fourth wife, Trish Van Devere, for over 10 years. His desire now is to retire from acting for good. He says that he would have done so years ago were it not for the

burden of taxes and alimony. "I've just had it. Acting has been very good to me, but it can mess you up. Acting should carry a government health warning: 'This can damage your psychological health'. It is very difficult. It is very dangerous. It is very destructive."

A way with the ladies: going through his paces with Tracey Reed (below) in **Dr. Strangelove** *(1963) and discussing* **Patton** *(1970) with this wife, the actress Trish Van Devere (below).*

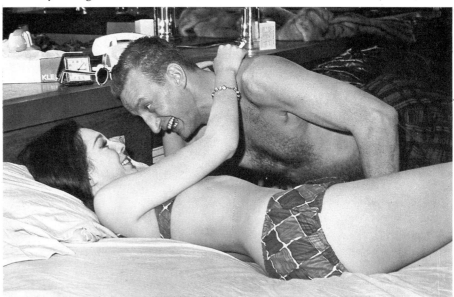

Peter Sellers

It had always been Peter Sellers' ambition to become an international star, yet even when he achieved this status, he suffered insecurity and fear of failure. Reputedly difficult to work with, this man of a thousand faces and countless voices was not popular in Hollywood; his unending quest for perfection upset fellow actors, directors and technicians alike.

Revelation

As is often the case with funny men, Sellers led an unhappy life. Christened Richard Henry Sellers, he was born in the English coastal resort of Southsea in September 1925. His parents were in the theater and spent their working lives touring the provinces with their comedy routine. Sellers later revealed that he hated the constant traveling and ever-present smell of grease paint that played such a large part in his formative years.

His career as a comic impressionist began in the Royal Air Force, when he joined ENSA in 1942. While in the Royal Air Force he toured India and the Far East—entertaining the troops with an apparently endless repertoire of impersonations. It was his skill as a mimic that won him his first work in radio—for the British Broadcasting Corporation. Impersonating two well known comedians of the day, Sellers recommended his talents over the telephone, thus quite literally talking his way into a job.

Royal Fans

His first film was *Penny Points to Paradise* (1951), and he also began working on the long-running classic radio comedy series *The Goon Show*. It was as a Goon that Sellers became a household name in Britain; even members of the Royal Family could be numbered among his fans.

During the 1950s and early 1960s he firmly established himself as one of Britain's brightest stars, appearing in such classics as *The Ladykillers* (1955), *I'm All Right Jack* (1959), *Two Way Stretch* (1960), *The Wrong Arm of the Law* (1962) and *Doctor Strangelove* (1963), which took him to Hollywood. There he made a succession of commercially successful, if artistically disastrous, films.

His highly successful *Pink Panther*

Above: *A natural comedian at work, as the egocentric, amorous concert pianist in* **The World of Henry Orient** *(1964).*

films came about almost by chance. In the first of the series, *The Pink Panther* (1963), his role was only to act as a foil for David Niven's gentleman jewel thief, but Sellers as the lovable, incompetent, accident prone Inspector Clouseau stole the film and paved the way for four sequels.

Sellers loved women and spent much of his time searching for a wife who could be both mother and lover. He married four times—to Anne Hayes, Britt Ekland, Miranda Quarry and Lynne Frederick. Three marriages

Forever on the marriage market: kicking a ball around with Britt Ekland (right), and accepting comfort from Lynne Frederick (bottom right).

ended in divorce and at the time of his death he was living apart from his actress wife Lynne Frederick.

Sellers was prepared to blame himself: "... I'm impossible to live with—it was entirely my fault that my first marriage broke up—I had an affair with someone I was working with. The second time (with Britt Ekland) it was just a mis-match. The third time with Miranda, well that was wrong again, probably me, I don't know ..."

Near fatal attack

In 1964 Sellers had a near fatal heart attack and, when he returned to work after a period of convalescence, suffered long bouts of depression. Convinced that he had lost the use of part of his brain, he became forgetful, irritable and increasingly difficult to work with. He once took a full page magazine advertisement to deny that he was "an ungrateful limey and rat fink".

The sad truth was that he was over-critical of his own work and would spend hours on a film set trying to achieve perfection. Sellers was a true professional; even when mis-cast, he would strive to give of his best.

After a particularly bad spate of films, he commented, "I hate everything I do so much that I think I'd better go one better before I die because I don't want to be remembered for all that lot." This ambition he managed to fulfill: he received some of the best notices of his career for his exceptional performance in the film *Being There* (1979), released shortly before he died of a massive heart attack in 1980, when he was only 54.

Complex man

The whole truth about Sellers will probably never be known. Since his death, friends have painted totally contradictory pictures of this complex man. Clearly however, Sellers was both emotionally vulnerable and unhappy. Though loved by millions, he never felt at ease playing himself, often taking refuge in the funny voices of his screen and radio characters.

He remained a joker to the end, however. Unknown to anyone he had arranged his own funeral music— Glenn Miller's *In The Mood*.

Sissy Spacek

In a world where starlets wear their charms up front, Sissy Spacek has proved that there's more to be gained by keeping hers under wraps. Her tiny physique and her washed out freckled face, with those luminous light green eyes, give her an elusive elfin presence that is strangely compelling.

Tomboy

Despite her Czechoslovakian name, Spacek is as American as blueberry pie. She was born on Christmas Day, 1949, into a happy Texan family living in Quitman (north-east of Dallas), a place that she describes as having "one of everything: one doctor, one hardware store, one dairy queen."

Her father was the county agent for the US Department of Agriculture, and she had two older brothers who naturally called her Sissy. The name stuck through a tomboy childhood. Spacek learned to ride so she could compete in rodeos and she was expert at baiting her own fishing lines. While she was at school she became a cheerleader, a majorette and a homecoming queen. You can't get much more Texan than that.

Shattered idyll

The idyll was shattered when she was 18 and her brother, Robbie, died of leukemia. "I went to New York to seek my fortune. I don't think it was only because of Robbie, but his death changed my parents' attitude. They realized you have to live your life every day because you don't know how long you'll be around."

She first tried to build herself a career as a singer/songwriter, hawking her country ballads around a town that didn't want to know. Undeterred, Spacek took lessons at the Lee

Above: *An Oscar winner, as Loretta Lynn, in* **Coal Miner's Daughter** *(1979).*
Below: *The terrified child-woman in*

Carrie (1976), *the film that made her.*
Right: *On her first visit to the Cannes Film Festival in 1977, accompanied by her newly-wedded husband, Jack Fisk.*

Strasberg Actors' Studio. "Acting was the first profession I ever came into contact with where I wasn't too short, too freckled or too Texas," she recalls. Her efforts were rewarded with a bit part in *Prime Cut* (1972), a drama about the white slave trade made in Canada with Gene Hackman and Lee Marvin. When the film failed, no one hurried to re-employ her so it was back to playing the guitar in an East Side steak house and selling clothes in a Madison Avenue boutique, a routine broken occasionally by brief TV appearances.

Her luck changed when she was cast opposite Martin Sheen in *Badlands* (1973). Not only did her performance alert the moguls to the fact that here

Above: *Conversation, as the main guest on the* **Dick Cavett Show**.

was an actress in her twenties who could play a 15-year-old girl with total conviction, but she met her husband, art director Jack Fisk. They were married shortly afterwards, with Jack's dog as witness.

Success, at last

Spacek's next film, again exploited her ability to look 10 years younger than she was, and put her name up in lights. It was *Carrie* (1976), Brian de Palma's creepie about a high school student who uses her telekinetic powers to exact a terrible pseudo-religious revenge on her classmates.

Later de Palma attempted to analyze her success. "When she makes contact with celluloid, there's a transformation. She is fearless. She'll try anything. She is not inhibited by persona, ego, image, none of those things. She is in lots of ways a primitive."

Robert Altman who produced her next film, *Welcome to L.A.* (1977), in which she plays a topless housewife and part-time hooker, added, "She is as good an actress as I've ever seen work. She is able to become whatever you ask her to do." He franked his opinion by casting her in his next film, *Three Women* (1977).

Ambition to sing

Spacek's ambition in the cinema was to sing as well as act, and the opportunity came in *Coal Miner's Daughter* (1979), the story of country and western singer, Loretta Lynn. She starts out in the backwoods as a child bride, has four children before she is 18 and becomes a grandmother before she reaches 30. The Spacek portrayal

includes 12 of Lynn's most famous numbers, thumped out on the guitar and sung with appropriate verve. Not surprisingly, it won her the Oscar for Best Actress.

Marriage comes first

In the early 1980s her career has wound down temporarily while she establishes her family. Her first daughter was born in 1982, and she is expecting another child. In between, she took the lead in *Raggedy Man*, (1981) and turned in a brilliant performance in Costa Gavras's *Missing* (1982).

Nearly 10 years after their wedding, the Fisks are living up to Spacek's dream of a different kind of marriage. "When we were first together, I was boggled by the idea of forever. I put $30 into a special bank account because that's what it costs to file divorce papers in California. Now it's different. Jack is more important to me than anything, including acting. If I had to, I'd choose Jack in a second because he's stayed with me through thick and thin."

Their lifestyle is simple and casual. They don't believe in dressing up and going downtown in Los Angeles to spend several hundred dollars on dinner with a crowd of movie folk. Instead Spacek will make a huge salad and invite a bunch of artists and sculptors over to share it, after a communal soak in the gas-heated redwood hot tub in the garden. "It's a good way to loosen people up," Spacek once claimed.

Sylvester Stallone

The story of Sylvester Stallone and his *alter ego*, the punch-drunk boxer, Rocky Balboa, is one of Hollywood's nicer fairy-tales. It began uncompromisingly in New York's Hell's Kitchen, in 1946, when Sicilian immigrant Frank Stallone's wife Jacqueline gave birth to a son in a charity ward. The forceps delivery severed a nerve in the baby's face, paralysing one side of his lip, chin and tongue so that he grew up with a lopsided appearance and indistinct speech.

When he was 10, his parents divorced and his father gave him a piece of advice: "You weren't born with much brain, so you'd better develop your body." As it coincided with his own inclinations, Sylvester took it and started using weights to such good effect that he won an athletics scholarship to the American College in Switzerland.

Later, he decided he would rather be an actor and enrolled at the University of Miami, where his lecturers were united in declaring him useless. This opinion was shared by agents and casting directors in New York where Stallone moved with the intention of breaking through on Broadway.

Instead, he found himself working as an usher in a movie house, alongside Sasha Czack, the girl he married.

Nude debut

When he did get a part in an Off-Broadway play in 1970, he had to perform in the nude, and the same was true of his first film, a soft-core porn number called *A Party At Kitty's* (1971).

His move to Hollywood brought him bit parts in *The Lords of Flatbush* (1974), *The Prisoner of Second Avenue, Death Race 2000, Capone* and *Farewell, My Lovely* (all in 1975), but barely enough money to pay the rent—and he was down to his last few dollars when he saw a screening of a Muhammad Ali fight.

Fired with enthusiasm, he rushed home and wrote a script in three days. Both Burt Reynolds and James Caan offered $360 000 for it, but not with

Right: *Putting the full weight of his Italian American machismo behind* **Rocky** (1976), *which made him rich.*

Stallone in the title role. However, he stuck to his guns and *Rocky* (1976) eventually got made for $1 million by United Artists. The film earned 10 Oscar nominations and the Best Picture Award.

Life exploded

Stallone became rich and famous overnight. "I made *Rocky* when I was 29½ years old and broke. When I was 29¾ I was a millionaire." Despite the obvious autobiographical parallels, his immediate future was not to be so rosy as Rocky's. His next picture *F.I.S.T.* (1978), which he co-scripted, and *Paradise Alley* (also in 1978)—which he wrote and directed, flopped. Worse, his character deteriorated into bullying arrogance.

"My whole life suddenly exploded. There it was, success, the nine-headed Hydra… I had everything, money, power. No one had taught me how to cope. I think I went a little crazy."

He bought bigger and bigger cars, more luxurious houses, dressed in flashy clothes and talked incessantly on chat shows about subjects of which he was ignorant.

He also discovered that playing a screen tough guy tempts people met casually to throw down gauntlets. "A man makes a comment about my wife and I lay one on him and chip his tooth. When he shows up in court, he's developed ambitions to be a model

Life after Rocky included a light romance (below) *during* **Escape to Victory** *(1980), a stint behind the cameras* (bottom left) *for* **Rocky II** *(1979), and directing John Travolta* (bottom right) *in* **Staying Alive** *(1983).*

specializing in toothpaste commercials!" Such close encounters cost Stallone $400 000 and prompted him to hire two body guards. Even today he never goes out without them.

Back to reality

His new status also caused a rift in his marriage, but Stallone eventually returned to Sasha and his two sons, Sage Moonblood and Sergio. "I wanted all the fun, the women, the revelry. But then I realized it was so repetitious. The same people, the same parties, the same jokes. So I went back home, and it was wonderful. Quiet, peaceful, happy."

There have been two extremely successful *Rocky* sequels—in 1979 and 1982—which Stallone wrote and directed as well as starred in. A fourth is in the pipeline.

Other Stallone projects have been *First Blood* (1981), his attempt to out-Eastwood Eastwood in the vigilante stakes, and *Staying Alive* (1983), the follow-up to *Saturday Night Fever* (1977), in which he directed John Travolta. Since then he has appeared in a curiosity called *Rhinestone Cowboy* (1984) in which he sings opposite Dolly Parton.

He has also embarked on a new career as a boxing impresario. His contender is 6ft 5in Lee Canalito, a great white hope for the world heavyweight crown that shall be forever Rocky's.

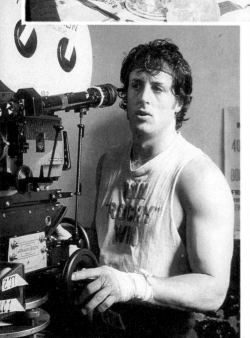

Barbara Stanwyck

Hardly anyone has been better regarded by their fellow-workers in the movie business than Barbara Stanwyck, a consummate professional if ever there was one. She was always word-perfect, always on time, never grumbled, never lied about her age and always considered those behind the camera to be her equals rather than inferiors.

She was born on July 16, 1907, the last of five children, and christened Ruby Stevens. The family, of Scots-Irish stock, lived in the Brooklyn slums and Ruby—orphaned at the age of four—spent her childhood in no less than 14 foster homes and attended as many schools. At 13 she went to work in a series of menial jobs, at the same time taking dancing lessons. At 15 she was riding an elephant for Ziegfeld, at 16 touring with the Follies.

Serious affair

At 18 she got a bit part in a play, *The Noose*, and when this hit trouble in the preview stage one of many changes promoted her to an important role.

Re-christened with names from a theater poster, she opened to rave reviews and played a 9-month run during which she had a serious affair with the play's star Rex Cherryman. The sudden death of Cherryman in 1928 distressed her greatly and it was perhaps on the rebound that she married vaudeville star Frank Fay.

In 1929 Stanwyck accompanied her husband to Hollywood. After two unfortunate movies and a failed screen test for Warners, she was spotted by Frank Capra who turned her fortunes around in *Ladies of Leisure* (1930) for Columbia. Warners and Columbia both duly placed her under contract and, for her first Warner picture, *Illicit* (1931), she enjoyed the distinction of billing as "Miss Barbara Stanwyck".

Highest paid woman

The following year, Warners upped her rate to $50 000 a picture and when Columbia refused to do likewise, she went on strike. Although she lost the ensuing court case, subsequently

Right: A true professional. The Brooklyn-born actress whose good humor and egalitarian principles became a legend.

Left: A scene with Robert Taylor, her second husband and frequent co-star. Below left: A kiss for Fred MacMurray, in Double Indemnity *(1944).*

Columbia matched Warners' fee. Stanwyck was always a shrewd judge of her own worth. She went freelance in 1935 because she knew she could win more favorable terms.

Meanwhile, Frank Fay's career had slumped and, seeking solace in alcohol and spite, he became impossible to live with. Stanwyck finally sued for divorce, but the settlement took years with Fay disputing custody of their adopted six-year-old son, Dion.

Spurned by son

"I want my son to be happy," she told reporters. "I want him to have that sure sense of security in his home that I missed so much in my own childhood." Although she prevailed, Dion, years later, had different ideas.

Meanwhile, Stanwyck went into the business of breeding thoroughbred horses, at Northridge in the San Fernando Valley. Soon afterwards the handsome and very eligible young MGM star Robert Taylor became her neighbor and "Overnight", observed a gossip columnist wryly, "he turned into a country squire."

The couple did little to hide their involvement, and MGM—ever ready to exploit private happiness—cast them together in *His Brother's Wife* (1936).

But it was not until 1939 that she and Taylor married, sold their ranches and settled in Beverly Hills.

Stanwyck's peak years were from *Annie Oakley* (1935) to the superb *Double Indemnity* (1944), and beyond to her fourth Oscar nomination role in *Sorry, Wrong Number* (1948). Thereafter, though she worked regularly, her career was at a lower level. Her marriage was in trouble by 1947 and divorce came in 1952. But she and Taylor remained on good terms and even made another picture together—*The Night Walker* (1965).

Since then Stanwyck has found a regular and lucrative home in television where, she says, "you work a little harder and a lot faster." Her successes range from the 1960s Western series *The Big Valley* to the 1980s melodrama *The Thorn Birds* and, as Frank Capra wrote, "In a Hollywood popularity contest, she would win first prize hands down."

James Stewart

When Universal teamed Jimmy Stewart with Marlene Dietrich, to film *Destry Rides Again* (1939), she "took one look at him and wanted him at once!" according to producer Joseph Pasternak. "He was just a simple guy: he loved Flash Gordon comics—that was all he would read. So, as a surprise, she presented him with a doll which she'd had the studio art department make up for him—a life-size doll of Flash Gordon, correct in every detail. It started a romance!"

Just a simple guy… when he appeared on England's long-running radio show *Desert Island Discs*, Stewart's choice of music was typically unpretentious. It is the same with his politics: an instinctive reactionary patriot and puritan, he consistently supports the Republican ticket. You always know where you stand with James Stewart.

Appealing vulnerability

Easy certainties do not always appeal to the public but Stewart always had a certain vulnerability that did touch the heart—a star for 50 years, he never lost public support.

James Maitland Stewart was born May 20, 1908 in Indiana, Pennsylvania, the son of a hardware store owner.

Educated at Princeton, he graduated in architecture, before following classmate Joshua Logan to Falmouth, Massachusetts where Logan had formed a troupe called the University Players. Class of 1932 was pretty talented: also in the troupe were recently married Henry Fonda and Margaret Sullavan.

Stewart was a beanpole of 6ft 3½in with a slow, hesitant drawl that would become famous but must then have seemed a handicap. But people took to him. By 1933, he was appearing on Broadway. Then he got a seven-year-contract with MGM.

Good guy's reward

There were 15 fairly insignificant roles before Stewart made the first of three unforgettable movies with Frank Capra, *You Can't Take It With You* (1938). Ironically, Stewart the right-wing fundamentalist embodied Capra's liberal

Screen action (right) into reality; Stewart was the first star to enlist in World War II (below).

humanism. In that adaptation of the Broadway hit—and later in *Mr Smith Goes to Washington* (1939) and *It's a Wonderful Life* (1946)—he epitomized human values over capitalist interests, and the image has stayed with him.

Having proved his worth with Capra, Stewart worked with many more of Hollywood's top directors:

Right: *Hot shot in* **Firecreek** *(1968)*
Below right: *The 41-year-old bachelor marries leading socialite, Gloria Hatrich – and lives happily ever after.*

Ernst Lubitsch, Frank Borzage, George Cukor, King Vidor, Cecil B. DeMille, Billy Wilder, Otto Preminger and especially Anthony Mann, John Ford and Alfred Hitchcock.

For Cukor he played his Oscar-winning Mike Connor in *The Philadephia Story* (1940)—Cary Grant, who had the choice of the male leads in the movie, chose the wrong one and never did win an Oscar in his entire career.

Patriot in action

In 1941, powered by his high-octane patriotism, Stewart led the Hollywood invasion of the armed forces, serving in the USAF and flying 20 bomb-runs over Germany. He ended the war a full colonel. Thereafter he remained in the Reserve, retiring in 1968 as a brigadier-general, the highest rank that has ever been attained by a member of American Equity.

Returning to Hollywood as a freelance, Stewart took various roles and, at 41, he also took a wife. Previously linked with Lana Turner, Ginger Rogers, Olivia de Havilland and Alice Faye as well as Sullavan and Dietrich, he now married Gloria Hatrich, a 31-year-old socialite. To her two sons, Mr and Mrs James Stewart added twin daughters, and remain happily married to this day.

Accomplishing something

Middle age did not diminish Stewart's popularity—indeed he remained in the box-office top ten throughout the 1950s and began working for a percentage of the profits. Among the movies adding to his wealth were *Harvey* (1950), a tall story he enacted several times on stage, *The Glenn Miller Story* and *Rear Window* (both in 1954), *The Spirit of St Louis* (1957), *Vertigo* (1958) and *Anatomy of a Murder* (1959).

Still active on film, television and stage, Stewart says, "I don't want to retire. I love making movies … it's rewarding and exciting to me. I feel that I'm accomplishing something, as when someone comes up to me and says, 'I don't know if it means anything to you, but you have given me and my family a great deal of enjoyment over the years'."

Meryl Streep

With her elegant, luminous face, lofty cheekbones and slightly corrugated nose, Meryl Streep is every casting director's first choice. She has shot to the top with lightning speed, collecting two Oscars, two nominations and numerous other awards in plum roles chased by Hollywood's leading ladies, all unseated by this cool blonde with a particular talent for accents.

A New York trained and based actress, Streep lives a very quiet and private life, wearing her freedom comfortably, while her face can be seen on the cover of nearly every magazine in the country.

Coloratura voice
Christened Mary Louise, one of three children, she was born in 1951 into an affluent New Jersey family: her father was a pharmaceutical executive, her mother ran her own graphics business.

At 12 her promising coloratura voice merited singing lessons with voice coach Estelle Liebling, and Streep savored her first taste of performing. Later, accepted by the Yale Drama School on a three year scholarship, she received the most thorough stage training, averaging 12 to 15 roles a year and specializing—ironically for one who has made her name in tragi-drama—in the art of comedy.

Tragedy strikes
On graduating she headed to New York, where she made her debut in Joseph Papp's production of *Trelawny of the Wells*. Next she played two roles a night in Arthur Miller's *A Memory of Two Mondays* and Tennessee Williams' *Twenty-seven Wagons Full of Cotton*, winning several awards before moving straight into a season of Shakespeare in The Park. There, Streep met actor John Cazale and they lived together until Cazale died of bone cancer two years later.

Before his death they worked on Michael Cimino's *The Deer Hunter* (1978), Streep's second film—her first was in a bit part as Jane Fonda's friend in *Julia* (1976). As Christopher Walken's steel-town sweetheart she won both an Oscar nomination and the Film Critics Award and was rushed into the TV series that *everybody* saw—*Holocaust*. Her brilliant performance as the Catholic girl resulted

in an Emmy for Streep, who refused to collect it on the grounds that performances should not be put up against each other for awards.

Keeping busy
Her next film role was playing Woody Allen's walk-off wife-turned-lesbian in *Manhattan* followed by *The Seduction of Joe Tynan* (both in 1979), playing a Southern rights attorney who has an affair with a married senator running for president.

It was her Oscar-winning performance as Joanna Kramer, the wife who deserts her family in *Kramer Vs Kramer* (1979), that took her to Hollywood. Her role garnered several other awards and co-star Dustin Hoffman predicted that she would

become "the Eleanor Roosevelt of acting".

Leaving the accolades behind, she returned to the theater in an off-Broadway production of *Alice in Concert*—a musical revue, before taking the title role in *The French Lieutenant's Woman* (1981), which required her to adopt an English accent for the British-made film that no British actress proved suitable for. This brought her another Academy nomination.

Streep then reunited with her

Below: *As Sarah Woodruff in* **The French Lieutenant's Woman** *(1981).*

Above: *A moment of anguish in the harrowing TV drama,* **Holocaust.**

Kramer director, Robert Benson, for a glamorous part in the thriller *Still Of The Night* (1981) with Roy Scheider.

Fight for Sophie

Her second Oscar-winner was Alan Pakula's *Sophie's Choice* (1982), as the doomed Polish heroine, Sophie. Untypically, Streep had to fight for the role.

"I really wanted that part and actually went to Alan's office and more or less threw myself on the floor and begged him to let me play Sophie," she says.

Pakula, who had already cast an unknown Polish actress, reconsidered and cast Streep who, for three months, studied Polish with her usual perfectionist zeal.

By now commanding $2 million a movie, she then headed for Texas to star in *Silkwood* (1983), as Karen Silkwood, the plutonium plant worker who died mysteriously in 1974.

"She is a lot like me," the actress comments, "my real personal self, a little sassy, and a lot of people get mad at her!"

Family life

Between movies Streep spends time with her family, husband sculptor Don Gummer and their son and daughter, on her 92-acre tree farm in Upstate New York or their modest converted loft in New York City.

Her next project reunites her with long-standing friend Robert de Niro in a modern love story which is entitled *Falling In Love.*

Above: *Playing with Justin Henry as the woman who leaves her family in* **Kramer Vs Kramer** *(1979).*

Below: *Keeping her feet on the ground between pictures, thanks to a happy marriage to sculptor, Don Gummer.*

Barbra Streisand

Outstanding, even among the growing number of Hollywood female stars who have proved themselves just as capable and versatile as their male counterparts, Barbra Streisand has made film history as the first woman to produce, direct, co-write, star and sing the songs in a film.

An intriguing mixture of glamor and power, her blunt approach and spine of steel have earned her some less than complimentary descriptions ranging from "superbrat" to "a cross between Groucho Marx and a Sherman tank".

Now always totally in control when she makes a film or a record, the fiery superstar is estimated to be worth around $100 million, making her Hollywood's richest tigress and the world's top paid singer.

Talons and talent

Yet Streisand was born in one of Brooklyn's roughest areas on April 24, 1942, a poor little Jewish girl brought up by her grandmother.

As a teenager, working in a local Chinese restaurant inspired her to grow her nails to the now traditional Streisand/Fu Manchu length. Then, at 18, she won a talent contest organized by a Greenwich Village nightclub, and was on her way to stardom.

Her very first Broadway appearance in *I Can Get It For You Wholesale* won her the New York Critics' Circle Award. Then *Funny Girl* put her on the international map as both an actress and a singer of mesmeric power, followed in swift succession by two more stage musicals: *Hello Dolly!* and *On A Clear Day You Can See Forever*. The film version of *Funny Girl* (1968) won her an Oscar.

Surrounded by awards which also numbered a Grammy for her first album *The Barbra Streisand Album* and an Emmy for her first television special, *My Name is Barbra*, by the time she made her fourth film—*The Owl and The Pussycat* (1970), with George Segal—she was already counted among the top ten film stars. She went on to make the madcap comedy *What's Up, Doc?* (1972) before trying her hand at producing.

Her first effort, a bizarre fantasy called *Up The Sandbox* (1972), failed, but she bounced back to play opposite the all-American idol, Robert Redford

in *The Way We Were* (1973). This was followed by the comedy *For Pete's Sake* (1974), with Michael Sarrazin, and the musical *Funny Lady* (1975), co-starring James Caan and Omar Sharif, before she felt ready to produce another movie.

This time she worked with her boyfriend, Beverly Hills hairdresser Jon Peters, whose only previous film experience was as a child extra in *The Ten Commandments* (1956). Together they produced a remake of *A Star Is Born* (1976). A star vehicle for Streisand, it co-starred Kris Kristofferson and became a box-office triumph in spite of volcanic ructions on the set.

Her next film, *The Main Event* (1979) did not, however, live up to its title. Teaming her with *What's Up,*

Below: *A song and dance girl to the very last spangle, in* **Hello Dolly!** *(1969)*.
Right: *Staring into Ryan O'Neal's eyes in the wild comedy* **What's Up Doc?**

Doc co-star Ryan O'Neal, it was the last Streisand/Peters co-production.

Her twelfth film in as many years had her playing a "minor" role to Gene Hackman's lead in *All Night Long* (1981), but it was a sophisticated performance—as Hackman's off-beat, platinum blonde lover.

Major challenge
Then she was ready to make film history, controlling every aspect of *Yentl* (1983), a project she had bought the rights to in 1974 and spent years hawking round Hollywood only to be turned down by every major film studio. The story of a young Jewish girl in Eastern Europe at the turn of the century who disguises herself as a boy (played by Streisand at the age of 41) in order to study the Talmud and become a rabbi, struck deep to her Jewish roots. She dedicated the film to her father, a teacher and scholar, who died when she was 15 months old.

"It was only through *Yentl* that I had a chance to make a father the most important man in my life," she explained.

Although the epic film was ignored when it came to the Oscars, it proved to be enormously successful worldwide.

Marriage to Elliott Gould, her co-star in her Broadway debut, **I Can Get It For You Wholesale,** *didn't last.*

Son and lovers
Other important men in her life have been ex-husband Elliott Gould—with whom she has a son, Jason—and her seven-year relationship with Jon Peters, with whom she shared her 20-acre ranch in Malibu, California and her Beverly Hills Mansion. There have also been "flings" (her word) with Omar Sharif, Canada's former Prime Minister Pierre Trudeau, co-stars Ryan O'Neal and Kris Kristofferson, Warren Beatty and, most recently, Steven Spielberg.

Workaholic
In response to accusations of being difficult to work with, Streisand says: "Most of that is pure sexism. I'm a workaholic who always considers the entire conception of a motion picture, not only my role. I'm not comfortable with my success and I never was."

Nor, does it seem, are her co-stars, many of whom have said biting things about her, one of the most moderate being Walter Matthau who has said he would only work with her again on a production of *Macbeth* . . .

Gloria Swanson

"Long before Hollywood made stars, there were stars who made Hollywood"—so ran a program accompanying a season of Gloria Swanson films in New York.

Swanson was one of the few stars who survived the initial transition from silent to sound films. Modern audiences probably know her best for her role as the aging movie queen Norma Desmond in *Sunset Boulevard* (1950).

She was born in Chicago on March 27, 1897 (the year is disputed). In 1913 a chance visit to the Essanay Studios in Chicago led to work as an extra and in bit parts. While there, Swanson met actor Wallace Beery and appeared with him in a number of shorts. They married in 1916, but the state of matrimony was not all she had hoped for and they were divorced three years later.

Swanson married for the second time in the same year, 1919. Film company executive Herbert Somborn was twice her age and though she had wanted security there was no excitement in the marriage. When it broke up she commented: "I not only believe in divorce, I sometimes think I don't believe in marriage at all."

Slavishly copied

Swanson rose to fame under the wing of director Cecil B. DeMille, making six films for him and becoming the highest paid star at Paramount. Her yearly clothes bill was estimated at $125 000 and everything she wore—from shoes to hairstyle—was slavishly copied by her thousands of adoring and loving fans.

She had a shrewd recognition of the value of publicity and no time for false modesty, declaring: "I have decided that when I am a star, I will be every inch and every moment the star! Everybody from the studio gateman to the highest executive will know it."

Royal welcome

When she returned to the United States from making *Madame Sans-Gêne* (1925) in France, she was given a royal welcome complete with motorcade, a brass band, her name up in lights in Times Square and 10 000 ecstatic fans. And she brought a new husband back with her—French nobleman Henri

Marquis de la Falaise de la Coudraye, thus achieving the ultimate Hollywood fantasy—marriage to an aristocrat.

Summing up that era later, Swanson explained: ". . . the public wanted us to live like kings and queens. So we did – and why not?"

When her Paramount contract expired, she refused the $1 million per annum the studio offered her to renew it. Instead, in 1926, she joined United Artists as an owner-member, producing her own films. Joseph P. Kennedy, father of John, Robert and Edward, provided the financial backing, and more. He arrived on her doorstep one day and, according to Swanson's account, seduced her.

After a couple of minor successes as producer-star, she chose the eccentric

Above: *Silent movie star. The demure facade hides a real Chicago toughie.*

Erich von Stroheim to make *Queen Kelly* (1928), with herself in the title role, but fired him when production costs soared and backers withdrew.

Censored

Rumors had been rife about just how realistic the sex scenes were, and the whole exercise was sheer extravagance—most of the original material would not have passed the censor. Swanson tried to salvage the project by pouring in her own money, but the final version was never released commercially in America.

Her first "talkie", *The Trespasser* (1929) was a smash hit, however, and initially she appeared to be one of the few silent stars to transfer successfully to the new medium. Unfortunately, her frivolous image did not appeal to Depression audiences.

The Marquis was also disillusioned and they were divorced in 1930.

Swanson then met Irish playboy Michael Farmer while yachting off the coast of France but, after reluctantly agreeing to marry, she lasted only three years with her fourth husband.

Meanwhile her star was fading. Swanson worked for various studios on projects which were abandoned, and she decided to retire from the screen in 1934.

In 1945 she married the wealthy William Davey but this time it lasted only a month. Swanson discovered that he was an alcoholic and he resented her attempts to reform him.

Outstanding comeback

Then came Swanson's outstanding comeback in Sunset Boulevard (1950), Billy Wilder's black look at Hollywood. For the third time Swanson was nominated for, and failed to get, an Oscar.

She made only three more films, her final appearance being in *Airport 1975* (1974), but she remained remarkably youthful until her death on April 4, 1983.

Perhaps it was inevitable that she never rekindled the adulation her silent screen appearances inspired. Opulence of that kind was sure to burn itself out and, anyway, in the words she utters as Norma Desmond: "I am big—it's the pictures that got smaller."

Above: *A third divorce before she was 35, from aristocrat, The Marquis de la Falaise de la Coudraye in 1930.*

Below: *As Norma Desmond, an aging movie queen, in* **Sunset Boulevard**

Above: *Her final appearance, as herself approaching 80, in the large-scale suspense drama* **Airport 1975** *(1974).*

Elizabeth Taylor

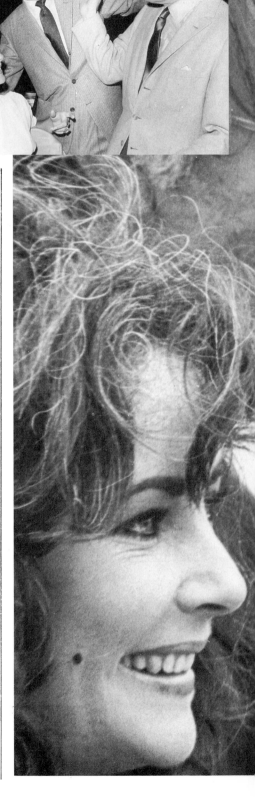

Elizabeth Taylor is indisputably the Hollywood megastar who has lived the most public of private lives. Right from the start, as a beautiful, violet-eyed child star at the age of 10, through four decades of film-making—including two Oscars and four nominations—and seven marriages of front-page proportions, the Taylor Tale has been covered in minute detail.

Born in North London, England in 1932 and christened Elizabeth Rosemond, she studied dancing with the great Vacconi, dance teacher to the British Royal Family, before being evacuated with her parents, art dealer Francis Taylor and actress Sara Southern, to California.

As a result of an informal conversation between her father and film producer Sam Marx, she became an MGM baby, attending the Little Red School House with Judy Garland and Mickey Rooney, and growing up in pictures like *Lassie Come Home* (1943) and *National Velvet* (1944).

Sensual actress

By the 1950s Taylor had blossomed into a sensual and powerful actress, starring in films like *A Place In The Sun* (1951), *Giant* (1956), *Raintree County* (1957), *Cat On A Hot Tin Roof* (1958) and *Suddenly Last Summer* (1959), with the hottest leading men of the time: Montgomery Clift, James Dean, Rock Hudson and Paul Newman.

The 1960s augered well for Taylor, with her first Oscar for her performance in *Butterfield 8* (1960) followed by *Cleopatra* (1963), the blockbuster on whose trouble-plagued

Above left: Velvet Brown, with fellow MGM baby, Mickey Rooney, in the heart-warming **National Velvet** *(1944).*
Above right: Marriage to Mike Todd in 1957, with next-in-line Eddie Fisher in attendance as best man.
Right: Richard Burton, the man she married twice, made her one half of the world's most spectacular couple.

shoot she met and fell in love with co-star Richard Burton. It was also the film for which she demanded, and received, her first mega-salary.

Spectacular couple

Taylor and Burton became the world's most spectacular couple, and later the world's most spectacular intermittently married couple.

Together they revived the dying star system. Their names guaranteed an audience for any film they appeared in and their private life went on public display too: romance, passion, raging rows and fabulous gifts like the $1 million Cartier-Burton diamond.

By the time *Cleopatra* finally came out, audiences no longer expected to see Antony or Cleopatra but simply Burton and Taylor in historical costume.

Married in Mexico in 1964, Taylor's marriage to Burton lasted 10 years. They remarried the year after their divorce but were at each other's throats almost immediately and divorced again in 1976.

During their years together Taylor and Burton made *The V.I.Ps* (1963), *The Sandpiper* (1965) and the film that brought her a second Oscar, *Who's*

Afraid Of Virginia Woolf? (1966), a film that showed her real acting abilities to the full. It also required her to age to 45, wearing a double chin and rubber bags under her eyes. The couple went on to make *The Taming Of The Shrew* (1967) together followed by *Doctor Faustus* and *The Comedians* (both in 1967), *Boom!* (1968), *Under Milk Wood* (1971) and *Hammersmith Is Out* (1972).

Other preconceptions

In the 1970s Taylor made very few films and some of those were less than memorable.

During that period she was more occupied with her seventh marriage to US Senator John Warner (from 1976 to 1981), her own ailing health (she has survived more than 30 major and minor operations to date) and her battle to beat the bulge.

Playing bitches

After a four-year break from films she made *The Mirror Crack'd* (1980), in England, before branching out late in life into a stage career. On the threshold of her fiftieth birthday she made her debut in Lillian Hellman's play *Little Foxes*, commenting of her role as Regina: "I am wonderful at playing bitches!"

Taylor made a triumphant tour of the United States with the play, ending up on Broadway before taking it to London.

In 1983 she and Burton reunited, but only professionally, to do Noel Coward's *Private Lives* on Broadway and on tour around America. The production did not garner great critical acclaim.

More recently Taylor, now a grandmother, has been under medical supervision once again—receiving treatment for her chronic addiction to diet pills.

Tipped to become her seventh husband is Mexican millionaire and lawyer, Victor Luna. He will succeed the playboy son of the hotel magnate, Conrad Hilton Jnr; British actor Michael Wilding; showman Mike Todd; singer Eddie Fisher; Richard Burton (twice), and John Warner.

A woman of enormous wealth, Taylor lives in America where she has several homes. She has already composed her own epitaph which reads: Here lies Elizabeth Taylor. Thank you for every moment good and bad. I've enjoyed it all.

Below: *Mixing jeans with mink on the eve of her fiftieth birthday, the woman who will try anything once prepares for her stage debut in* **Little Foxes.**

Spencer Tracy

"This mug of mine is as plain as a barn door. Why should poor people want to pay 35 cents to look at it?" asked Spencer Tracy—unlikely star material, not least to himself.

He had a gruff, uncompromising manner that often spilled over into drunken aggressiveness, giving colleagues cause to fear his bad temper. But a star he was, one of the most revered of actors. He was also one half of a remarkable 25-year partnership on screen and off, that was by common consent not subjected to the usual speculations of the gossip columns.

Destined for priesthood

Tracy was born on April 5, 1900 in Milwaukee, and after a Jesuit education was intended for the priesthood. But that was not to be: instead, he enrolled at New York's Academy of Dramatic Arts in 1922, and made his first Broadway appearance as a robot.

Most of his stage work was in stock companies and it was in one of these that he met actress Louise Treadwell, whom he married in September 1923. Although in later years they often lived apart, the couple never divorced: Tracy was a devout Catholic and fell back on his religion when he discovered that his son was deaf. He was determined to earn whatever money was necessary for medical treatment. Thus he tried, but failed, to find good acting jobs at the end of the 1920s—"They said I had no sex appeal. The matinées were strictly for the women and nobody was coming to my matinées."

He was 30 when he finally went to Hollywood, after director John Ford spotted his potential in a lead role on Broadway and cast him in *Up the River* (1930). Because he was not considered attractive enough to succeed as a romantic lead, Tracy then played a succession of "tough guys" for Fox Studios, until *The Power And The Glory* (1933). The movie provided him with his first big break.

He had kept a low profile—showing

a marked disinterest in the Hollywood social life—but suddenly, along with success, he hit the headlines.

For years his publicists had suppressed stories about his drinking and his bad temper, but his affair with 20-year-old actress Loretta Young became national news. They fell in love on the set of *A Man's Castle* (1933) and Tracy left home. The romance generated a lot of public interest and was serialized in the fan magazines. But the following year Young announced

1935, he was arrested in a hotel for drunkenness and destroying private property. He made the headlines again.

Tracy then began his 20-year stint with MGM, who dubbed him "a man's man" in their publicity. When he starred with Joan Crawford in *Mannequin* (1938), they were rumored to be having an affair, but this time he did not leave his family, appearing to be settled both personally and professionally. His fame steadily grew: he won Oscars two years running—the

Hollywood. He also traveled abroad with her.

There was no question of them marrying however; he because of his Catholicism and she because she did not believe in it anyway. When Hepburn was away on location for *The African Queen* (1951), Tracy took to drink again, deeply affected by her long absence.

Illness and isolation
His health was not good and when he

Left: *Up for an Oscar for the first time in the screen adaptation of Kipling's* **Captains Courageous** *(1937).*
Above: *At his grouchiest best when the festivities are over in the sharp comedy,* **Father of The Bride** *(1950).*
Above right: *With Katharine Hepburn, on his last film,* **Guess Who's Coming To Dinner?** *(1967).*

that she and Tracy were parting as his religion prevented their marrying. He returned to his wife.

Plagued by drink
His years with Fox were plagued with problems over drink and time-keeping. Once, when sleeping off a drinking session, he was accidentally locked in the studio overnight. Early in the morning a terrible row could be heard from the set—Tracy was busy demolishing it!

While making his last film for Fox in

only actor ever to do so—for *Captain Courageous* (1937) and *Boys Town* (1938).

Very private affair
Always wary of the press, when a reporter once questioned him about his private life, he replied: "Private life? Now you're kidding me. There's no such thing as a private life in this town. It isn't allowed."

But he was wrong. His life with Katharine Hepburn was very private and generally treated with respect. *Woman of the Year* (1942) was their first film together. They already admired each other's work and their professional collaboration was a happy one.

Their personal relationship had far-reaching effects on Tracy: he drifted away from many of his old friends and began to mix in Hepburn's circle, which had no connection with

failed to co-operate at work, MGM ended their 24-year association. He seemed bitter, dismissing the new screen heroes in a few words: "Pretty-faced no-talents are always around in this business. They don't last and they're not missed, for a new crop comes in and it's the same asparagus." Tracy felt strongly about acting and always missed his work on the stage.

Throughout the 1960s, Tracy became increasingly isolated and was said to be so difficult that only Hepburn could handle him; she cut back on her own work to look after him as his health deteriorated.

Despite speculation that he was too ill to work, Tracy and Hepburn made *Guess Who's Coming To Dinner?* (1967), the last of their seven films together. On June 10, 1967, two weeks after its completion, he died of heart failure. Ironically it was to become the most successful picture of his career.

John Travolta

The magic ingredient in the meteoric rise of John Travolta is that every teenage boy wants to be like him and every teenage girl falls in love with him. For this he can thank the winning combination of sleek black hair, blazing blue eyes and dazzling smile he inherited from his Italian father and Irish mother.

The youngest of six children, Travolta was born in Englewood, New Jersey, in February 1954, and as his mother was an actress and drama teacher, he had showbiz in his blood. Indeed, four of his siblings are in the profession that John was introduced to at 9, in the musical *Bye Bye Birdie*.

At 16 he signed on for dancing lessons with Gene Kelly's brother, Frank. He also learned to sing well enough to make a single, *Let Her In*, which reached the US Top Ten.

Autumn-spring romance

The well-built six-footer learned to face the cameras in commercials before moving to Hollywood. A string of television bit parts led to his first break, the role of Vinnie Barbarino in the series, *Welcome Back, Kotter* (1975). He then established his promise in the cinema with *Carrie* (1976).

The same year he appeared in *The Boy In The Plastic Bubble*, a television film, playing the son to Diane Hyland's mother. Off screen, their relationship blossomed into an autumn-spring romance that ended tragically a year later when the 41-year-old actress died of cancer. By then, he was enmeshed in the role that rocketed him to international fame, the disco dancing Tony Manero, in *Saturday Night Fever* (1977), but he still had time to grieve.

"I felt the breath go out of her when she died in my arms," he said at the time. "The 18-year gap in our ages never made any difference . . . Part of me was ripped away when she was taken from me . . . if she'd lived, it's very possible I'd have married her."

Travolta consoled himself with a frenzy of work for *Grease* (1978), the biggest money-making musical of all time and the film that confirmed him as the hottest male lead in Hollywood. The world's teenagers slicked back

Right: *Flashing feet and sinuous hips in* **Saturday Night Fever** *(1977)*.

Above: *Sweating it out as disco dancer Tony Manero, in* **Staying Alive** *(1983)*.

their hair, turned up the volume and writhed in frenzy as they tried to emulate him.

Despite the loud-mouthed extroverts he played, the real Travolta proved to be an honorable, if none too bright, ambassador for his generation. "Everyone was waiting for me to go on some drinking binge or to end up on a drugs charge," he commented in an interview, "but I knew from the start that wasn't the way to go."

Trauma

When his mother died shortly after Diane Hyland and his next film, *Moment by Moment* (1978), attracted vicious reviews, Travolta turned to psycho-analysis and scientology.

As a result of his reflections, he diversified into parts that showed his talent for acting rather than his double jointed pelvis. *Urban Cowboy* (1980) and *Blowout* (1981) went some way to restoring his dented status and his self-confidence, before he allowed himself to be tempted into the lucrative follow-up film *Two of a Kind* (1983). This re-united him with *Grease* co-star, Olivia Newton John, but the film was so bad that its distributors in London decided it would be a bad idea to show the product to the critics.

Re-shaped by Stallone

Staying Alive (1983) wasn't much better, but joined the skills of Travolta to the iron discipline and uncanny eye to the main chance of Sylvester Stallone in a money-making venture. Stallone wrote and directed it, and re-shaped his star with six months of weight-lifing and dancing. By the end of it Travolta had the rippling chest, trim waist and muscled legs he displayed so overtly as the scantily, loin-clothed Manero.

Now the two men plan to work together on a musical, and provided Francis Ford Coppola will direct it, on *The Godfather III*.

Below: *On and off set with Olivia Newton John, in* **Grease** *(1978)*.

Erotic dream

At 30, Travolta still clings to his freedom, though he admits to losing his virginity aged 13 and to having a demon sex drive. "I like being with women who have the same sexual appetite because it's frustrating being the coach in bed."

Names that have been linked with his are co-stars Olivia Newton John and Debra Winger, Priscilla Presley—one-time wife of Elvis—and Brooke Shields. His longest running affair has been with Marilu Henner, whom he first met in 1972. Will it be marriage this time? Who can say? Certainly not Travolta.

"Most of my friends are family people. I look at them and see their perfect relationships and realize that's what I am looking for, a wife with whom I have a complete rapport." But at night, he dreams his recurring erotic dream and the face is always the same. It belongs to Jane Fonda.

Lana Turner

According to a leading columnist, Lana Turner is "All the Hollywood legends rolled into one . . ." She has married seven times and in the late 1950s was involved in one of Tinseltown's most grisly scandals ever.

Turner's rise to fame has become part of cinema mythology, although the popular account of her discovery in Schwab's Drugstore on Sunset Boulevard has been amended. She *was* spotted by Billy Wilkerson, publisher and editor-in-chief of *Hollywood Reporter* but it was a year before she appeared in a small but key part in *They Won't Forget* (1937), and earned her "Sweater Girl" title.

Father murdered
She was born on February 8, 1920 in Idaho and, following a tough childhood (her father was murdered when she was 10), was eager to embrace the film colony's fantasy lifestyle. One of the nation's favorite pin-ups, she enjoyed countless affairs.

Her first romance to attract big publicity was with handsome attorney Greg Bautzer. It was assumed they would marry but bandleader Artie Shaw, her co-star in *Dancing Co-ed* (1939), eloped with her on her twentieth birthday. After the Las Vegas ceremony she kissed him for the first time. The impulsive marriage lasted barely four months, and Bautzer handled the divorce.

By 1941, Hollywood's "Nightclub Queen" was established as a star and partnered by a string of admirers, including millionaire Howard Hughes. She was clearly enjoying life.

First scandal
Then, in July 1942, she suddenly married the unknown Stephen Crane. In December she announced she was pregnant and was promptly hit by scandal: Crane's first wife declared her divorce from him was not yet final. Turner sued for annulment and at first did not wish to remarry him, but the prospect of bearing an illegitimate child finally persuaded her and the couple made a decidedly unromantic second marriage in February 1943. Baby Cheryl Crane was born in July and her parents were divorced the following April.

After that, a string of romances kept Turner almost permanently in the headlines, but Tyrone Power was the great love of her life. For once, *she* did the chasing and Power was the one to back out.

Below: *With fourth husband, Lex Barker;* The Sea Chase *(1954)*.
Right: *Still beautiful in her fifties, opening a portrait exhibition in 1976.*

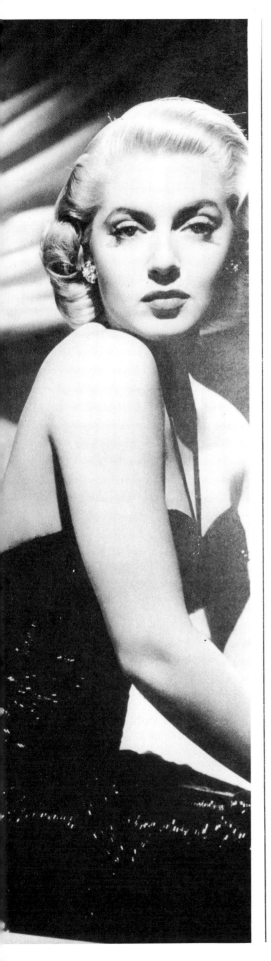

Hurt by this, Turner coped by throwing herself into further rounds of partying. Then, in April 1948, she married millionaire Bob Topping. The couple were hounded by the media and suffered hostility on their highly publicized trip to England.

With these pressures and the burden of two miscarriages, Turner's third marriage also failed. Undeterred, before her divorce in December 1952 she had already set the scene for wedding number four, with Tarzan star Lex Barker, whom she married in September 1953.

After a number of box office failures, MGM dropped her and she formed her own production company, happy to be independent and enjoying her most peaceful marriage to date. Even so, they divorced in 1957 by which time Turner had embarked on the affair that would turn into a nightmare.

Stabbed to death
Johnny Stompanato, a small-time crook with reputed gangland connections, attracted Turner initially, but soon began to plague her with his jealousy. He even came to blows with her co-star Sean Connery on the set of *Another Time, Another Place* (1958).

Turner's career was flourishing again—she had received an Oscar nomination for *Peyton Place* (1957)— but she was upset by the turmoil of the 14-month relationship, which came to a violent end on April 4, 1958. 14-year-old Cheryl overheard threats to her mother, herself and her grandmother and, before anyone realized what was happening, stabbed

Above: *Watching John Garfield work on the set of* **The Postman always Rings Twice** *(1946).*

Stompanato to death with a knife.

Famous attorney Jerry Geisler was hired to defend her but the case never came to trial. The inquest verdict was justifiable homicide.

Meanwhile, however, revealing letters from Turner to her dead lover were stolen from his apartment and given to the press. Many were printed in full. The sheer volume of publicity was overwhelming. In the aftermath of this scandal little Cheryl was made a ward of court and placed in her grandmother's custody.

Most dangerous
Amazingly, Turner's career survived and she went on to make *Imitation of Life* (1959), her biggest box office success.

There were also three more marriages – to ranch-owner Fred May, businessman Robert Eaton and hypnotist Ronald Dante. She has since "found God" with the aid of hairdresser companion Eric Root, whose spiritual guidance, she claims, has steered her away from alcoholism.

With her fluctuating professional and personal fortunes, Turner is well aware of the dangers of living out her own image. As she once said: "It is unfair to blame this on Hollywood. It is due to everything that goes with big success and sudden success. Such success is the most dangerous thing that can happen . . . there is nothing more devastating."

Rudolph Valentino

Rudolph Valentino was the major sex symbol of the silent screen; his explicitly sensual appeal inspired erotic fantasies in women, and envy and derision in men. Known as the screen's "Great Lover", in real life his first marriage was unconsummated, and he allowed himself to be dominated by women throughout his career.

Valentino's eloquence was expressed by his eyes and his supple body for he did not live long enough to make a talking picture. Dying at 31 he became identified for all time with his romantic screen image.

Casanova image

He was born in Italy on May 6, 1895 and came to New York in 1913, making a living by partnering women in dancehalls. His dislike of the "Casanova" image he thus acquired was not helped by his arrest in 1916 in connection with a blackmail case. He was also a witness in a divorce hearing which led to a murder.

Feeling unsafe in New York, he went to Los Angeles in the hope of finding work in films and appeared in a number of minor films between 1918 and 1920. Then Metro screenwriter June Mathis got him the lead in *The Four Horsemen of the Apocalypse* (1921), in which his talent as a dancer was put to use in a tango scene that electrified audiences. Valentino had arrived.

His personal life was less successful. He married actress Jean Acker in November 1919—when they had only known each other for a few days—and she locked him out on their wedding night. For her, it was very much a marriage of convenience.

Strong-willed women

Acker was one of a group of camp-followers to Metro's leading female star, lesbian Alla Nazimova who considered Valentino the "perfect Latin lover" and wanted him as her leading man in *Camille* (1921). The film's production designer was another strong-willed woman, Natasha Rambova (born Winifred Shaughnessy). Valentino was soon in love with her.

These women (including Mathis) encouraged Valentino's interest in the supernatural; he received "messages"

Above: *A well-muscled view of Valentino at the height of his fame, in 1922.*

and consulted spirits before making any important step. This left him open to exploitation and went hand in hand with his love of dressing up and being photographed in historical costume, whether or not it had any relation to work.

He was in his element as *The Sheik* (1921), which really established him. The mixture of cruel sadist and tender lover was a heady one for female audiences, who identified strongly with Valentino's willing victims.

His divorce case coincided with the film's release, but the story of his impotent marriage did not harm his image. On the contrary, his wife's claim that Valentino "hit me with his fist and knocked me down" increased his erotic appeal.

Breach with studio

After their marriage in March 1923, Rambova wanted to manipulate her husband's career at Paramount, causing bad feeling. She demanded full artistic control. As the breach with the studio widened, Valentino declared: "I cannot work for this motion picture corporation . . . I cannot forgive the cruelty of the company to Mrs Valentino."

He was, however, greatly in debt. His personal expenditure reflected the extravagance of Rambova's production ideas: he furnished his mansion with antiques from Europe, ordered custom-built cars and kept a stable of horses. Eventually he was obliged to settle with the studio. When subsequently United Artists signed Valentino, Rambova was banned from the set. She left for New York ostensibly on good terms with her husband, but they never saw each other again.

Valentino made *The Son of the Sheik* (1926) to cash in on his earlier success, as he was now hopelessly in debt. He did not live to see its release; instead, he had to endure media taunts about his masculinity. Shortly before his death a leading newspaper called him "Rudy—that painted pansy".

Ultimate tribute
On August 15, 1926 he was rushed to a New York hospital with a gastric ulcer and ruptured appendix, and there began an hysterical media countdown to his death on August 22. Mobs flocked round the funeral parlor where his body lay in state and 100 000 people filed past the open coffin. Actress Pola Negri sent 4000 roses – their names had recently been linked—and rushed to the scene swooning with grief. Fans attempted suicide as the inevitable cult sprang up around the dead star.

But the ultimate tribute for Valentino was that as his funeral service began on August 30, work in every film studio and location in California stopped for two minutes.

Above: *In* **Son of The Sheik** *(1926), with Vilma Banky, he inspired mass eroticism and oriental mania.*

Below: *A second marriage to Natasha Rambova resulted in strained relations with the studios and a bigamy charge.*

John Wayne

The 1979 Oscar ceremonies were dominated by a giant of a man with an easy, swaying gait and a gravel-voiced drawl familiar from over 250 films. The man was John Wayne or "The Duke", as he was known for most of his life. "I'm mightily pleased I can amble down here tonight," he said, to a crescendo of applause. "Oscar and I have something in common. Oscar first came to the Hollywood scene in 1928. So did I. We're both a little weatherbeaten, but we're still here and plan to be around for a whole lot longer."

For once, he could not keep his word. Wayne's ill health was one of the world's worst kept secrets and within two months cancer had finally beaten the man who had towered over the film industry for 50 years.

Wayne was raised with the unlikely name of Marion Michael Morrison. Born in May 1907, the son of a pharmacist in a small town in Iowa, he eventually won a football scholarship to the University of Southern California, where his involvement with Hollywood started when the coach of the famed "Thundering Herd" gave western star Tom Mix a box at the stadium in return for a job for his hard-up star player.

Singing cowboy

Wayne stayed on at the studio shifting props until John Ford gave him a small part in *Mother Machree* (1927). But despite this early break Wayne's career did not come easily: there were false starts as a singing cowboy (the voice was dubbed), and a whole string of undistinguished westerns, including *The Big Trail* (1930).

Eventually, however, Ford gave him the part of the Ringo Kid, in *Stagecoach* (1939). The film launched Wayne's career and cemented a partnership that was to produce some of America's most acclaimed westerns, including *She Wore a Yellow Ribbon* (1949), *The Searchers* (1956), and *The Man Who Shot Liberty Valance* (1962). "He was more than a father," Wayne was to say. "Not all kids love their fathers."

Big sonovabitch

As the years went by, Wayne's screen image grew and matured. No more a slim, cocky, young gun-slinger, he began to play gruff, older-statesman roles. "I never knew that big sonovabitch could act," Ford exclaimed after seeing Wayne in *Red River* (1948).

Wayne, the man and Wayne, the screen star, were almost indistinguishable. Both were hard-drinking, tough-fisted and, though gallant to women when the occasion demanded, were at their happiest with plenty of liquor, a deck of cards and like-minded male companions.

It was the real Wayne who launched with zest into the ultra-right McCarthy witch-hunts, but it could just as easily have been the irascible one-eyed Marshall Rooster Cogburn he played in *True Grit* (1969), winning an Oscar for Best Actor.

"Not everything is black and white," a liberal-minded aquaintance once told Wayne, only to be greeted with a roar of "Why the hell not?"

But like the best of his roles, Wayne's toughness was diluted with a dash of sentimentality. His patriotism could verge on the mawkish: "If you played my favorite song everyone would have

Left: *The making of a super hero: the Duke in his youth honing his gutsy all-American image in* **Conflict** *(1936).*

Left: *Working on* **The Green Berets**
(1968); he directed and starred.
Below left: *Something of an alter ego –
the tough marshal in* **True Grit** *(1969).*

to stand up," he told a band-leader
who asked for his request. He adored
his seven children—offspring of his
three marriages.

"He was as tough as an old nut and
soft as a yellow ribbon," was Elizabeth
Taylor's apt appraisal.

The "Big C"

It seemed impossible to imagine him
ever being ill, but in 1964 Wayne was
diagnosed as having cancer and had a
lung removed. Typically he was
quickly back on set, proud of having
beaten the "Big C"—almost as though
only a *really* majestic disease was a
suitable opponent for "The Duke". But
there was purpose to all the interviews:
Wayne turned his misfortunes into a
courageous crusade. "I decided that if
I, John Wayne, came out and said
something about cancer it might stop
some poor slob putting a gun in his
mouth and blowing his brains out."

In 1978, however, Wayne became ill
again and had open heart surgery,
followed by severe hepatitis. Again he
recovered faster than anyone imagined
possible. It seemed that he had once
more swaggered past death until
doctors discovered that his stomach
was riddled with cancer and were
forced to remove it. According to Pat
Stacy, Wayne's last love, there was a
time when he could not bear the pain
and the humiliation any longer and
demanded a pistol so that he could
"blow my brains out". Stacy refused
and Wayne lived to receive his special
award at the Oscar ceremony.

In the final film the actor appeared
in, *The Shootist* (1976), he tells a boy
"I won't be wronged, I won't be
insulted, I won't be laid a hand on. I
don't do these things to others and I
require the same of them."

A fitting epitaph

Admirers suggested that this could
stand as a fitting epitaph, but Wayne
had other ideas. During the making of
the film in which he plays an aging
gunfighter dying of cancer, he was
asked how he would like to be
remembered. He replied, "The
Mexicans have an expression *Feo,
fuerte y formal*—'he was ugly, he was
tough, but he had dignity'. If they say
that about me I'll be happy."

Orson Welles

There are many tales, apocryphal and otherwise, about modern Renaissance man Orson Welles, who has been active in so many fields—from bullfighting and sherry commercials to theater production and cinema. His single greatest achievement however, has to be his first feature film, *Citizen Kane* (1941), made when he was only 26. It regularly tops critics' personal polls.

However, when it was first released *Citizen Kane* provoked the wrath of newspaper tycoon William Randolph Hearst—on whom it was based. He tried to suppress it and when this failed sabotaged its release in major outlets. The film was a financial flop and Welles' subsequent efforts were subjected to rigorous studio scrutiny.

Infant prodigy

An infant prodigy, he was born on May 6, 1915 in Wisconsin and took up music, acting, painting and writing in his very early childhood. By the age of 5 he was presenting his own magic and puppet shows, and was acquainted with the works of Shakespeare.

Below: The showman "levitates" his assistant, in his night club act.

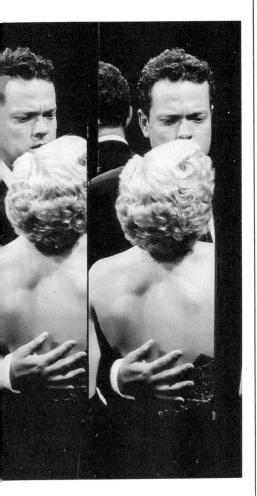

When he was 16, he bluffed his way into the Gate Theatre, Dublin where he made his debut as a professional actor, later saying of this achievement, "I played a star part the first time I ever walked on the stage and I've been working my way down ever since."

The itinerant Welles then tried, unsuccessfully, to find work in London, then on Broadway, before going to Morocco, then Spain—where he worked for a time as a picador. He returned to America in 1934 and there embarked on a stage career which embraced production, writing and directing, as well as acting.

Sexually precocious

Welles was very precocious sexually, too, and claimed to have been making love from the age of 11. Reputedly a womanizer—hence the tag "King Leer"—he was only 19 when he

Left: A genius at work. Welles making screen history as he directs his first film, the legendary **Citizen Kane** *(1941).*

married his first wife, actress Virginia Nicholson. She divorced him on the grounds of incompatibility after five years.

Welles once said that he hates women but he also needs them. This ambiguous view emerged symbolically in the early stages of his relationship with second wife, Rita Hayworth: he used to saw her in half on stage as a highlight of his magic act.

The couple wed in 1943 but were clearly ill-matched and Hayworth later complained that it was impossible to live with a genius. In vain she tried to curb his appetite for travel and work, but he resisted—pointing out that he did not try to change her.

They divorced in 1947, after making *The Lady From Shanghai*(1948), in which director Welles was felt to have mutilated the image of sex goddess Hayworth: he had her long red hair cropped and dyed a brash blonde. Like so much of his work it was not a box office success at the time, but has since become a classic.

Essentially a hack

Welles did not however, see himself as a poor, struggling artist: 'I am essentially a hack, a commercial person. If I had a hobby I would immediately make money on it—or abandon it.'

If not money, he certainly made news. His most sensational exploit was an American radio broadcast in October 1938 in which he enacted H.G. Wells' *The War Of The Worlds* so realistically that listeners really believed that Martians had invaded the United States. Thousands of people fled their homes in panic and CBS were obliged to make a public apology.

Welles barely avoided even worse notoriety for an incident during a performance of *Julius Caesar*. Playing the part of Brutus, he accidentally stabbed Caesar (Joseph Holland) with a real knife. The actor lost a lot of blood as he lay stoically on stage until the act ended. He was then rushed to hospital where he recovered.

Too much, too soon

In the eyes of some, Welles had too much, too soon. On arrival in Hollywood in 1939, his contract with RKO was so indulgent (complete artistic freedom and a guarantee of no studio interference) that there was inevitable resentment from other members of the film colony. Welles reacted with typical disdain—"Hollywood is a golden suburb, perfect for golfers, gardeners, mediocre men and complacent starlets."

He was also smart enough to realize the value of his youth in that medium. Years later, speaking of his legendary Hollywood deal, he said, "I got it because I was young and if you're young in America they'll give you the world."

He never lost the "boy wonder" tag although in recent years he has spent more time acting in other director's films than in completing his own. Married for a third time in 1956, to Italian actress Paola Mori, Welles thereafter spent most of his time in Europe. He made a triumphant return to Hollywood in 1975 when he was awarded the American Film Institute's Life Achievement Award.

Although not touched with the wild brilliance of his early work, his creative output continues to impress. As was said of him when he first arrived in Hollywood: "There but for the grace of God, goes God."

Mae West

Never a conventional sex symbol, you might say that it wasn't the idea of Mae West's delivery that counted; it was the delivery of her ideas. She was an original in that her performance was both an act and its own critique; no one could send her up better than she did herself. And her self-parodying certainly paid off—in 1935 she was the highest paid woman in the US.

Baby Vamp

She was born in Brooklyn on August 7, 1892 (some sources say 1888) and, in November 1980, she was buried there—next to her parents. Her father, Battling Jack West, was a sometime heavyweight boxer and private detective. Mrs Matilda West, ever regretful she didn't go on the stage herself, was delighted when her buxom daughter played burlesque as "The Baby Vamp".

Looking back West remembered: "I never had much time to mix with other children ... I was so carried away with myself, my dancing, my singing. Besides, growing up in show business

makes you a lot smarter and it gave me a standing in the neighborhood."

On the vaudeville circuit she worked up an act with song-and-dance man Frank Wallace, and they were married in Milwaukee in April 1911, when Mae was 17 (or perhaps 23). By the end of the tour, the marriage was over too "I wasn't in love with this man," she later declared, "I realized how much I loved my mother and I had done this without telling her." Mae went back to her mother and stayed with her until Matilda's death in 1929.

Begging letters

The marriage remained a secret until 1935, when Wallace, mindful of the community property laws, sued West for his share of her spoils of stardom. Counter-petitions flew and, before he could wrest a settlement, he found himself divorced and without a case. She ignored his subsequent letters.

Years later, she said: "Marriage and one man for life is fine for some people, but for me it wasn't good. Every time I look at myself I become absorbed in

Below: *Come up and see me sometime; what man could refuse?*

Above: *Instructing studs in deportment, for* **Myra Breckinridge** *(1970).*

myself and I didn't want to get involved with another person like that." She never married again.

Cashing in on fantasy

West channeled her energies into creating her stage persona, playing vaudeville on Broadway. But it took time to succeed. Said one review: "Unless Miss West can tone down her stage presence in every way, she just as well might hop right out of vaudeville into burlesque."

She was supporting a pair of comics when she decided to adapt the shimmy she had seen danced in the black jazz dives. It worked. But it wasn't until she started writing her own material—indulging her sexual fantasies in dialog—that she took off.

Above: *The spirit of America, in the satirical* **Belle of the Nineties** *(1934).*

Her first play had the all-time no-nonsense title: *Sex*. It had a naval lieutenant hero and was about extortion among Trinidadian prostitutes. Mae's experience of prostitutes was confined to having had one pointed out to her on a street corner.

Charged with obscenity

The play opened in 1926 to little interest and less critical support but it was taken up by sailors on leave and then won a cult following among Manhattan's sensation-seekers. This attracted the best publicity of all, a puritan backlash with police busting three theaters and arresting 41 performers on obscenity charges, Mae among them.

Also raided was a serious play about lesbianism, *The Captive*, starring Basil Rathbone and Helen Menken—not, of course, written by West. She loved gay men—her second play, *The Drag*, was about them and her fifth, *Pleasure Man*, about drag artists—but she had a blind spot about lesbians. She roundly abused *The Captive* and the resulting fracas with Menken resulted in West being fined $500 and sentenced to 10 days imprisonment.

From then on her notoriety assured success. *Diamond Lil*, her hit of 1928, became the movie *She Done Him Wrong* (1933) for Paramount. Single-handedly she saved the studio from bankruptcy.

Her one-liners were now for the world. Her movie appearances—only 12 in all—were always scripted by herself and maintained the throwaway *double entendre* and the shimmy-walk that were her trade-marks. At 86 (or perhaps 90), she shimmied out again, somewhat embarrassingly, with her usual entourage of muscle men, in the movie of her play *Sextette* (1978).

Self-cultivated myth

West was a self-cultivated myth, encouraging preposterous tales of her sexual appetite and endurance. Around her, notions multiplied: she was really a man, a virgin, even older. By her own account, she was pathological about "health", obsessive about ESP, totally absorbed in her own fantasy.

But however unreal her life may have been, she taught us that sex was fun. She was a life-saver in that she saved us from self-destructive guilt and it seems only appropriate that an inflatable life jacket should be named after her.

INDEX

Absence of Malice 131
Adam's Rib 87
Adventure 67
Advise and Consent 109
Affair in Trinidad 83
African Queen 25, 87, 177
Agatha 91
Airport 89
Airport 1975 173
Algiers 104
Alias Jesse James 93
All About Eve 44, 129
All My Sons 107
All Night Long 79, 171
All the President's Men 90-91
American Citizen 18
American in Paris 99
Anastasia 23
Anatomy of a Murder 167
Anchors Aweigh 99
And God Created Woman 16
And Justice for All 138, 139
Angels With Dirty Faces 30
Angry Hills 103
Annie Hall 9
Annie Oakley 165
Anniversary 45
Another Time, Another Place 36, 181
Apartment 113
Apocalypse Now 29
Arch of Triumph 22
Around the World in Eighty Days 97, 135
Asphalt Jungle 129
Assassination of Frank Wilson 29
Atlantic City 107
Author! Author! 138
Autumn Sonata 23
Babes in Arms 155
Babes on Broadway 155
Babette Goes to War 17
Baby Face Nelson 155
Badlands 161
Bad Man's River 123
Bananas 8
Band Wagon 13
Barabbas 145
Barbarella 65
Barber Shop 59
Battling Butler 96
Beast of Berlin 102
Beau Brummel 19
Bedlam 95
Before the Mast 103
Being There 159
Belle of New York 13
Bells Go Down 122
Bells of St Mary's 22
Beloved Infidel 141
Ben Hur 88
Best Friends 149
Best Little Whorehouse in Texas 149
Beyond the Rainbow 26
Bible 156

Big Broadcast 42
Big Broadcast of 1938 59, 93
Big Clock 109
Big Country 88, 141
Big Sleep (1946) 14, 25; (1978) 127
Big Trail 184
Big Wheel 155
Bill of Divorcement 19, 86
Birdman of Alcatraz 107
Birth of a Nation 72
Black Gold 144
Black Knight 103
Black Orchid 117
Blonde Venus 76
Blood Alley 127
Blood Feud 117
Bloodline 85
Blowout 178
Blue Angel 52
Bobby Deerfield 138
Body Snatcher 95
Bold and the Brave 155
Bonnie & Clyde 20, 54, 78
Boom! 175
Boy on a Dolphin 103, 116
Boys from Brazil 123, 141
Boys' Town 155, 177
Brass Target 117
Brave Bulls 144
Bride of Frankenstein 95
Bridge Too Far 79
Bringing Up Baby 86
Broken Blossoms 72
Bronco Billy 56
Buccaneer 88, 145
Buddy, Buddy 113
Bullitt 125
Buster Keaton Story 97
Butch Cassidy and the Sundance Kid 131, 147
Butterfield 8 174
Caine Mutiny 25
Calamity Jane 47
Cameraman 96
Camille 182
Candidate 147
Cannonball Run 149
Capone 162
Captain Blood 60
Captain Horatio Hornblower 140
Captains Courageous 154, 177
Carnal Knowledge 132
Carpetbaggers 103
Carrie 161, 178
Casablanca 22, 23, 25, 105
Casino Royale 9
Cat and the Canary 93
Cat Ballou 119
Cat on a Hot Tin Roof 131, 174
Charge of the Light Brigade 134
Children of Divorce 38
Children of Sanchez 145
China Syndrome 113
Chinatown 54, 132
Cincinnati Kid 124

Citizen Kane 186
City Lights 33
City Streets 27
Cleopatra 174
Coal Miner's Daughter 161
Come Back, Little Sheba 107
Comedians 175
Comedy of Terrors 95
Condemned of Altona 117
Conversation 79
Cool Hand Luke 131
Coquette 143
Counsellor-at-Law 19
Country Girl 43
Count Your Blessings 35
Cover Girl 82, 99
Criminal Code 94
Crimson Pirate 107
Cruising 138
Curse of the Pink Panther 135
Daddy Long Legs 13
Dancing Co-ed 180
Dangerous 44
Dante's Inferno 82
Dark City 88
Dark Victory 44
David Copperfield 59
Dawn Patrol 134
Day at the Races 121
Days of Glory 140
Days of Wine and Roses 113
Death Race 2000 162
Deer Hunter 50, 168
Deliverance 148
Dentist 59
Desert Fox 123
Desire 52
Destry Rides Again 53, 166
Devil is a Sissy 154
Dial M for Murder 100
Dinner at Eight 19, 80
Dirty Dozen 119
Dispatch from Reuters 150
Doc 54
Dr Ehrlich's Magic Bullet 150
Doctor Faustus 175
Dr Jekyll and Mr Hyde 18
Dr No 36
Dr Strangelove 156, 158
Dog Day 119
Dog Day Afternoon 138, 139
Domino Principle 79
Don Juan 17
Double Indemnity 165
Double Whoopee 80
Down Argentina Way 74
Down to the Sea in Ships 26
Dracula 95
Duel in the Sun 73, 140
Duet for One 55
Earthquake 89
East of Eden 48
Easter Parade 13
East Side of Heaven 42
Easy Rider 132, 133
Easy Street 33

Ecstacy 104
Effect of Gamma Rays on Man-in-the-Moon Marigolds 131
El Cid 88
Electric Horseman 147
Elephant Walk 111
Elmer Gantry 107
End 149
Eureka 79
Ex-Lady 44
Facts of Life 93
Falling in Love 168
Family Affair 155
Family Reunion 45
Fanny by Gaslight 122
Farewell, My Lovely 127, 162
Farmer Takes a Wife 62
Fatal Glass of Beer 59
Femme et le Pantin 16
Femmes 17
Film 97
Fire Down Below 113
Fire Over England 110
Firepower 117
First Blood 163
F.I.S.T. 163
Fistful of Dollars 56
Five Easy Pieces 132
Five Fingers 123
Five Star Final 94
Flame and the Arrow 107
Flesh and the Devil 69
Flying Down to Rio 12, 152
Folies Bergère 35
For a Few Dollars More 56
For Me and My Gal 99
Formula 29
For Pete's Sake 170
42nd Street 152
For Whom the Bell Tolls 22, 38
Fountainhead 39
Four Horsemen of the Apocalypse 182
Fourteen Hours 100
Francis in the Haunted House 155
Frankenstein 94, 95
Free Soul 67
French Connection 78, 79
French Lieutenant's Woman 168
Friends of Eddie Coyle 127
From Here to Eternity 107
Fugitive Kind 29
Funny Face 13, 85
Funny Girl 170
Funny Lady 170
Funny Thing Happened on the Way to the Forum 97
Gaslight 22, 105
Gator 149
Gauntlet 57
General 96
Gentleman's Agreement 140
Gentlemen Prefer Blondes 129
Getaway 125
Ghoul 95
Giant 48-9, 174

Gigi 35
G.I. Joe 126
Gilda 82, 83
Girl Friday 77
Glenn Miller Story 167
Godfather 29, 139
Godfather Part II 50, 51, 139
Going My Way 42
Goin' South 132-3
Gold Diggers of 1933 152
Gone With the Wind 38, 67, 110
Good, the Bad and the Ugly 56
Gorky Park 119
Go West 96
Graduate 79, 90
Graft 94
Grand Hotel 19
Grapes of Wrath 63
Gray Lady Down 89
Grease 178, 179
Great Escape 125
Greatest Show on Earth 88
Great Gatsby 103
Great Profile 19
Great Sinner 140
Greek Tycoon 145
Green Mansions 85
Guadalcanal Diary 144
Guess Who's Coming to Dinner?
    87, 177
Gunfighter 140
Guns of Navarone 141
Guys and Dolls 29
Hamlet 136
Hammersmith is Out 175
Hands Across the Table 115
Happening 54
Harry and Son 131
Harvey 167
Hatter's Castle 122
Heaven Can Wait 20
Hell in the Pacific 119
Hell's Angels 80
Henry V 136
High Noon 39
High Sierra 25
High Society 43
Hill 37
His Brother's Wife 165
His Majesty the American 94
Holiday 87
Holiday Inn 42
Home from the Hill 127
Honky Tonk Man 56
Hooper 149
Hoopla 27
Houseboat 117
How to Be Very, Very Popular 75
How to Marry a Millionnaire 75
Hudd 131
Hunchback of Notre Dame
    (1939) 108; (1956) 144
Hurry Sundown 54
Hush . . . Hush Sweet Charlotte 45
Hustler 131, 156
Iceman Cometh 119
I Could Go On Singing 71
Illicit 16
I'm All Right Jack 158
Imitation of Life 181

Immortal Battalion 134
I Never Sang for My Father 79
Innocents of Paris 35
Inn of the Sixth Happiness 23
Interiors 9
Intermezzo 22
International House 59
In the Wake of the Bounty 60
Intolerance 96
Irma La Douce 113
Isle of the Dead 95
It 26
It Happened One Night 67
It's a Gift 58, 59
It's a Mad, Mad, Mad, Mad
    World 97
It's a Wonderful Life 166
It Should Happen to You 112
Jezebel 44
Joan of Arc 22
John and Mary 90
Johnny Guitar 41
Joyless Street 69
Julia 168
Julius Caesar (1949) 88;
    (1953) 29
Key 117
Key Largo 25
Keys of the Kingdom 140
Khartoum 88
Kid 33
Kid Auto Races at Venice 33
Kiki 143
Killers 106
King of Comedy 51
King of Jazz 42
Kitty Foyle 153
Klansman 119
Klute 65
Kotch 113
Kramer Vs Kramer 91, 168
Ladies of Leisure 164
Ladies of Washington 144
Lady from Shanghai 83, 185
Ladykillers 158
Lassie Come Home 174
Last Detail 132
Last Tango in Paris 29
Late Extra 122
Legend of the Lost 116
Lenny 90
Leopard 107
Let's Go Places 74
Let's Make Love 129
Life and Times of Judge
    Roy Bean 131
Lilith 78
Limelight 33, 97
Little Big Man 90
Little Caesar 150
Little Foxes 44
Little Lord Fauntleroy 154
Little Women 86
Local Hero 107
Lolita 123
Lord Jeff 154
Lords of Flatbush 162
Love 69
Love and Death 9
Love in the Afternoon 35, 85

Love Laughs at Andy Hardy 154,
    155
Love Me or Leave Me 47
Love Me Tonight 35
Love Parade 35
Lucky Lady 79
Lust for Life 144
MacArthur 141
Madame Sans-Gêne 172
Madame Sin 45
Mad Genius 94
Magnificent Seven 125
Main Event 170-71
Maltese Falcon 25
Mandingo 123
Manhattan 9, 168
Manhattan Melodrama 154
Man in Grey 122
Mannequin 41, 177
Man on the Flying Trapeze 58
Man's Castle 177
Man Who Knew Too Much 47
Man Who Loves Women 149
Man Who Shot Liberty Valance
    184
Marathon Man 91
March or Die 79
Marnie 37, 101
Marriage, Italian Style 117
Marseilles Contract 123
Mary Poppins 10, 11
Mask of Fu Manchu 94, 95
Mask of Virtue 110
Mean Machine 149
Mean Streets 51
Meet Me in St Louis 71
Me, Natalie 138
Message 145
Midnight 19
Midnight Cowboy 90
Midsummer Night's Dream 155
Midsummer Night's Sex
    Comedy 9
Midway 88
Mildred Pierce 41
Mirror Crack'd 175
Misfits 67, 129
Missing 113, 161
Missouri Breaks 29
Mister Roberts 63, 112
Mr Deeds Goes to Town 38
Mr Smith Goes to Washington
    166
Moby Dick 141
Modern Times 33
Moment by Moment 180
Mommie Dearest 41, 55
Monsieur Beaucaire 93
Monsieur Verdoux 33
Monte Carlo Baby 85
Monte Walsh 119
Morning Glory 86
Morocco 52
Mother Lode 89
Mother Machree 186
Mountain Men 89
Mummy 94, 95
Murder by Decree 123
Murder on the Orient Express 23
Mutiny on the Bounty 29

My Fair Lady 85
My Lady of Whims 26
My Little Chickadee 58
My Man Godfrey 115
Naked Jungle 88
Nanny 45
National Velvet 155, 174
Navigator 96
Nederland in 7 Lessen 85
Network 54
Never Give a Sucker an Even
    Break 59
New Kind of Love 35
New York, New York 51
Niagara 129
Night at the Opera 121
Night Moves 79
Night of the Hunter 73, 109
Night Walker 165
No Limit 27
No Man of Her Own 115
North by Northwest 123
Nothing Sacred 115
Notorious 22
Not to Be Trusted 154
Nun's Story 85
Objective Burma! 61
Odd Couple 113
Odd Man Out 122
Offence 37
Of Human Bondage 44
Old Dark House 94, 95
Old-Fashioned Way 59
Old Spanish Custom 96
Omen 141
Once in a Lifetime 102
Once Upon a Wheel 131
One-Eyed Jacks 29
One Flew Over the Cuckoo's Nest
    132
One Hour With You 35
On Golden Pond 63
Only Angels Have Wings 82
On the Beach 140
On the Town 99
On the Waterfront 29
Open and Shut 79
Orchids and Ermine 154
Ordinary People 147
Our Dancing Daughters 40
Our Hospitality 96
Outlaw Josey Wales 57
Out of Towners 113
Owl and the Pussycat 170
Ox-Bow Incident 63
Paint Your Wagon 119
Paisan 22
Paleface 93
Panic in Needle Park 138
Papillon 90, 124
Paradise Alley 163
Parole! 144
Party at Kitty's 162
Pat and Mike 87
Patton 156
Pawnshop 33
Peer Gynt 88
Penny Points to Paradise 158
Perfect Crime 114
Petrified Forest 25

191

Peyton Place *183*
Pharmacist *59*
Philadelphia Story *87, 167*
Picnic *131*
Picture Mommy Dead *105*
Pièges 35
Pink Panther *158*
Pirate *71, 99*
Place for Lovers *54*
Place in the Sun *174*
Plainsman *144*
Planet of the Apes *89*
Plastic Age *26*
Platinum Blonde *80*
Pocket Money *119*
Point Blank *119*
Pollyanna *143*
Pony Express *88*
Pool Sharks *59*
Poppy *59*
Possessed *40*
Postman Always Rings Twice *132*
Power and the Glory *176*
President's Lady *88*
Pride and the Passion *77 116, 117*
Prime Cut *119, 161*
Primrose Path *153*
Prince and the Showgirl *129*
Prisoner of Second Avenue *162*
Prison of Zenda *123*
Private Life of Don Juan *122*
Private Life of Henry VIII *108*
Professionals *119*
Public Enemy *30, 80*
Puzzle of a Downfall Child *54*
Queen Christina *68, 69, 136*
Queen Kelly *172*
Rachel Rachel *131*
Raggedy Man *161*
Raging Bull *50, 51*
Ragtime *31*
Rainmaker *87*
Raintree County *174*
Raven *95*
Reaching for the Moon *42*
Rear Window *100, 167*
Rebecca *137*
Rebel Without a Cause *48*
Reckless *81*
Red Dust *81*
Red River *184*
Reds *20, 79, 132*
Revenge of the Creature *56*
Rhinestone Cowboy *163*
Richard III *136*
Road to Singapore *42, 93*
Road to Utopia *92*
Roaring Twenties *30*
Robin and Marian *85*
Rocky *163*
Roi Des Champs Élysées 96
Roma Citta Aperta 22
Romance on the High Seas *47*
Roman Holiday *84, 85, 141*
Roman Spring of Mrs Stone *111*
Ronde, La 65
Rooster Cogburn *87*
Rough Cut *149*
Sabrina *85*
Saga of Gösta Berling *69*

Samson and Delilah *105*
Sand Pebbles *124*
Sandpiper *174*
Saratoga *81*
Saskatchewan *103*
Saturday Night Fever *163, 178*
Savage *88*
Savage Innocents *145*
Save the Tiger *112, 113*
Sayonara *29*
Scarecrow *79, 138*
Scarface (1932) *95*; (1983) *139*
Scarlet Street *150*
Sea Beast *19*
Searchers *184*
Secret Call *27*
Secret Mission *122*
Secret of the Incas *88*
Secrets *143*
Seduction of Joe Tynan *168*
Semi-Tough *149*
Separate Tables *83, 107, 135*
Sergeant York *38*
Serpico *138, 139*
Seven Chances *96*
Seventh Veil *122*
Seven Year Itch *129*
Sextette *189*
Shalako *17*
Shampoo *20*
Shane *103*
Sharky's Machine *149*
She Done Him Wrong *76, 189*
Sheik *182*
Sherlock Junior *96*
She Wore a Yellow Ribbon *184*
Shining *132*
Ship of Fools *119*
Shootist *185*
Shout at the Devil *119*
Silence Est d'Or 35
Silkwood *168*
Silver Chalice *130, 131*
Singin' in the Rain *99*
Sing, You Sinners *42*
Skyward *45*
Smokey and the Bandit *149*
Snows of Kilimanjaro *141*
S.O.B. *10*
Somebody Up There Likes Me *125*
Some Like It Hot *113, 129*
Something Blonde *117*
Son of Frankenstein *95*
Son of the Sheik *183*
Sophia *117*
Sophie's Choice *168*
Sorry, Wrong Number *165*
Sound of Music *10, 11*
Special Day *117*
Spellbound *22, 140*
Spirit of St Louis *167*
Splendour in the Grass *20*
Stagecoach (1939) *184*; (1966) *43*
Stage Fright *53*
Stalking Moon *141*
Star *44*
Star! *11*
Star is Born (1954) *71, 123*;
(1976) *170*
Starting Over *149*

Staying Alive *163, 179*
Still of the Night *168*
Sting *131, 147*
Strada, La 144
Straight Times *91*
Strangers *45*
Straw Dogs *90*
Streetcar Named Desire *28, 29, 111*
Stromboli *23*
Sudden Impact *56, 57*
Suddenly Last Summer *174*
Suds *143*
Sun Also Rises *61*
Sunflower *117*
Sunset Boulevard *172, 173*
Supergirl *55*
Superman *29, 79*
Superman II *79*
Sweet Smell of Success *107*
Sylvia Scarlett *77*
Take the Money and Run *9*
Tall Story *64*
Taming of the Shrew (1929) *143*;
(1967) *175*
Tarantula *56*
Targets *95*
Taxi Driver *51*
Teahouse of the August Moon *29*
Temptress *69*
Ten Commandments *88, 151, 170*
Terms of Endearment *133*
Terror *95*
Tess of the Storm Country *143*
Test Pilot *66*
That Hamilton Woman *110*
That's Entertainment II *13*
They All Laughed *85*
They Won't Forget *180*
Things Are Looking Up *110*
Thomas Crown Affair *124*
Three Ages *96*
Three for the Show *75*
Three Musketeers *54*
Three Women *161*
Three Violent People *88*
To Be or Not to Be *115*
To Catch a Thief *100*
Today We Live *41*
To Have and Have Not *14, 25*
To Kill a Mockingbird *141*
Tom Horn *124, 125*
Tootsie *91*
Torn Curtain *10*
Torrent *69*
Touch of Evil *88*
Tramp *33*
Treasure of the Sierra Madre *25*
Trespasser *172*
Trail of the Catonsville Nine *141*
Tribute *113*
Trip *132*
Trog *41*
Trop Credule 34
True Grit *184*
Twelve Angry Men *63*
Twelve O'Clock High *140*
Twentieth Century *19, 115*
20,000 Leagues Under the Sea *123*

Two-Faced Woman *68*
Two of a Kind *181*
Two-Way Stretch *158*
Two Women *117*
Ultimate Solution of Grace Quigley *87*
Under Capricorn *22*
Under Fire *79*
Under Milk Wood *175*
Under Two Flags *27*
Unseen Enemy *72*
Up the River *176*
Up the Sandbox *170*
Urban Cowboy *178*
Verdict *131*
Vérité 17
Vertigo *167*
Victor/Victoria *10*
V.I.P. *174*
Virtue *114*
Viva Zapata! *29, 144*
Voyage *117*
Wait Until Dark *85*
Walk, Don't Run *77*
War and Peace *85*
War Hunt *147*
Warrior's Husband *86*
Watcher in the Woods *45*
Way Ahead *134*
Way Down East *72*
Way We Were *147, 170*
Wedding *73*
Welcome to L.A. *161*
Whatever Happened to Baby Jane? *41, 45*
What's New Pussycat? *8*
What's Up, Doc? *170*
When a Man Loves *19*
White Cargo *104*
White Christmas *43*
White Mama *45*
Who's Afraid of Virginia Woolf? *174-5*
Wicked Lady *55*
Wild One *29*
Wild Party *26*
Will Penny *88-9*
Winning *131*
Winning of Barbara Worth *38*
Witness for the Prosecution *109*
Wizard of Oz *70*
Wolf Song *38*
Woman in the Window *150*
Woman of the Year *87, 177*
Wrong Arm of the Law *158*
WUSA *131*
Wuthering Heights *134, 137*
Yankee Doodle Dandy *31*
Yearling *140*
Yentl *171*
Yesterday, Today and Tomorrow *117*
You Can't Take It With You *166*
Young Frankenstein *79*
Young Lions *29*
Young Man of Manhattan *152*
Young Mr Lincoln *63*
You're in the Navy Now *119*
Zelig *9*
Zorba the Greek *145*